IVONNE HAASE

Beth Galí

Diseño y Arquitectura

1966 - 1998

TEXTOS DE JAAP HUISMAN
ORIOL BOHIGAS
ANTONI LLENA
ANTONI MARI

Contents

Presentation *Yvònne G.J.M. Joris*	7
Introduction Un itinerario profesional, cultural y político A professional, cultural and political itinerary *Oriol Bohigas*	8
Un toque del sur en una ciudad del norte A touch of the South in a Northern City *Jaap Huisman*	14
Beth Galí el milagro de Barcelona Beth Galí and the Miracle of Barcelona *Jaap Huisman*	26
Proposals, works and projects **1966-1971**	38
Arquitectos y pintores Architects and Painters *Antoni Llena*	46
Proposals, works and projects **1976-1994**	52
Respeto a la tradición y sutil irreverencia Respect for subtle irreverence towards tradition *Antoni Mari*	124
Proposals, works and projects **1994-1998**	128
Biography	169
Bibliography	174
Collaborators	176
Photographers	177

Presentation

's-Hertogenbosch Municipal Council has commissioned the Spanish architect and designer Beth Galí to refurbish the public space of a large part of our town centre.

Her ideas have certainly transformed the appearance of central 's-Hertogenbosch. It looks lighter, more airy and contemporary. The atmosphere has even taken on a dash of the Mediterranean. Galí changed the townscape, chose an 'un-Dutch' type of paving and designed stainless-steel bike racks and unorthodox street lighting. She also conceived a striking building – the Stoa – on Burgemeester Loeffplein.

Her interventions in the historic town centre are at once understated and refreshing, contrasting yet seamlessly merging with what was there before.

The completion of her projects in 's-Hertogenbosch provides an ideal opportunity for an exhibition and a book focusing on a wider survey of her work. The context of other projects adds relief to each individual achievement and does full justice to Beth Galí's qualities as an architect and designer of public spaces.

Yvònne G.J.M. Joris
Director
MUSEUM HET KRUITHUIS

Introduction

A professional, cultural and political itinerary

It is not easy for me to write a short note about Beth Galí and her work, because I know her life and work far too well – through public appearances, personal correspondence and professional collaboration. It is far too tricky a task for me to sort out from such an extensive panorama what might be essential for a reader coming to this whole wealth of personal anecdotes as an outsider. For the same reason, if I had to write a long essay – something which would no doubt be considerably easier – I would set out to observe the subject from a variety of points as diverse as Beth Galí herself. In this way, I could weave a simple fabric of facts and arbitrary references from which readers might fashion their own overall understanding of her life and work, bringing to bear their own healthy cultural prejudices. A crucial thread in this fabric would be the one explaining her commitment – cultural, social and professional – to the strengthening of design, architecture and urbanism in her immediate context. Even now that she has established an international reputation, the key to understanding Beth Galí lies in the intensity of her professional, academic and on occasion political itinerary in a Barcelona which, in the space of a few years (coinciding with her working life), has transformed itself into a key point of reference.

The first stage of this itinerary might be termed an affirmation of young industrial design in Catalonia. In 1966 – the year in which the Sindicato Democrático de Estudiantes, a clandestine, democratic students' union, was founded – Beth Galí won one of the annual prizes awarded by the industrial design section of the ADI FAD architecture and design association, having played an active role as student and promoter of the first design schools. I remember her as the revolutionary student of the Escuela Elisava, supporting

the split that led to the creation of the new Escuela Eina, calling for a new set of cultural – and even political and moral – criteria in the conceptual development of design. She created products whose aesthetic and functional qualities were submitted to a radical manifesto aimed at the promotion of new social values. The latter were a powerful gesture of renewal in relation to the design of the 1950s, in which my own generation had chiefly concerned itself with faithfully resurrecting the formal and productive methodologies of the Modern Movement, which had suffered severe repression during the early years of the Franco regime.

The EINA School was a cultural adventure of the greatest importance. From its first beginnings it attracted tutors of exceptional quality from a wide range of fields, including Alexandre Cirici, Albert Ràfols Casamada, Román Gubern, Federico Correa and Manolo Sacristán. It was also involved with foreign artists and intellectuals like the Italian Gruppo 63, which included Nanni Balestrini, Furio Colombo, Gillo Dorfles, Umberto Eco and Vittorio Gregotti. It was in this fertile soil that Beth Galí cultivated a way of understanding culture and craft that undoubtedly provided her with one of the key foundations for her future development.

I then remember her between 1973 and 1982, as a student in the Faculty of Architecture in Barcelona, and in particular during my time as Head of Faculty, which coincided with the long-hoped-for transition to democracy after General Franco's death. In the space of just a few months, Spain's universities changed radically. A generation of academics and intellectuals now came to the fore who were still fired by the combative spirit of years of political struggle, yet who understood that that same spirit now had to be applied to cultural needs.

Beth Galí was a conspicuous member of that new university generation. Barcelona's ETSAB school of architecture reinstated the tutors and professors removed from their posts by the Franco dictatorship. Together with colleagues who had managed to cling on during the years of darkness, they were able to offer for the first time a specialist education of the highest quality. The teaching of Rafael Moneo, Federico Correa, Esteve Bonell, Xavier Rubert de Ventòs, Manuel Ribas i Piera, Eugenio Trias, Félix de Azúa, Albert Viaplana, Joaquim Bassó, Oscar Tusquets, Jordi Garcès, Helio Piñon, Ignasi, Manuel de Solà-Morales and others was complemented by regular visits by figures like Alvaro Siza, Mario Botta, James Stirling, Nicolau M. Rubií i Tuduri, Peter Eisenman, Lodovico Quaroni, Giancarlo de Carlo, Carlo Aymonino and Mario Manieri Elia. A series of memorable international forums were organised, all of which were consistently supported and in a number of cases suggested by the students. The result was a new programme of studies that set out to restore the hierarchy of values to architecture teaching and design practice in order to give the discipline a real professional status and identity.

That group – usually referred to as the eighties generation – completed its studies in incomparably better conditions and went on to contribute to the task of renewing the urban design of Barcelona and all of Catalonia. In 1980, Narcís Serra, Barcelona's first democratically elected mayor in 50 years, was responsible for implementing the new urban-planning methods that were destined to achieve such significant results. These included the city's nomination to host the Olympic Games, urban projects rather than general and partial plans and specifically local architectural solutions rather than indicative and purely normative planning. Even before they had graduated, thirteen of the students belonging to the eighties generation had been recruited by Barcelona City Council to form the first 'Urban Projects Workshop'. Between then and 1992, they helped mark out the entire operational system for the transformation of Barcelona, showing their ability to contribute to an exceptionally high level of quality. Subsequently, as qualified architects, they continued to work for the City Council, and a group of them set up the 'Municipal Organisation for Urbanistic Promotion (IMPU)', an effectively autonomous body that took charge of the most important operations for the forthcoming Olympic Games.

Beth Galí played an outstanding part in the Urban Projects Workshop, and above all at IMPU – not only because she was personally involved in many of the projects but also because she contributed so much to the enthusiasm of the whole group, the first of its kind to be set up by a local authority in Spain. It boasted all the advantages of a private studio, while at the same time benefiting from systems of collaboration and a commitment to a deeper social engagement that were undoubtedly the product of their student experience and were nourished by the grassroots civic enthusiasm of the time. The works of that period most directly attributable to Beth Galí include the Parc del Migdia, which reclaimed the mountain of Montjuïc for the city and the Fossar de la Pedrera – a monument to the victims of the Spanish Civil War, presided over by the tomb of Companys, the president of Catalonia shot here on Franco's orders. Then there is Parc de l'Escorxador, featuring the Joan Miró Library, and a great many public spaces that slowly but surely have helped weave the new structure and image of the city.

Beth Galí now works independently with her own office. There is no doubt that her recent international successes in the fields of architecture and urban design are bound up closely with all these crucial earlier experiences. She is one of the most characteristic representatives of the eighties generation in Barcelona – a generation that also includes excellent architects like Enric Miralles, Carme Pinós, Moisés Gallego, Franc Fernández, Tonet Sunyer and Olga Tarrassó. Her achievements have enabled her to enter the debate concerning new ways of understanding urban control – the imposing of urbanity onto the *urbs*.

For that reason, the series of episodes I have summarised here strikes me as highly important to the course of Beth Galí's professional and cultural itinerary – a crucial thread in that fabric to which I referred at the outset. It is a fabric against which the reader can lay out and fit together the whole body and pattern of her work.

Oriol Bohigas

A touch of the South in a Northern City
Un toque del sur en una ciudad del norte

A casual stroller entering Kerkstraat from the Markt might not notice anything unusual. The street might seem a bit cleaner than before, a bit tidier. Perhaps the shopkeepers have agreed to cut back on their pavement displays. But by the time our pedestrian reaches Kerkplein, a hundred metres further on, something is beginning to dawn. The Dutch Reformed Church, which used to be tucked away on a square hardly worth the name, somehow appears to have moved forward. A low, unobtrusive staircase, halfway between a raised pavement and a platform, adds a touch of class to the church. It has suddenly become eye-catching, having once been passed by without a second glance.

Let's go a little further. What's this? A few signs in 's-Hertogenbosch have been moved. Not much, but it's enough. The cycle-rack in front of the post office – did you ever see such a gleaming specimen anywhere in the Netherlands? Not the usual dull rack in which one lot of scrap metal meets another. These are stainless steel, and if we turn around, we can take in the entire scene: the racks, the granite paving slabs and the lighting on Kerkplein – lampposts upgraded into searchlights, which cast a filtered light onto the ground while brightly illuminating the church. An object lesson in how to turn a public interior into a domestic one.

Was it necessary, this grand clean-up of Noord-Brabant's provincial capital? The Municipal Planning Department believed it was. The city centre was felt to be stifling, its public space long neglected. The symbols of this neglect are the same everywhere in the Netherlands – a forest of traffic signs, bollards to stop parking, boards advertising local traders, bottle-banks and litter bins. The municipal council also contributed by installing advertising hoardings, which are an attractive source of revenue. Ad-hoc solutions were found for

Un paseante que anduviera casualmente por la Kerkstraat desde el Markt podría no notar nada extraño. La calle podría parecer algo más limpia que antes, más aseada. Tal vez los tenderos hayan decidido retirar un poco sus anuncios pero cuando nuestro peatón llegue a Kerkplein, cien metros más allá, algo empieza a nacer. La iglesia Reformista Holandesa, que se encogía en el rincón de una plaza que apenas merecía ese nombre, parece como si se hubiera desplazado hacia adelante. Una escalera libre, suave, a medio camino entre un pavimento levantado y una plataforma, le da a la iglesia un toque de distinción. De pronto se hace vistosa cuando antes pasaba desapercibida.

Avancemos un poco más. Algunas señales de 's-Hertogenbosch han sido desplazadas. No mucho, pero sí lo suficiente. El aparcamiento de bicicletas frente a correos ¿se había visto nunca algo tan reluciente en Holanda? Esto no es un viejo hierro retorcido, es acero inoxidable y si nos volvemos, captamos la escena entera: los parkbikes, las losas de granito del pavimento y la iluminación de Kerplein - postes de luz ascendidos a iluminarias que arrojan una luz filtrada hacia el suelo mientras dan brillo a la iglesia. Una lección de cómo convertir lo público en doméstico.

¿Era necesaria esta gran limpieza de la capital de Nord-Brabant? El departamento de proyectos urbanos creyó que sí. El centro de la ciudad resultaba bochornoso, sus espacios públicos largo tiempo descuidados. Los símbolos de este descuido son los mismos en toda Holanda - un bosque de señales de tráfico, postes para impedir el aparcamiento, carteles con anuncios de los comerciantes, cubos de basura y de reciclaje de vidrio. El consejo municipal contribuía instalando paneles de anuncios, una atractiva fuente de ingresos. Soluciones ad. hoc se iban improvisaban para cada nuevo

each new problem, resulting in the gradual fragmentation of 's-Hertogenbosch's centre.

Bakker and Bleeker, a firm of landscape architects from Amsterdam, were called in to analyse the situation,. The first thing that needed to be done, they concluded in their 1993 report, was to draw up a traffic and transport policy. The only way to save the city centre was to strictly reduce the weight of traffic. The inner city was being crushed by its own popularity. Day-trippers, people from the suburbs, and café and restaurant-goers all descend on the Markt and the Parade, half of them from out of town, and a quarter of these from outside the region. An expression – the 'geranium market effect' – has been coined to describe this undesirable congestion. When, once a month, the Sunday market sells geraniums for the special price of NLG 7.50 for three, the public turns up en masse, ignoring an even cheaper offer on Friday and Saturday. People like to have something to do on a Sunday, preferably in an attractive and historic town centre.

The municipality declared war on dilapidation with the triple battle-cry of 'safe, clean and attractive'. In that order. What's more, town planning and market research revealed that the city centre could use more shopping space. More specifically, an extra 8,000-9,000 square metres were needed in the Tolberg district, conditional on the boosting of existing space. Tolberg, with its uninspiring 1960s architecture, was ripe for transformation. It was a forgotten and poorly exploited section of 's-Hertogenbosch's triangular city centre, which is odd considering its strategic location next to the Markt.

's-Hertogenbosch was not the first city to tinker with its centre. Eindhoven had already brought in the German architect Walter Bruhl, Groningen had banned traffic from its old centre and even in the Brabant countryside, villages have been using their public space to raise their profile. The explanation for this is fairly pragmatic – with municipal reorganisa-

tion on the horizon, each municipality is keen to use up its reserves and 'street furniture and lighting' is the perfect cost item.

Even without this impulse, however, the refurbishment of public space has become a hot item. There wasn't a municipality in the country that failed to send its representatives on a pilgrimage to Barcelona. In 's-Hertogenbosch's case, the journey to Catalonia was not a direct one. A delegation of councillors, contractors and town planners first visited cities like Luxembourg, Eindhoven, Maastricht and Cologne in search of precise ideas of how Bakker and Bleeker's report could be put into practice. Luxembourg was rated very highly, but the final result was considered too sterile, with a granite carpet running through the city that you could eat your dinner off. Nevertheless, the group came away from Luxembourg convinced that effective refurbishment stands or falls by the quality of the finish.

Bakker and Bleeker's masterplan serviced as the blueprint for the refurbishment. Three parties were to compete for the commission: Bakker and Bleeker, the architect Borek Sípek and, following a visit to Barcelona, the Spanish landscape architect Beth Galí. The council's decision to drop Bakker and Bleeker was logical. Their ideas were familiar and it was time for something new – someone who could add a dash of the unexpected. Sípek, who had earned his spurs as architect of the castle in Prague, came up with an intriguing new philosophy, suggesting during a day-long session that the city be refurbished step by step – a conquest that would advance from street to square.

This approach was very appealing. Meanwhile, the Municipal Planning Department had put forward another name, following some reconnaissance work

17 A touch of the South in a Northern City

abroad. Beth Galí was a surprising choice. Barely 40 years old at the time, she had not realised that many projects. The large Parc Joan Miró, in collaboration with Marius Quintana and Antonio Solans, the Fossar de la Pedrera cemetery, the Parc del Migdia on the hill of Montjuïc and one building, the library in Parc Joan Miró – all in Barcelona. The planners couldn't quite remember who had first come up with the name Galí, the project developer or the civil servants.

There was no doubt, however, as to why she had been picked out. Galí had demonstrated her ability to deliver modest and high-quality work with a contemporary touch in a historic environment. Above all, it was her simple, almost obvious interventions in Barcelona's little squares that convinced the delegation. This is not an architect of the grand gesture or extreme views, but one with a chameleon's ability to find the right appearance for any environment. What's more, if 's-Hertogenbosch was looking for touch of the Mediterranean, what better than to import a little bit of Catalonia?

Galí was initially surprised at being approached. If ever there was a country that had recognised the importance of public space at an early stage, surely it was the Netherlands? During her studies, the Lijnbaan in Rotterdam had been held out as the ideal model of a promenade, destined to be imitated by other cities for decades. Moreover, landscape architecture was a separate discipline in the Netherlands, whereas it is only a sideline for the Spanish. Trainee architects in Spain study architecture and link it effortlessly to industrial design, public space and theory. Architects have to be at home in all markets and it is not unusual for them to produce a chair one minute and a building the next. Nevertheless, she knew what was lacking in the Netherlands. Too little has been invested in durable materials. Parks and squares have not been treated as autonomous assignments but as part of general town planning.

She knew the Netherlands in another way, too. Shortly after the war, her parents fled into exile in Hilversum, before moving on to London a few years later. She returned during the Provo era of the late 1960s, drawn by the magic of Amsterdam, hitchhiking to the Dam, like so many other young people. It was a particular paradise for those who came from a totalitarian society. Even now, she cherishes the memory of Amsterdam as an enchanting city with a unique centre.

's-Hertogenbosch is different from both Amsterdam and Barcelona. It is a small, pleasant city with a historic centre in which large-scale transformations might be inappropriate. Such injections might have been necessary in Barcelona to restore the city to life, but in 's-Hertogenbosch? A more discrete approach was needed. 'As if someone went round one night with a magic wand to make a few small adjustments?' Something like that.

'Can I really improve things,' she thought when she first came to the city and experienced its light. Obtrusive design was the last thing 's-Hertogenbosch needed. The priority instead was the structuring of space. Fortunately, she was preceded by Bakker and Bleeker's masterplan, which prescribed a major clean-up. This extended not only to fairly obvious areas like street furniture and lighting, but to advice on refuse collection, the nuisance caused by drug addicts and the rerouting of traffic. By the time Beth Galí arrived, the ground had been well and truly prepared.

The nature of the assignment and the decision-making process suited her down to the ground. The 'less is more' principle in architecture is not just a cliché as far as Galí is concerned – her work focuses on the issue of space. She begins each project by removing ballast, frills and superfluous detail. And she approaches the client's wishes in a similar way. What's left forms the nucleus of the design, which has to be tested and explored over and over again. Nothing can be left to chance. Her purified landscape architecture is a response to what she encounters outside – public spaces that have been left to themselves and have discovered their own expression.

Her approach is certainly impressive, but it is more than that. 's-Hertogenbosch wanted someone who could introduce a different culture. Barcelona may be a place of fashionable pilgrimage, but few Spanish architects had worked in the Netherlands. Joan Busquets had been active in Haarlem and The Hague, while Oriol Bohigas once acted as consultant to the municipality of Rotterdam. That was pretty much it. Galí's assignment was initially limited to two streets – very different in character – which were to serve as the starting point for 's-Hertogenbosch's facelift. She was also expected to work closely with the city's management and maintenance services. At the end of the day, you can lay all the expensive tiles you want, but if they are immediately snowed under with chip-packets, the effect is destroyed.

The two streets were Kerkstraat and Karrenstraat. The first, a refined connecting road between the Markt and the Parade, and the second the Cinderella of the town centre. If you want to persuade the public of the effectiveness of your plans, you don't just have to arrange the shop-windows beautifully but the toilets, too. The same approach was applied to both streets and, ultimately, for the whole city centre. Ironically, the centre of gravity is underground. After all, there's no point in replacing the carpet if the floor beneath is in poor condition. A layer of granulate, 20 cm deep, was laid, followed by a 5 cm layer of sand. The paving was laid on top of this and jointed with more sand.

Just as we run pipes beneath or along the skirting board in our living rooms, the drains, piping and electrical cables here were placed to the side, to show off the central section with its one-piece granite slabs to best effect. The special

Before / After

underground support was needed to prevent the Norman slabs from cracking. The council realised that the refurbishment was luxurious – more so than many people are used to in their own homes. And that entails certain duties, beginning with consistent cleaning and decent management.

Galí was well aware that 's-Hertogenbosch is not Barcelona. The squares in the Catalan city were designed for people who had thrown off the yoke of tyranny after half a century, and were now finally able to talk freely. Public space there is an expression of democratic feeling, of people drinking in and celebrating their liberty. Such feelings could not be transferred to a provincial capital, however distinguished. But in spite of the marked political and climatic differences, she found that public space in the Netherlands still has meaning. Nowhere in the world had she seen so many people on the street, strolling past the shops and hankering after a pavement café. That was the difference compared to Barcelona – Dutch people are always on the move.

Anything too provocative would clearly be out of place in 's-Hertogenbosch. If public space is anything, it is a human theatre. It is the people who lend it colour, aided in this instance by the pink granite. Take Kerkplein. What precisely is it, when all said and done? In Bakker and Bleeker's report, it was described as a 'confetti square' – a charming name for a secondary space – whereas the Parade, Markt and Stationsplein determine the character of the city. They are its calling card. And yet she had never come across a square like Kerkplein in Barcelona. A closed space with its simple Dutch Reformed Church, where weddings are sometimes held, where people of the Reformed faith attend Sunday ser-

Before / After

vice and which has a further function as a cultural centre.

She pulled out her magic wand and injected a sense of direction into that triangle. You no longer walk past the church without noticing it. The streetlights and the pattern of the granite floor now emphasise the axis on which the church stands in relation to the square. That in itself makes a big difference. A low staircase highlights the entrance to the church – an architectural addition that strengthens the space. Galí uses the word 'shelter', which ought probably to be understood in two ways: as a wall delineating space and a form of protection. An intimate feeling underscored by atmosphere and materials. 'I wanted to use the church as a façade and the steps as a genuine staircase – the kind newly-weds can have their photographs taken on.' The lampposts, a contemporary mixture of spotlights and mood lighting, added the finishing touch to the fairy tale.

What little criticism there was of the project was fairly easy to answer. Yes, it was an expensive operation (NLG 26 million), but it cost less than had been spent on Breda town centre, which is also paved with granite. Some felt it was out of character, but what is the typical character of 's-Hertogenbosch? The junk that used to litter the streets? Nor are the elements of the design obtrusively modern. Take the lights suspended over Kerkstraat. You could swear they'd been there for the past half century.

Galí's trial zone caught on. The police showed an intense interest in the new lighting in Karrenstraat, recognising the importance of good lighting for security. There are no parked cars to hide behind and the view remains clear at all times. The conquest of the city centre rolled on into Vughterstraat,

Hinthamerstraat and Hoge Steenweg, with lampposts lighting up a monument here and a crossroads there with an intensity matching the brightness of the refurbishment. There is certainly room for much bolder lighting, as the civil servants noted during their reconnaissance abroad. Paris lights up its squares brilliantly, giving you the feeling of walking on stage. In the Netherlands, by contrast, and 's-Hertogenbosch is no exception, city squares at night are like black holes that scare you away rather than drawing you to them.

Some elements of the assignment were new to Galí. She had never designed a cycle-rack, for instance, and what she saw didn't exactly encourage her. They accumulate dirt, are usually broken and are generally horrible artefacts. When there are no cycles propped up against them, they are one of the strangest and ugliest obstacles in the street scene. For that reason, she wanted to design something that would be an attractive object even when empty – something beautiful in itself. City Hall officials cautiously made the point that cycle-racks also had protect against theft, which Galí achieved using a thick pole to which bikes can be chained. So how did it work out in practice? The new rack in front of the post office was filled with bikes within half an hour – it clearly inspired confidence.

The city centre operation grew out of discussions at City Hall and the drawing up of a wish list. Galí didn't necessarily have to design everything herself. It was sufficient for her to create a 'school' – a 'how-to' guide for public space for the benefit of other designers and technical staff. Proof that such an approach can work was provided when Stationsweg and Stationsplein were redesigned in a similar spirit by the Khandekar and Van Aalderen firms, which followed the Catalan architect's system, keeping clutter in the street to a minimum.

It was the context that got Galí thinking. The couleur

locale. Whereas in Catalonia she would opt for materials like marble or travertine, the logical choice in 's-Hertogenbosch was brick. The Stoa, the elongated building she designed in the Tolberg district, also had to be unobtrusive, its form kinked halfway along. It is actually only the roof that grabs the eye – a serrated edge of pointed roofs that seem to float above the building, as if a red carpet had been installed between the Markt and Tusquets' Arena.

It was an awkward spot, as she had discovered during her visits – an unprepossessing transition between the historic Markt and the suburbs. Yet it had to house a prestigious shopping gallery. Whereas most of the streets in the town centre form part of a web, enabling pedestrians to wander from one passage to another until they reach the end of the shops, Loeffplein is a dead-end. Shoppers have to turn around, assuming they have bothered to explore this direction in the first place. It would take some pretty expressive architecture to transform this square.

The construction of the Stoa allowed Galí to do what she likes best – actual building. Landscape architecture can be too much like styling at times, one-dimensional. 'Building takes you to the core of architecture... Now I'm getting a bit older, I would prefer to design public buildings – libraries and museums. More so than private homes. Public buildings are really an extension of the street.'

No matter how different they may be, 's-Hertogenbosch and Barcelona share the fact that they have initiated a process in the improvement of their public space. The demolition of high-rise apartment blocks and the creation of squares in Barcelona were like throwing open the windows of a smoky room. The air suddenly cleared. A new spirit entered the city, prompting other initiatives. The atmosphere changed from stifling and conservative to open and dynamic. The increase over the past ten years in the number of hotels alone speaks volumes about the faith that now exists in the potential of the city. Foreign delegations came to sample this atmosphere, each picking up the baton in its own specific way. Barcelona was to become a training ground.

The process seems to be going the same way in 's-Hertogenbosch, both internally and externally. This can have its downside, like when other cities shamelessly copy its cycle-rack design, but in most cases the developments are more unexpected – such as the shopkeepers who, inspired by the refurbished street, have responded by upgrading their own businesses. Traders in Vughterstraat, for instance, took advantage of the restyling process to give their neighbourhood a facelift. In so doing, they fulfilled the original intention of improving the whole city by means of a few essential interventions – prods that have been felt in every corner of the 's-Hertogenbosch triangle.

In the meantime, the city has begun to draw delegations from other municipalities, just as Barcelona was a favourite destination ten years ago. Visitors are shown the impact of simple but effective changes like those on Kerkplein and Hinthamerstraat. And even in urban renewal zones well away from the centre, squares have been dug up and liberated from the railway-sleeper culture of the 1970s. Here too, the clear conception Galí developed for 's-Hertogenbosch has been taken to heart.

This just leaves the Markt and the Parade. For the time being, the primary roles of the two squares remain plain – the Markt as a genuine marketplace and the Parade as the ideal location for the 'Boulevard' festival and other cultural events. Although it has not yet been decided how they are to be paved and lit, the overall scheme is sure to be clear and simple.

Jaap Huisman

Beth Galí and the Miracle of Barcelona

The 'rediscovery of the city' happened at an identifiable time and place – Barcelona, 1980. It also had an identifiable guru in the shape of Oriol Bohigas, the head of town planning. Bear in mind that this was only ten years after the death of General Franco. A country that had rejected every cultural innovation for half a century, that had closed its borders and subjugated or exiled its creative talent suddenly emerged as a source of inspiration. It was as if the sun had suddenly been let into places that had remained in shadow for all those years.

Spain quickly set about making up for lost time on all fronts. It wanted to place itself on an equal footing with the rest of western Europe, obliging it to put right what had gone wrong – and that was a lot. The total neglect of Spain's inner cities – especially Barcelona's – was a particular problem. Barcelona's fate wasn't particularly surprising. Madrid had done its best to belittle the city in order to undermine Catalonia's nationalist aspirations.

A new mayor was appointed in Barcelona in around 1980. He wasted no time in sacking the entire planning department and appointing a new team headed by Oriol Bohigas from the architect's firm MBM. Bohigas can fairly be said to have made history. His ideas were to benefit not only Barcelona, but other European cities as well, including 's-Hertogenbosch.

Barcelona's story echoes that of every modern European city with one foot in a monumental past and the other hobbled by congested roads, demographic change and geographical location. Barcelona is squeezed between the hill of Montjuïc, Mount Tibidabo and the sea, leaving it with no room to expand. It also had a severe maintenance backlog in several fields. Little had been done in the Catalan capital in terms of planning and development since the 1929 World

Exhibition. The building of social housing, a key instrument for ensuring the continued vitality of a town, had been put on the back burner. As a result – and this is again not limited to Barcelona – urban-dwellers had been turning their backs on the city, having lost faith in its viability.

Bohigas didn't attempt to reinvent the wheel. Nor did he begin with a clean slate. A masterplan had been drawn up in 1976, a remnant of the Franco era. The plan contained a number of weaknesses, but it nevertheless set forth the philosophy that was to be pursued for Barcelona's refurbishment. Several 'quality zones' had been selected, from which the renovation of the city would be tackled. More important, perhaps, was the allocation of social housing and public facilities to certain districts of the city. What the plan lacked was any kind of coherence between urban planning and the design of the urban fabric. It simply failed to consider the design of public space.

Plans were all very well, but Bohigas wanted action. He came up with a slogan: 'not plans but projects'. He abandoned the model of integrated urban planning, which he viewed as too large in scale and metropolitan, and decided instead to divide the city up into sections, which were carefully mapped. The second decision he took was to pursue renewal in the existing city. The housing shortage was most acute in the old town, and the quality of accommodation left much to be desired. The idea was to make the city more liveable by building homes or creating parks on disused industrial sites and by moving or closing off streets. If these projects were to succeed, they had to meet the needs of local people – in other words, their social relevance was crucial. All too often in the past, town planners had come up with ideas that went straight over their citizens' heads.

Bohigas realised that the city was hopelessly split between two poles – a crowded inner city and suburbs that were too sprawling. What was the point, he asked, of placing cultural centres, say, in outlying districts that lacked any kind of city life? Greater unity could be achieved by giving those districts a more urban character and simultaneously creating more space in the inner city.

The key to Barcelona's revitalisation was a dual one: public space and public buildings. This represented a break with the history of the Modern movement in architecture, which had always emphasised the role of social housing as one of the engines that would drive society towards an eventual, supposed utopia. History had demonstrated, however, that this strategy had utterly failed to produce the desired result. Take the high-rise apartment blocks built in the greenbelt – the banlieue of Paris or Amsterdam's Bijlermeer. Their internal quality might be good, but they lack communication with their surroundings. They are neither town nor countryside.

Bohigas opened up the city by applying the philosophy that historical towns can only be preserved by strengthening them and stressing their identity. And that could only be achieved by eliminating weaknesses and emphasising strengths. One of Barcelona's weaknesses, for instance, was the way its traffic was managed. In the 1960s, the city had been heartlessly sliced up by urban motorways that have ruined the picturesque Barri Gòtic. It strongly resembles 's-Hertogenbosch in this respect. Here too, it was congestion in the inner city – located off-centre in relation to the suburbs, like its counterpart in Barcelona – which prompted the recovery operation. It was necessary in both cities to get planners and operational staff to pull together. At the end of the day, you can come up with all the utopian ideas you want – if they are not properly implemented, they will always remain a distant dream.

Bohigas gathered a group of young students – talented people who had never been given the opportunity to prove themselves during the Franco era. It felt like Spain was waking from hibernation and that mountains suddenly had to be moved. The days of paper projects and architectural competitions that would never be put into practice were over. One of the young talents that Bohigas plucked from the Academy of Architecture was Elisabeth Galí i Camprubi, or Beth Galí for short. Born in 1950 and every inch a Catalan.

Galí recalls how the new dynamism was exploited. 'We formed a team at the city hall. That in itself was unprecedented, as the building had never been used in such a way before. Bohigas brought together a team of 14 architects and organised workshops in which we had to come up with plans. What could we do on a neighbourhood by neighbourhood basis? What investments, what improvements? Because Barcelona was bursting at the seams.' The team worked like people possessed. There was an explosion of creativity. The architects split the city into ten districts and set to work in pairs – one to each sector. In each district, they identified ten strategic locations for which new designs were to be drawn up. They included parks, chains of small squares, avenues and churchyards.

Barcelona was taken in hand in a remarkably short period. Nor was the activity limited to the old town on either side of the Ramblas, the central axis linking the Plaça de Catalunya with the harbour. Housing blocks were demolished all over the city to create space for small parks and squares. Traffic circulation was tackled and, last but not least, patches of land and former industrial sites were reclaimed.

'We became convinced during the workshops,' Beth Galí says, 'that an immense amount could be achieved even through small interventions.' Things like squares that improve the quality of life in a particular neighbourhood and which would spread like a chain reaction into the surrounding districts.

The award to Barcelona of the Olympic Games really put the wind into the Bohigas team's sails. Suddenly, there were a thousand things to do, a deadline and a pressing need. All these were heightened by the decision of the civic authorities that the Games were to be held inside the city proper rather than outside it. This meant, for instance, that a solution had to be found for the traffic problem in a city whose motor vehicles had become hopelessly tangled up in a grid pattern of housing blocks, conceived in the nineteenth century by the planner Cerda.

Wide boulevards were laid out as elongated strips of greenery, the city centre was girdled by two ring roads – Cinturión 1 and 2 – and, even more essential perhaps, Barcelona was given a structure that was clear in its hierarchy and focused attention on both the periphery and the city centre. The layout of the public space formed a crucial link in the revitalisation of the city. Not only did the municipal planning department establish a high standard, it also pursued a certain homogeneity, to ensure that squares, promenades, public gardens and playgrounds would form a recognisable and coherent chain running through the city. They were no longer to be treated as an afterthought, but as the vehicle for all other investment.

Barcelona was in a whirl. Construction work wasn't so much large in scale as spread all over town. A total of 160 projects were carried out between 1980 and 1992, ranging from cemeteries to avenues, courtyards to quaysides. Dilapidated urban spaces were transformed into lively public stages. The huge square in front of Sants station, for instance, was given a pavilion for people to shelter from the sun, complete with a long, undulating bench, and paving that subtly distinguished between pedestrians, strollers and rail passengers in a hurry. It is a fine example of how a shapeless expanse can be given a clear and attractive appearance.

Bohigas set his apprentices to work on a dizzying number of new projects. The young Beth Galí was given the assignment, together with Marius Quintana and Antoni Solans, of designing the Parc de L'Escorxador on the site of a former abattoir, not far from the strategically located Plaça d'Espanya – the eastern gateway to the inner city.

Galí combined a square with an L-shaped park – hard elements with soft ones. The hard parts are the courts for basketball and boules players, with the soft area made up of the more enclosed green space of the park, which is also located a little further away from the road. It is something of an unapproachable space at first sight, because of the empty stone area. This is reserved from time to time for special events and so tends to be empty more often than full. On closer inspection, however, we begin to discern the park's different layers.

Five years ago, the name of the park was changed to Parc Joan Miró and a building – a library – was added as the design's finishing touch. It forms a thick, full wall that separates the park from the chaotic city. The library protects the park's back – something it needed. The building functions, in other words, as a filter.

Galí remembers this first project as a long process. The location was not an easy one and the budget was minimal. The money for the library was initially lacking. And when it was finally made available, the designers were confronted by an unexpected assault by local youngsters. She had never seen a wall so plastered with graffiti as that of her library. Vandalism, she confesses, is one of the most serious threats to attractively laid out public spaces. It has the capacity to demolish all good intentions.

Parc Joan Miró, with the artist's towering Woman and Bird sculpture as a beacon, has a meaning. It symbolises Barcelona's resurrection. It was the first park to be created after the restoration of democracy and was intended to give citizens the sense of being able to speak freely. The street had hitherto been a dangerous place. Your conversations could be overhead and you ran the risk of being arrested for illegal assembly. Citizens were never free. This park, with its different levels at which each activity has been provided with its own section and where young and old can exist alongside one another was designed to tempt Barcelona back out of doors.

Although completed a mere ten years ago, there are old people here smoking cigars on a bench next to the kiosk, while the youngsters practise skateboard moves up and down the steps. Gardeners have found their eldorado in the formally laid-out flowerbeds, pergolas and rows of box trees. People come here to play football and to stroll. It also had an unexpected effect. The special gate that Galí designed to separate the park and library, in the middle of a bridge, turned out not be watertight. Children squeeze or climb around the black metal child figures and make off with their library books.

The workshops bore fruit, plans became projects and Galí had to recruit personnel to staff her office, because she now received a new assignment – Parc del Migdia on Montjuïc, where much of the Olympic Games were to be held in twin stadiums. She was assistant manager at the time of the IMPU, the Institute for Urban Planning and Olympic Construction. The delegation from 's-Hertogenbosch was particularly taken by the multifunctional character of Parc del Migdia. It could service as a model in this respect for the refurbishment of the Parade, which also has a chameleon-like potential – one moment a space that invites us to meditate on its historic appearance, the next the stage for the 'Boulevard' festival. Del Migdia unites these two elements, the peace of nature on the slopes of Montjuïc and the spectacle of the theatre performances staged there, when the steps are transformed into seating.

As elsewhere in her work, Galí has both taken advantage of the location and given it an added impulse. This particular site is extremely uneven. It is a once forgotten corner of the city that has been made accessible again by a few interventions. It links the Olympic site – otherwise a dead zone on the western slopes of Montjuïc – with a residential area on the southern flank, transforming the area into a dynamic park. A long, undulating rambla (parade) leads past an old quarry that has been converted into a theatre for open-air performances. A pointed observation post, recalling the sharp bow of a ship, seems to burst out of the rock. From this vantage point, visitors can view the Olympic arena, Barcelona's old fortress and the harbour in the distance. The materials she used seem to have flowed from the spot itself. Strips of granite and concrete are like tamed chunks of rock. The groundplan betrays Galí's need for order and mathematical structure. The basis of her design is formed by a taut grid of radial lines and planes, as if she wanted to counterbalance the amorphous mountain.

From Parc del Migdia, you can see the Fossar de la Pedrera – another of Galí's designs, and the one she considers to be the clearest expression of her vision. She feels Catalan through and through and says that her region's rational culture gives her a greater affinity with the Netherlands than with centralist Madrid. In the Fossar, she says, she was able to achieve her ideal – to create a place of memorial for the Catalans. The site includes the tomb of Lluís Companys, the Catalan president who was executed during the Spanish Civil War on Franco's orders. 'When I first went there, it looked terrible. It was miles from anywhere and looked more like a rubbish tip, covered with weeds. It seemed like a forgotten place. You had the sense that it was a location no one wanted to have. I wanted to hold on to that initial impression, because it can be dangerous to change a place too fundamentally. If you intervene too much, you wipe out its history.' The great shortcoming of architects, she believes, is that they often march through cities with their seven-league boots, flattening tradition with their heavy, powerful buildings.

The mayor of Barcelona was very keen for the Fossar to be carefully refurbished, as he expected it to become a place of pilgrimage. And so it proved. Every Sunday, the car park is full as visitors flock to the cemetery in search of both their past and a little recreation. When laying out the site, Galí's mind turned to the military cemeteries found all over the world, with their horizontal tombstones in a sea of green. That's what she wanted, too — the same anonymous stones on a bed of greenery – so that visitors could walk through the graves, if they wanted to. Grass, she realised, is a precious commodity in Spain and one that is difficult to maintain. But maintain it they must, she believed, to make up for the inhospitable character originally radiated by the site.

As you enter the park, you are obliged to tread carefully. The blocks of stone on the slope focus the visitor's attention on the material itself and on the symbolism of the site. As she did at Parc Joan Miró, Galí has taken a location and unravelled it into a sequence of images and atmospheres, giving visitors the sense that they are walking from one scene to another. Parks as films. As you complete your ascent, the field of grass opens up, with its leaning or fallen tombstones. A little further on, the grass stops and there is a stretch of fine gravel, where a long wall with an awning provides some protection against the fierce sun. Behind this lies Companys' monument in the middle of an elongated basin, playfully surrounded by water plants and accessible via a wooden platform. Its sober and effective character has a Japanese air.

The same sequencing principle turns up again in Kerkstraat in 's-Hertogenbosch, although its perception is less strong because of the competing urban images of shop-windows, advertisements and illuminated signs. The change of scene in this case is indicated by the granite slabs that curve with the line of the street. As night falls, they are assisted by the streetlights, which draw corners and walls out of the darkness. The clinkers add unity to the whole, but more than that, they accentuate the turns of the corners. In this way, Galí shows how you can never take in the entire space at a single glance. Public spaces are more attractive when they only reveal themselves bit by bit. As you enter Kerkplein, you suddenly notice a new element in the composition – the surfaces of the steel tree-grilles that 'imprison' the old beech and the lampposts with their square plate screens that filter the light onto the pavement below.

This subtle change of image is expressed in Parc Joan Miró through the different levels and types of plant, while in the Fossar de la Pedrera it is achieved by the use of walls, central European and Mediterranean trees. In Kerkstraat it is done with the historical genius loci. However different each may be, they share the fact that they have been executed with the utmost precision, in the knowledge that only in this way can Galí's message of 'less is more' be done full justice.

The architect she actually wishes to be is expressed in her love of the wall. The bare wall of the Dutch Reformed Church on Kerkplein grows in its nakedness precisely because of the contrast with the granite steps and the low, stainless steel railing. The wall was already there but she has made it stronger. In Parc Joan Miró, the wall of the library – built in a flaming Andalusian travertine – functions as a screen, protecting the park from the noise of the city, while simultaneously shaping the space. For she realises that public space slips through your fingers if it is not delimited.

The library enabled her to make a statement – or, if one prefers, to be provocative. This was made possible, however, by the fact that the surroundings were so unapproachable. Generally speaking she prefers reticence, an approach that prompts the question of whether she can actually be called a proponent of a style and whether she is more of a follower than a trend-setter. She hates to be pigeonholed. 'When you're designing something, you don't have a particular style in mind. Style only comes when the work is complete. It is time that decides the style of a particular building, not architects. To my mind, that was the mistake of postmodernism – the notion on the part of architects that they could invent a style. That to me is the end of a process –something that can take years!'

She views her commission to redesign 's-Hertogenbosch city centre as both a highlight and the beginning of a new stage in her career. The period of experimentation, she believes, is now over. This is not the first time that Galí has embarked on a new chapter in her life. Her curriculum vitae reveals that she started out at the age of four as a musician, eventually becoming a concert pianist. Her musical career lasted until she was 31, when she enrolled at the Academy of Architecture. She played Bach, Schubert and, of course, Spanish composers like Albéniz and Granados. She still has a grand piano in her office for when she needs play Schubert – her current favourite – to unwind for a while. She doesn't think about architecture at those moments, as that would distract her from her music. What music has in common with architecture, she says, is that it is a precise science – rational, technical and structured. And what about lyricism? 'Yes, that too, of course. I'm constantly pursuing the line that links symbolism in music and that in architecture.'

Jaap Huisman

Beth Galí at the piano

Works and Projects
1966-1998

Year	Title	Page
1966	Textiles	40
1966	Jewellry	41
1966	Connectable furniture modules	42
1969	Portable shower	43
1969	Hi-fi amplifier AT 229	44
1971	Aladino; articulated book case	45
1976-80	Four houses in Selva de Mar	52
1982-89	Joan Miró Park	54
1984-90	Joan Miró Library	58
1984	Lamparaalta	62
1982-89	Casa Cases	64
1984-86	Fossar de la Pedrera	68
1985	Reyes house	72
1985	Bernad house	74
1987	EINA, 20 anys d'avantguarda	76
1987-90	Barcelona Film Festival	78
	"Hollywood-Hollywood"	78
	"La vie en rose"	80
	"L'occhio del diavolo"	81
	"Llum de lluna"	82
	"Atrapados"	82
	"Ritmo loco"	83
1987	Bercy Park	84
1988	Discotheque in Poble Espanyol	86
1989-91	Park at the southern end of Rovira tunnel	88
1990	Antwerpen - stad aan de stroom	90
1990-92	Jover - Sala house	92
1988-92	Migdia Park and Sot del Migdia	96
1991-92	Façade and new access to the South-West cemetery	102
1991-92	New accesses to the mountain of Montjuïc	104
1992	Habitaciones misteriosas; headquarters of a saving bank	106
1992	Spreebogen in Berlin	110
1995	Una nube sobre Berlin, two parcs at Potsdamer Platz	114
1994	Zafra Park	120
1994	Corberò a la Tecla Sala	128
1995	Monument	130
1994	Indumentària, women's clothes shop	132
1993-98	Remodelling of the historic centre of 's-Hertogenbosch	134
1994	Park bike	144
1993-98	Stoa building in 's-Hertogenbosch	146
1995-98	Remodelling of the historic centre of Roermond	154
1996	Veranda, urban spaces of Piet Smit plan in Rotterdam	156
1997	Pitmit outdoorlamp	160
1998	Neruda stool/Neruda bench	162
1998	Collserola; dwellings in Barcelona	164

Textiles

1966

My first fabric design commission came from a Barcelona firm, which asked me to create a new collection of bed linen. They wanted to launch patterned sheets onto the Spanish market – something that was then a complete novelty in this country. I asked myself why bed linen always had to be white, and I proposed a very simple type of pattern, but with the condition that it was only to be printed on black cotton. This was too daring for my clients, who rejected my designs. It then occurred to me that if they didn't want to make sheets, the next best thing would be headscarves. And few years later it became very fashionable to sleep between black sheets.

Monika Friden and Beth Galí by Antoni Bernad

Jewellery
1966

Beth Galí by Antoni Bernad

For a whole generation of young people, the second half of the sixties represented a period of reaction against everything connected with the establishment. These were the years of the Pop Art explosion. We embraced the phenomenon with enthusiasm as a direct and provocative international language that opted for an ironic yet positive approach to the contemporary world. I discovered the fascination of the Pop scene in the work of British artists like David Hockney, Allen Jones, R.B. Kitaj and Eduardo Paolozzi, and the Americans Jasper Johns, Robert Indiana, Robert Rauschenberg, Jim Dine, Roy Lichtenstein, Claes Oldenburg, D'Arcangelo, James Rosenquist and, it goes without saying, Andy Warhol, whom I was able to meet in person in 1969.

We questioned every aspect of our existence: why, for example, should women adorn themselves with gold and silver jewellery and false metallic imitations? I came up with a series of very inexpensive pieces of plastic jewellery which could be put together in endless different ways by the wearers themselves – transparent tubes, with strands of different coloured plastic inserted in them, which could be coiled around an arm or an ankle and stick-on bull's eyes on plastic discs to make earrings and bracelets. There were also sandals for going barefoot, with the protection – or obstacle – of the soles removed.

Connectable furniture modules
Manufactured by Tecmo G3

DELTA D'OR ADI-FAD AWARD 1966
1966

I am captivated by transparency in solid materials. This cubic module in Perspex offered the versatility we wanted to achieve in the organisation of the domestic environment and the new ways of living in it. The modules could be combined in a whole range of ways in the different spaces of the house. The elemental form of the module and the variability of its uses meant it could be used to store books, records or cassettes, to display objects in the living room, to keep odds and ends together in the kitchen or bathroom, and so on. Above all, however, it was a response to the almost imperative need to free the home from old habits and antiquated junk. More than a piece of furniture as such, it was a proposal, an attitude.

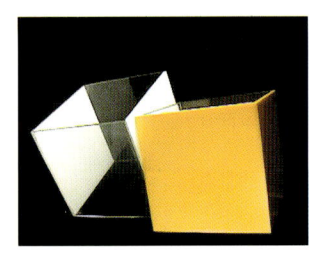

Portable shower

Manufactured by Raydor

DELTA D'OR ADI-FAD AWARD 1969 - WITH GEMA BERNAL AND RAMÓN ISERN

1969

This was a truly industrial design in that it was to be manufactured in a production run of thousands. I thought about how tricky it tends to be fit the shower handset onto its wall mounting – how difficult it is to put it in exactly the right place while you are actually showering, covered in soap, with your eyes closed.

I remember being surprised by the telephone shape of all existing handsets. Why should a shower look like a phone? After all, the only thing you need to be able to do is to direct the water onto every part of your body while holding the spray in one hand.

Our design set out to resolve these questions. The mounting system was significantly simplified by using a magnet – no great concentration would be needed to attach the magnetic spray to the steel plate attached to the wall. The shape was felt to be ideal for holding the handset in one hand and directing the jet of water at the desired area.

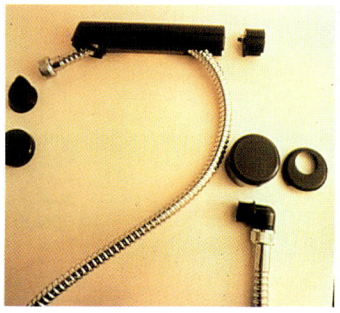

Hi-fi amplifier AT 229

Manufactured by Vieta Audioelectronica

Selecció ADI-FAD award 1969 - With Gema Bernal and Ramón Isern

1969

The sorry state to which Spanish industry had been reduced by the Franco dictatorship meant that everything had to be designed from scratch. The design of this hi-fi amplifier was an attempt to introduce a certain rationality into the finish of items of sound reproduction technology. We dispensed with almost all the unnecessary embellishments found so often on this kind of equipment, usually with the intention of creating a false image of technological ostentation.

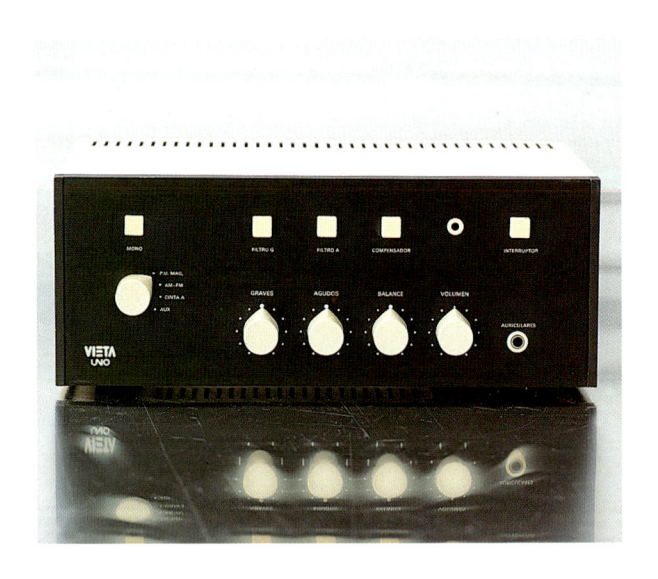

Aladino

Articulated book case - Manufactured by Tecmo G3

Selecció ADI-FAD award 1971

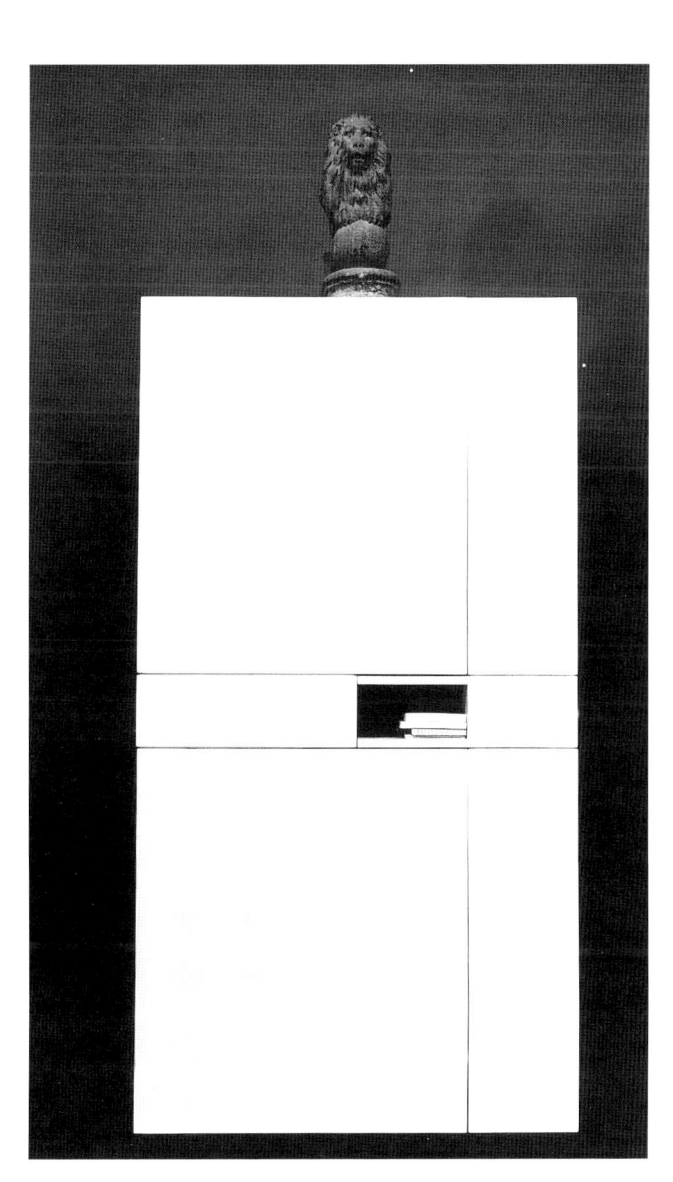

1971

This bookcase unit was designed to take account of the small surface area of most homes. In a flat of 90 m² – and often less – storage is frequently a problem. In response, I suggested this idea for a bookcase to the manufacturer for whom I was designing various pieces of furniture. It held a great number of books, and thanks to its rollers could be folded back on itself to occupy less space.

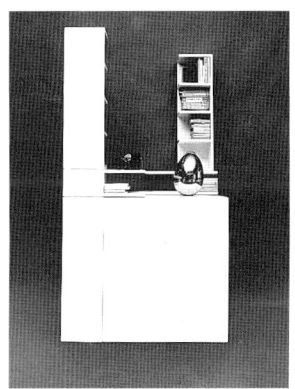

Architects and Painters

The bones support the body's flesh. Does that make them architecture? There is no doubt that without bones the body would be reduced to the condition of the slug, which instead of holding itself upright, slithers over the ground. It is true that what sustains things is architectural reason (even a poem has an architecture that bears it up), but that does not mean that the rationale of architecture is the structure that underpins it. Far from it. It is not the structure that underpins it, but art; and the fact is that if architecture is not art, then neither is it architecture. And it never will be art if it does not reinvent the human subject it sets out to serve.

All of us, architects and painters, make architecture. The boundary that separates the one from the other is simply that architects are governed by the discipline imposed by the law of gravity. If they were governed by the same laws as painters, their works would fall down rather than rise up in the air, because we painters follow the rule laid down for us by life, which is chance, and not the law of gravity. But let me insist on this – no-one is either an architect or a painter if they are not an artist, if they are not a poet, if they do not know how to transform a particular reality into cosmology.

And now three questions: what architecture do painters make use of? Which is the greater discipline, architecture or painting? And who is the pioneer, the architect or the painter?

We will let the paintings of Velázquez reply to the first question. His painting is held up not by the drawing, nor by the colour or the composition – the three pitfalls of painting, which, if the painter fails to transcend them, will prevent him from transforming it into art. Velázquez's painting is held up by the air he knew how to paint so well, an air that is the mirror of nothing, and of which he becomes the architect when

with Joan Miró and Joanet Artigas

he dresses us, reflecting us there, in emptiness.

Michelangelo Buonarroti will help us arrive at the second answer. What difference is there between his architecture and his painting? In my view, none at all. The distance that separates God's fingertip from Adam's on the ceiling of the Sistine Chapel – a distance it is impossible to span – not only holds in tension the titanic effort of his painting, it is the same distance that strives to liberate the Vatican dome from its own weight. A single obsession runs through Michelangelo's painting, his sculpture and his architecture: the urge that drives us to be what we can never be – an impossible aspiration, but one that causes us to be what we are. If in the 'Pietà' the light slides off the marble, polished to exhaustion, it is because the artist wanted the light to flow down like the water of a spring, to wipe away the form in which the sculptor imprisoned the figure. But can the water escape from the transparent prison that configures it?

In the dome that crowns the Vatican basilica, Michelangelo the architect throws himself into pure abstraction in order to liberate himself from the slavery of the form, and in this way convert it into light; in other words, into illusion. And it is illusion because all of the light is projected in negative, in the shadow that envelops us.

That leaves us with the question of who is the pioneer, the architect or the painter? It will be answered by a painter and by an architect: Piero della Francesca and Gaudí. Because in this race, from one end of history to the other, architects and painters have handed on the baton to one another without rancour.

With his painting Piero della Francesca surpasses Bramante, the architect of San Pietro in Montorio, the great round church in Rome and an indispensable landmark of the Renaissance. He does so, furthermore, without tracing a single curve in his painting. The invisible line of his pictures is the circumference, which draws the whole, at the same time as it christianises the concept of the eternal return that presided over the world of classical antiquity. Everything in his painting is circular: the sky is inside the earth thanks to the streams of water left by the rain, and the birds fly within it like fish. What is the light he paints? That which announces the morning or that which tells of the fall of evening? Which season does he portray, if a single picture evokes signs of them all? Where are his figures looking? So attentively does he present them to us that they seem passive, but what they perceive is the latent reality that is not seen. The 'Madonna del Parto' itself, so laden with fruit that the whole thing splits open, is the one that welcomes in, that receives – the fruit of life that is death in that great cemetery of San Sepólcro in Umbria. If Piero della Francesca, as a man of his time, makes use of perspective, he does not allow himself to be dazzled by the invention. He knows very well that reality is something deeper, much deeper than the illusion created by the mirage of perspective.

The architect Gaudí traced a bridge over a dried-up river. The great tradition of our culture having been interrupted, he linked it to the modern tradition, and did so by taking onto his shoulders everything that we had been denied (he is Gothic, Baroque, Romantic, Rationalist and even Surrealist). In building this bridge, he not only anticipated our painters but created the best architecture. He restored our culture to a state of normality

So what is the point of all these meanderings? Well, simply, to make apparent the manner we painters have of constructing. Because the fact is we begin the house with the roof. What does the Mother of God in Titian's painting 'The Assumption of the Virgin' have to do with the clouds that bear her aloft? What does Beth Galí have to do with all this swirling mass of clouds? The clouds are a way of indicating how close her architecture is to painterly intuition. The concept that shapes it – for all that it is governed by an architectonic rationale – is, in effect, an artistic instinct that renders it true. A natural instinct that comes from her family background: granddaughter of the noucentista painter Francese Galí, friend and revered teacher of Joan Miró, Beth has been surrounded by painters since she was a little girl. By painters and architects. So much so that the practice of architecture has become an entirely natural gesture to her. A gesture wholly free of those ties that so often reduce to banality the architecture of professionals nourished only by an architectural culture and diet.

When Salvador Dalí first heard the surname Galí it sent him into ecstasies. In his imagination he heard a perfect symbiosis of GAla and DaLÍ. I do not think that Beth Galí has anything to do with Gala or Dalí, but I do believe that if anything is connected with her surname it is painting and architecture. If she paints with her architecture, it is not because she uses colours, but because, through them, she modulates the sensations that give reason.

Antoni Llena

catalan Francesc Galí, amigo y maestro reverenciado de Joan Miró, Beth ha vivido desde pequeña rodeada de pintores. De pintores y de arquitectos. De modo que, en ella, la práctica de la arquitectura no es sino un gesto natural. Un gesto desprovisto de ese tic que tan a menudo banaliza la arquitectura de los profesionales que sólo se nutren de cultura -de cocina- arquitectónica.

Una vez, Salvador Dalí se mostró exultante de alegría al oir el apellido "Galí". En su imaginación veia una simbiosis perfecta de GAla y DaLÍ. Yo no creo que Beth Gali tenga nada que ver con Gala y Dalí, pero si que creo que si algo liga con su apellido es justamente esto: pintura y arquitectura. Si pinta con su arquitectura no es porque emplee colores, sino porque a traves de ella modula sensaciones que son razón.

Antoni Llena

Four houses in Selva de Mar

Selva de Mar, Girona

WITH ANTONI SOLANAS
1976–1980

Our brief was to construct four private houses as holiday homes for four friends and their families. The houses were to be sited next to one another but were to remain independent in the interests of privacy. The site, over a hectare in area, is on the side of the mountain of Sant Pere de Rodes, and most of the area of the plot is steeply sloping, with stone terraces that were once planted with vines. A grove of pines now stands here, with the remainder of the plot on the level ground on the banks of the Selva watercourse. The site has views of the little towns of Selva de Mar and Port de la Selva, and there are no other buildings in the vicinity.

The project responded to the conditions outlined above. The diagonal line of the façade, for example, ensures the privacy of each house. The layout of the little group sought to avoid the customary 'bittiness', and strove instead to achieve a volumetry designed to camouflage the complex, blending it in with the terrain amidst the pine trees and the bands of stone terracing.

The living area on the ground floor of each house opens onto the kitchen and a bedroom or bathroom, with a transverse flight of stairs leading up to the first floor, which is occupied by either three bedrooms or two bedrooms and a bathroom. One of the bedrooms serves as a study.

The materials employed include local stone for the 40 cm-thick walls, painted woodwork, roof slabs with exposed beams and small vaults of white-painted concrete, stoneware tiling on the floors, and plastered walls (with the exception of bathrooms and kitchens, which have 20 x 20 cm white Valencia tiles laid diagonally). The roof is flat.

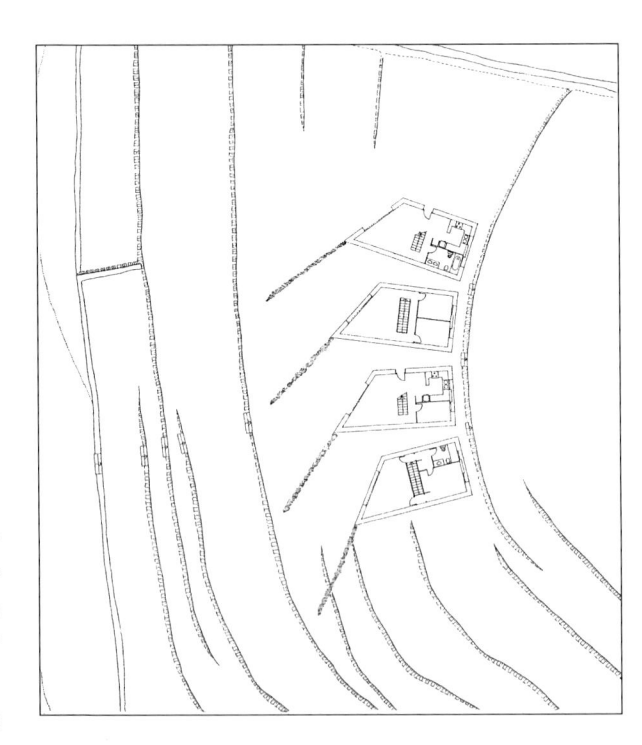

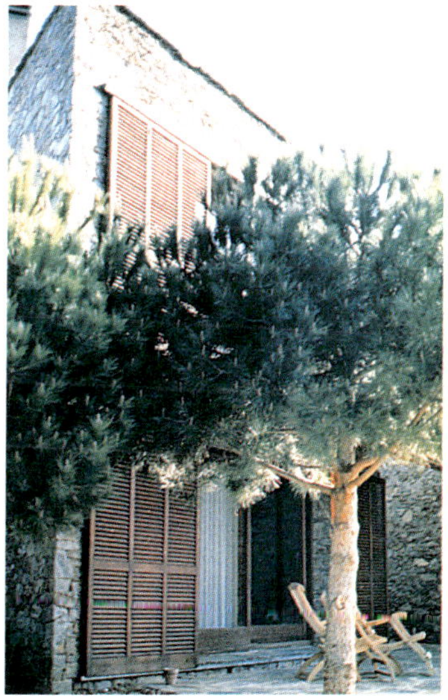
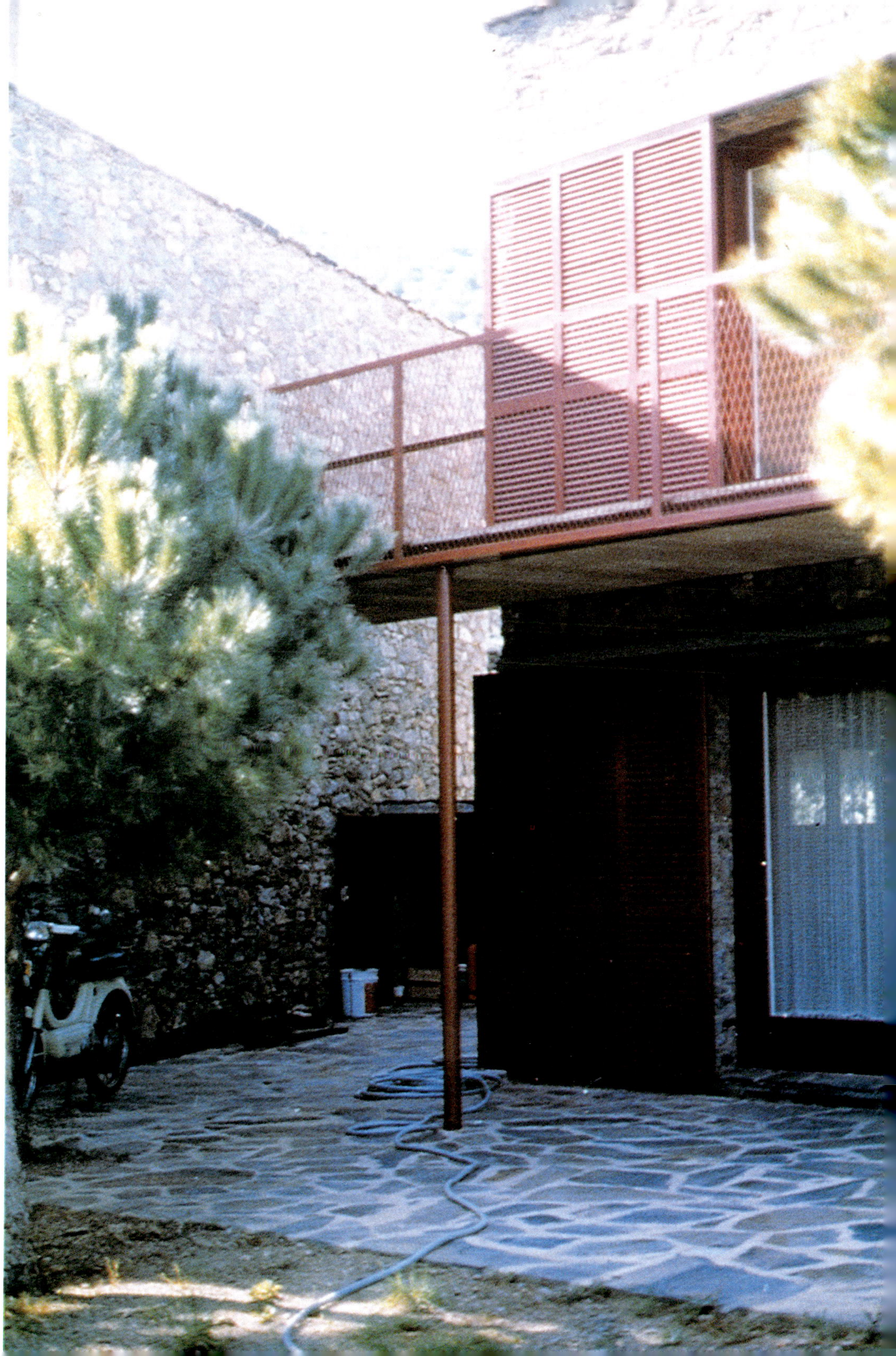

Joan Miró Park
Barcelona

WITH ANDREU ARRIOLA, MARIUS QUINTANA, ANTONI SOLANAS AND STUDENT: JORDI JANSÀ
1982–1989

The Parc del Escorxador and the Joan Miró Library are two different projects at the same site, although they are closely linked in terms of both the history and conception of the overall complex. The park was, in fact, designed in 1982, whereas the library, which had always been present as an undefined longitudinal building on the eastern edge of the park, only came into being in 1986. Placed in a strategic enclave for the city, between the geographical border of the *Eixample* (the Cerdà grid) and the old neighbourhood of Hostafrancs, the park responds to this border condition by assuming a morphology consistent with its context, while at the same time creating an internal, completely self-referential logic.

The relentless regularity of the *Eixample* block gradually gives way to a more fragmented order, in which axes of view and circulation are constantly created and interrupted. They never align with the city's street pattern and thus evoke the idea of a labyrinth and serve, perhaps, as a metaphor of the city itself. The park as metaphor of the city also offers a key to the reading of the sectional changes which, accommodating the site's actual topography, organise the park in three descending terraces. The highest terrace is the paved plaza with Miró's monumental sculpture hovering over a sheet of water. By its very emptiness, starkness and proportions, the plaza assumes a completely urban character. On the intermediate level there is a series of spaces for sports and social activities carved out of a regularly planted grove of palm trees. Among the columnar trunks of the palm trees, a monumental pergola frames one of the principal avenues of the park. The greater part of the park lies on the lowest level,

55 Joan Miró Park 1982-1989

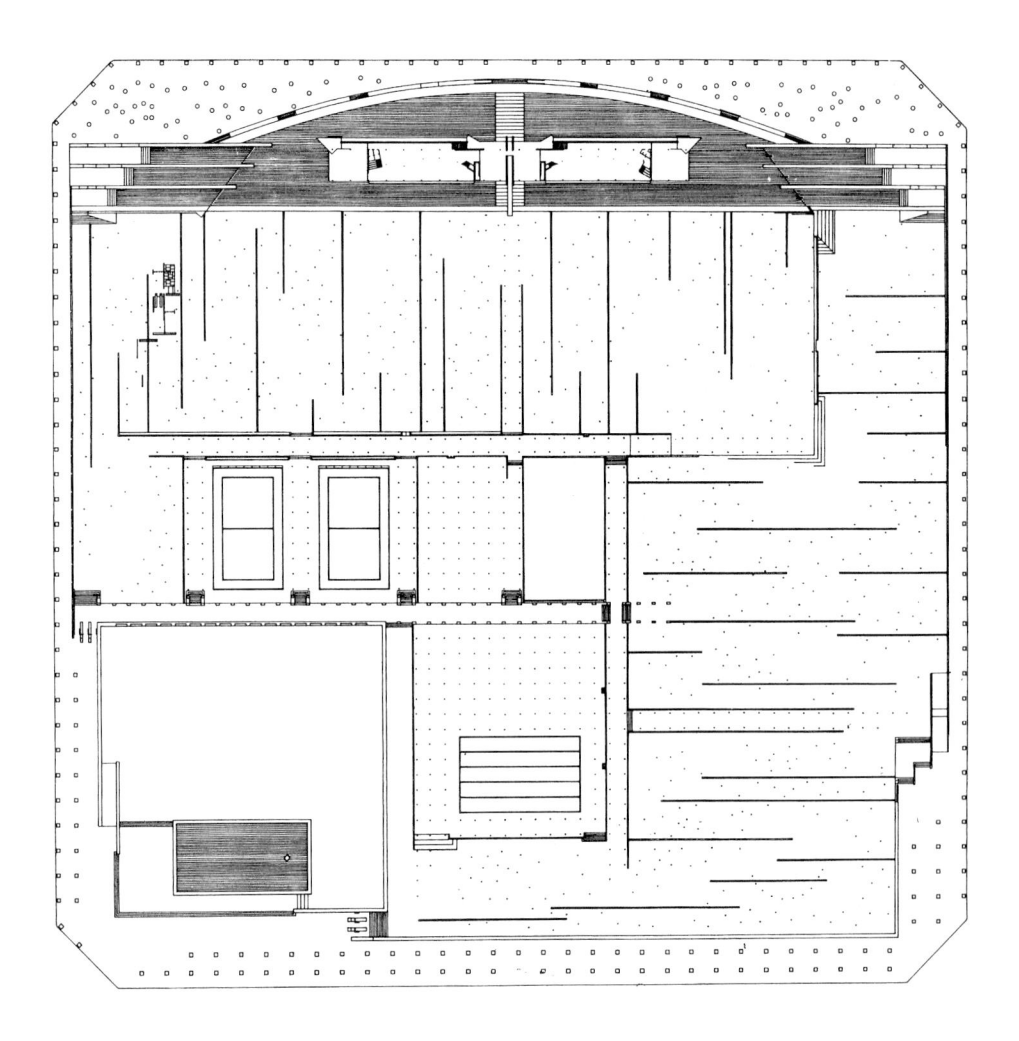

informally planted with pine trees, which create quieter, more intimate spaces. The Joan Miró Library rises in this section of the park – lower than the streets around it which border the Cerdà grid and hence physically and psychologically distant from noise and distractions – as a pivot and filter between city and park.

The building reveals itself between the pine trees which, continuing over the fence of the park, spread onto the pavement. Following the curve of the pond around the building, the trees thin out to unveil the play of stone walls which make up the main façade of the building and which, reflected in water, respond to the scale of the city that rises up in front them. This façade, defined by the blindness of the walls, originates from the orientation and section of the building, as well as from the placement, in plan, of the book stacks, which require an enclosing blind wall and a vertical light source above the mezzanine. By contrast, the southern façade, which faces the park, captures the light by means of a continuous glass wall along which the reading tables are placed. Outside, rows of cypress trees form green walls that border the pond and thicken between the waterfalls. These cypresses can be seen as a replica and natural extension, in vegetation, of the stone wall system. The main access to the park, the only instance in which it aligns with one of the streets of the Cerdà grid, divides the building into two symmetrical wings – one for adults and one for children.

The open space of the park is finally reached after crossing through a narrow passage of parallel walls. These walls are blank screens that reflect a transparent brightness onto the two entrance porches: here, the sound of waterspouts marks the threshold of a place in which silence is obligatory. The reading rooms in the interior, defined by radial bookshelves placed along a curve, open up towards the park while still maintaining a certain distance from it thanks to the sheet of water that lies between the trees and the building. Natural light is reflected off the water and filtered through the wide eaves designed to protect against direct sunlight. Bouncing off the interior walls and ceiling, this shimmering light becomes the main source of brightness, constant throughout the building.

Joan Miró Library

Barcelona

With Marius Quintana, Antoni Solanas
and students: Marcos Roger, Alfonso de Luna, Hubert van der Linden, Alessandra Dini,
Joaquim San Joan, Maura Monente, Jordi Jansà, Metchhild Stuhlmacher

1984-1990

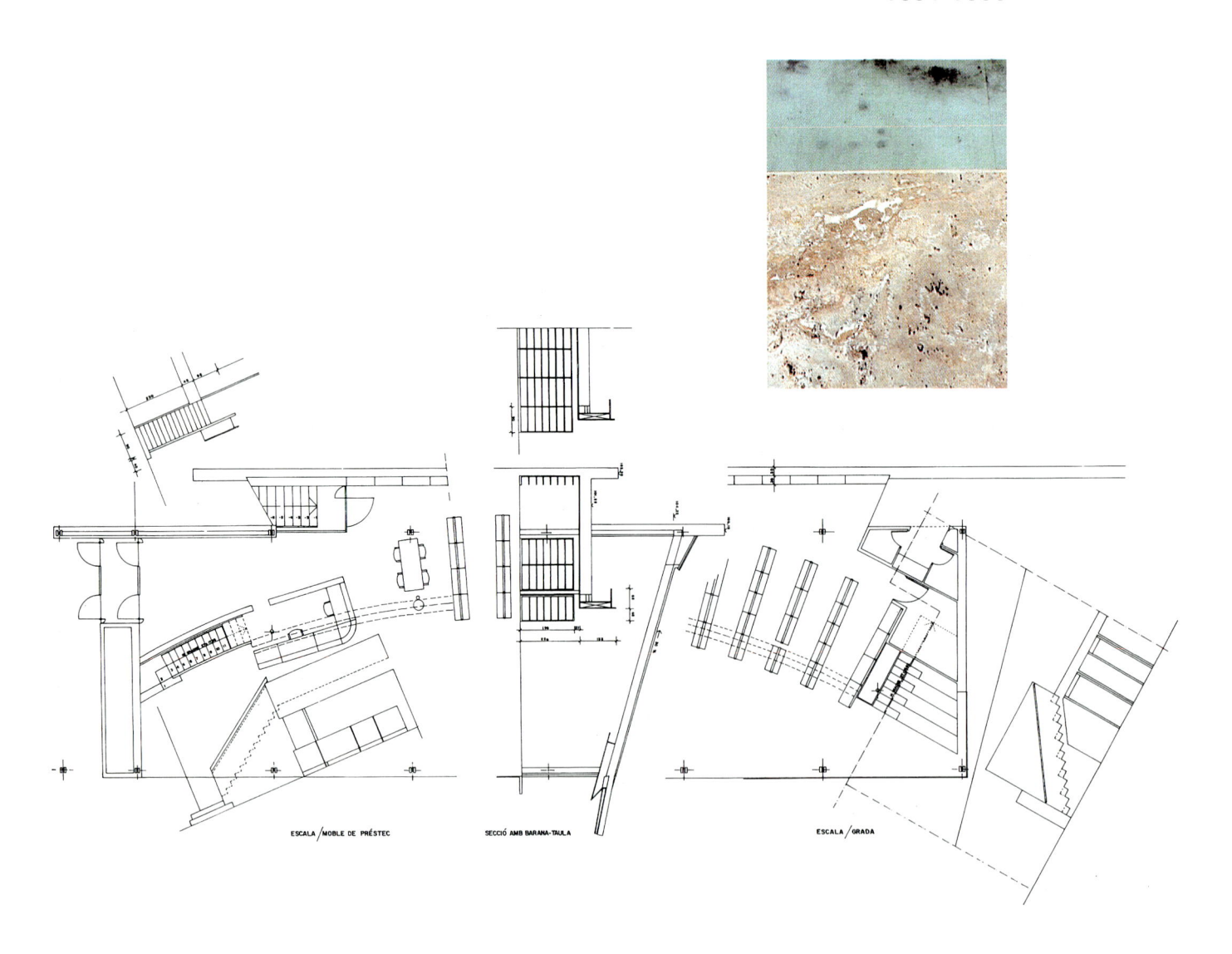

ESCALA/MOBLE DE PRÉSTEC   SECCIÓ AMB BARANA-TAULA   ESCALA/GRADA

59 Joan Miró Library 1984-1990

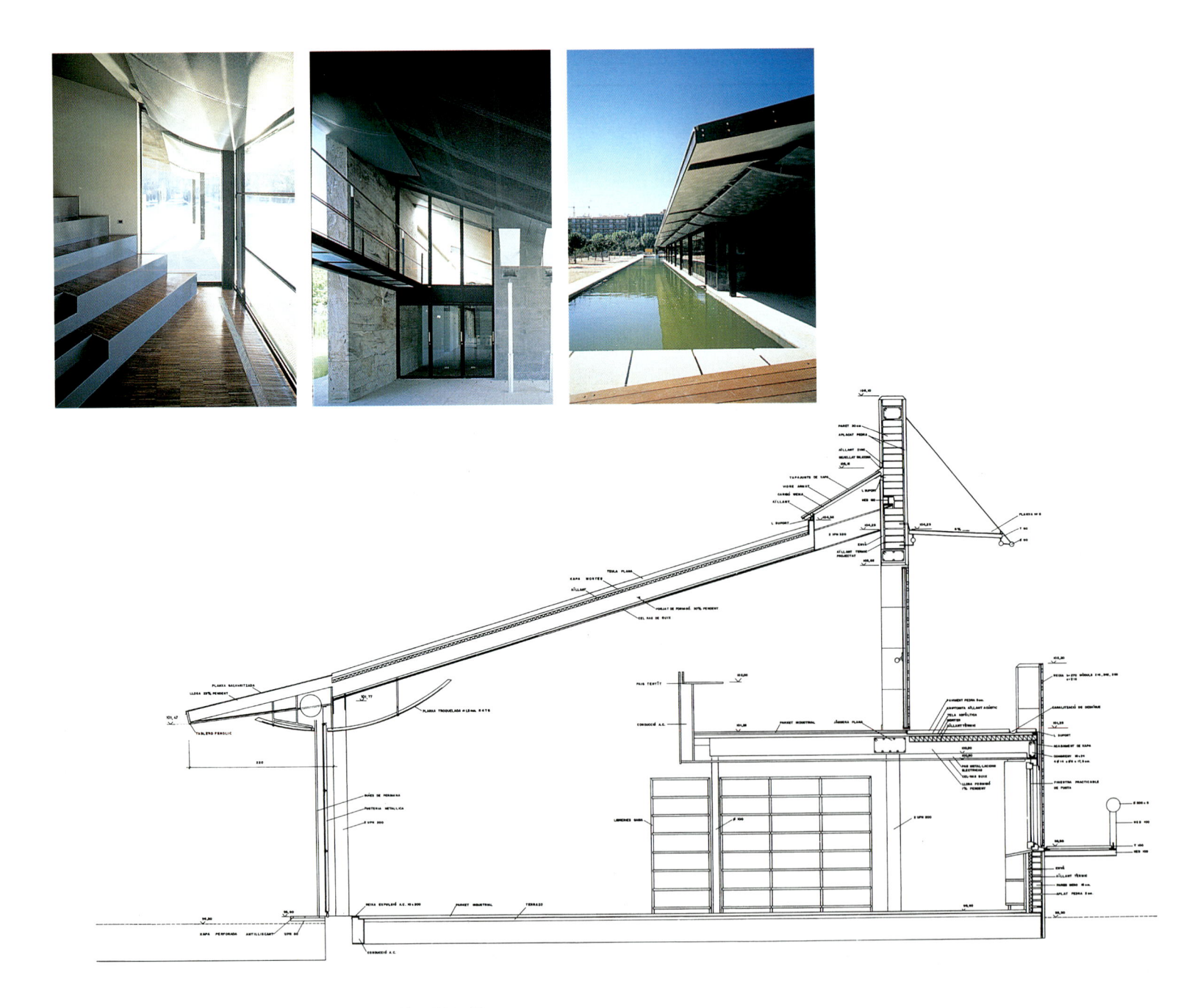

Joan Miró Library 1984-1990

61 Joan Miró Library 1984-1990

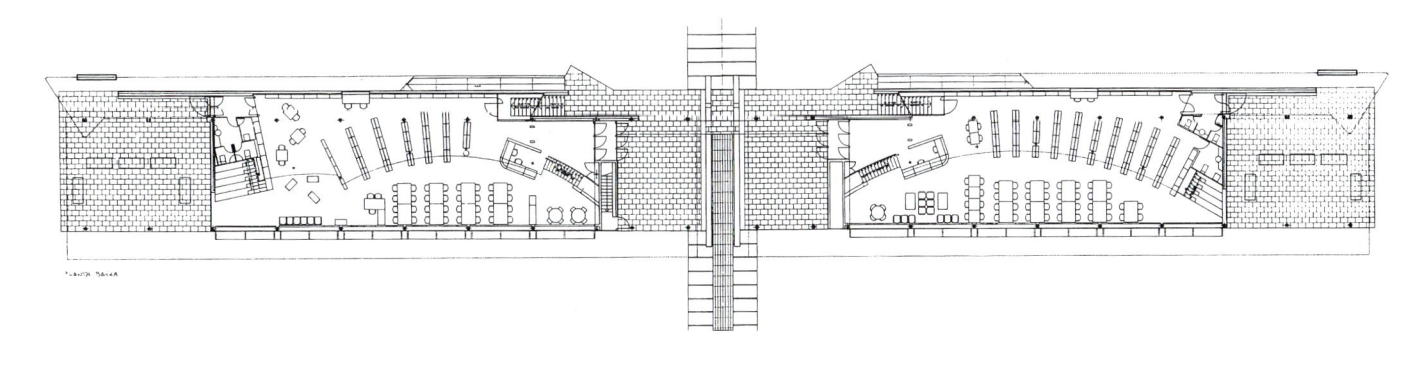

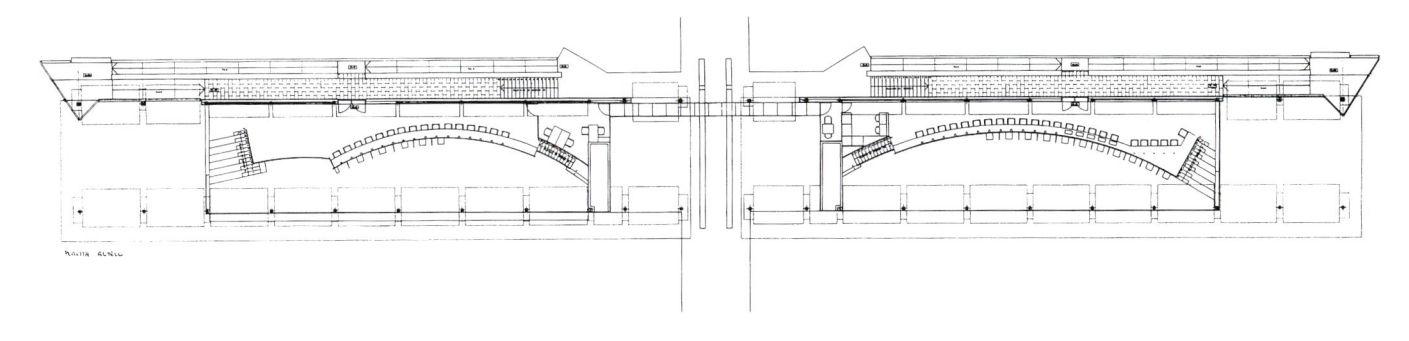

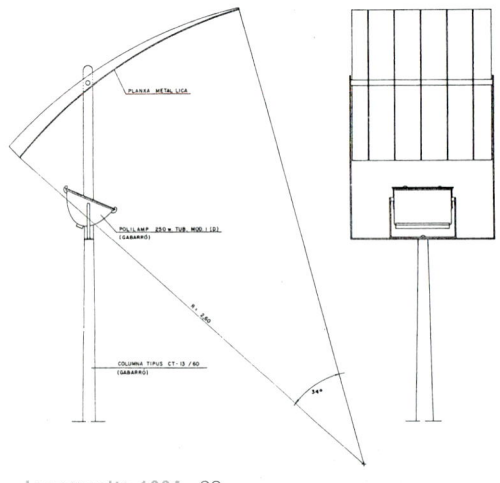

Lamparaalta

Outdoor lamp - Manufactured by Santa & Cole

DELTA D'ARGENT ADI-FAD AWARD 1984 - WITH MARIUS QUINTANA

1984

When I was commissioned to design a park in 1980, shortly after leaving architecture school, it was an absolutely new experience for me. The park in question was the Parc del Escorxador in Barcelona. In the midst of all my doubts and preconceptions, I recall that there was one certainty I carried with me to the end of the project. This was a conviction concerning the illumination of a natural setting – about the way trees, for example, should be lit. I hated those lamps with glass globes, where the point of illumination seems to make itself more important than anything else. I wanted to employ the same system of indirect light that is customarily used in the home. I thought of the magnificent lamps by Le Corbusier in the Unité d'Habitation in Marseilles, of the indirect light in the interior of Gunnar Asplund's Law Courts in Gothenburg and the invariably indirect light in Alvar Aalto's buildings. It was here that I found the key that brought me to the initial design idea.

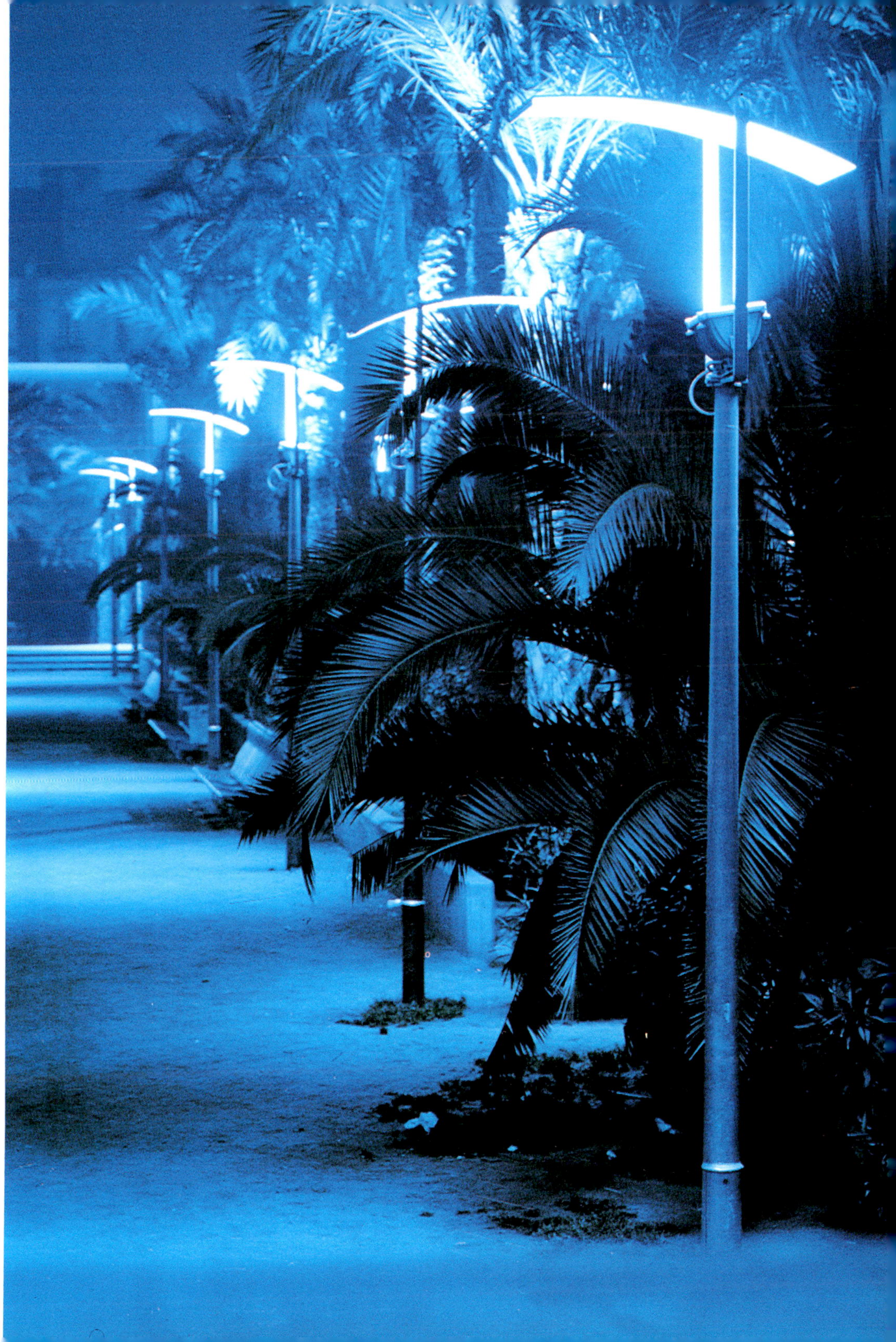

Casa Cases

Two-apartment building - Barcelona

WITH MARIUS QUINTANA AND STUDENTS: JORDI JANSÀ, ALESSANDRA DINI, MAURA MONENTE AND HUBERT VAN DER LINDEN

1982–1989

The Casa Cases is set on one of the hills behind Barcelona, with a magnificent view of the city and the sea. It is sited in the landscape according to an approach originally adopted by the Renaissance villa and subsequently reworked by modern architecture, whereby an object with a pure form is contrasted with the irregular forms of the natural objects around it. At the same time, the implantation reflects local planning regulations, which call for square or rectangular plots with a distance of at least three metres between the boundary of the plot and the walls of the house. The house has a square plan measuring 12 x 12 metres and is developed over three levels, standing on a platform that compensates for the slope of the terrain. We took advantage of the difference in level to accommodate the garage in the space beneath the platform. It is reached via a large arch on the street. The swimming pool, which occupies precisely the three-metre separation between the house and the perimeter, is located at the highest part of the plot, overlooking the valley. The platform is transformed here into a large terrace looking out over the city, while, on the hill side, the same horizontal plane is laid out in the form of a garden, densely planted with cypresses and fruit trees, which screen the house from the road running behind it.

The internal distribution is organised in plan around a central core with lift and services, which is crowned by a four-pitched roof. In section the house is divided into two duplex apartments, one occupying the ground floor, the other the second floor, with the first floor being divided into two parts to accommodate the bedrooms of both apartments. The internal organisation is reflected in the façade,

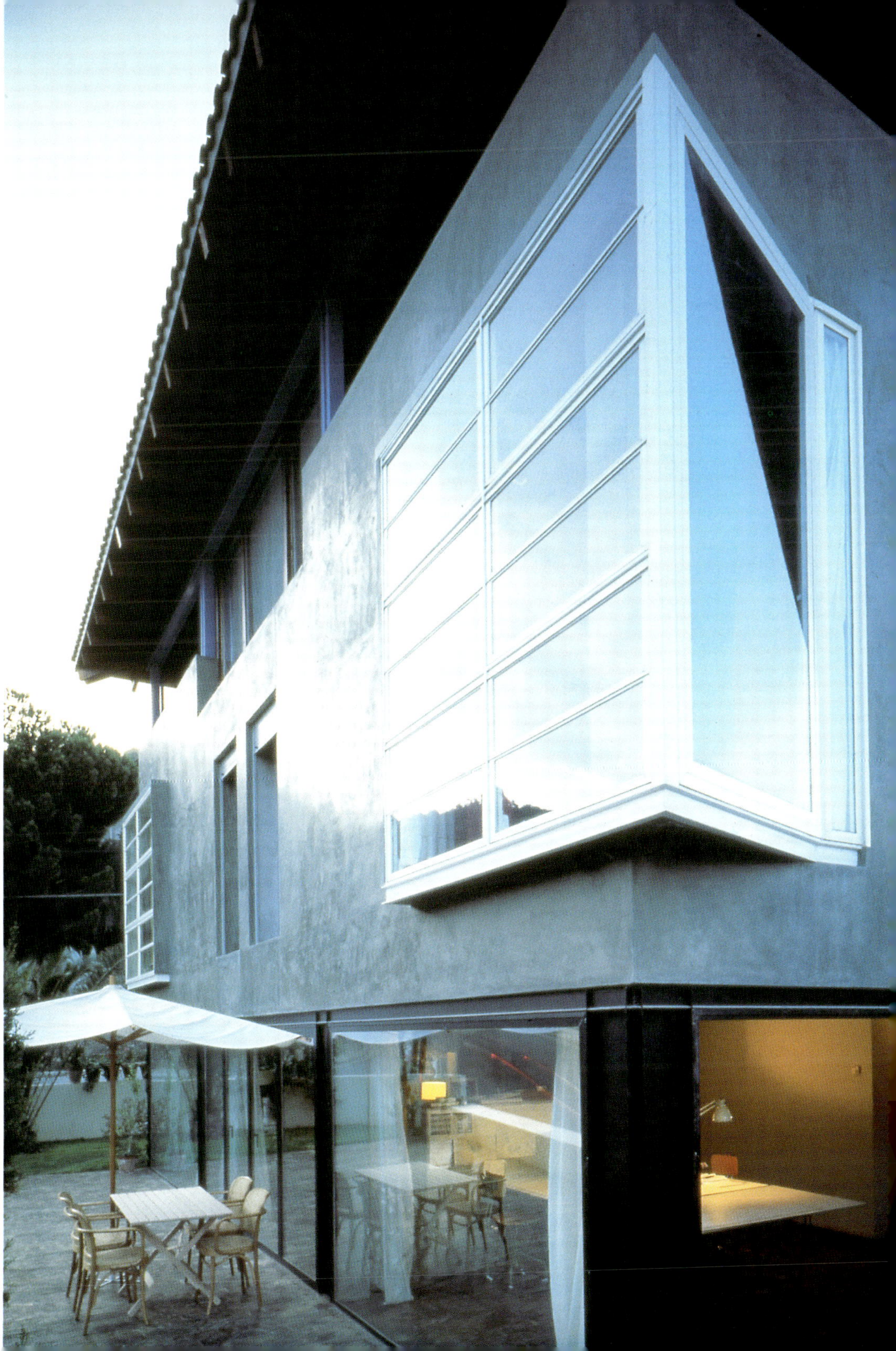

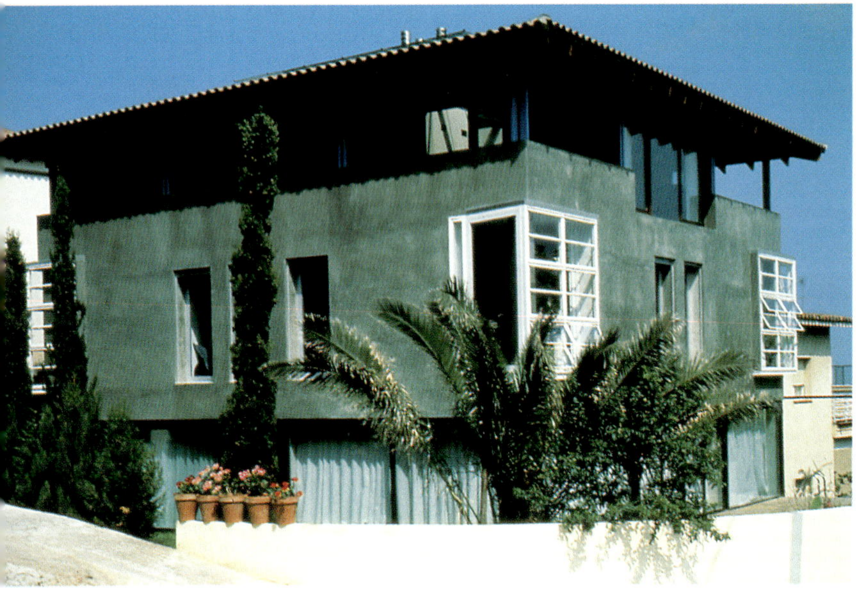

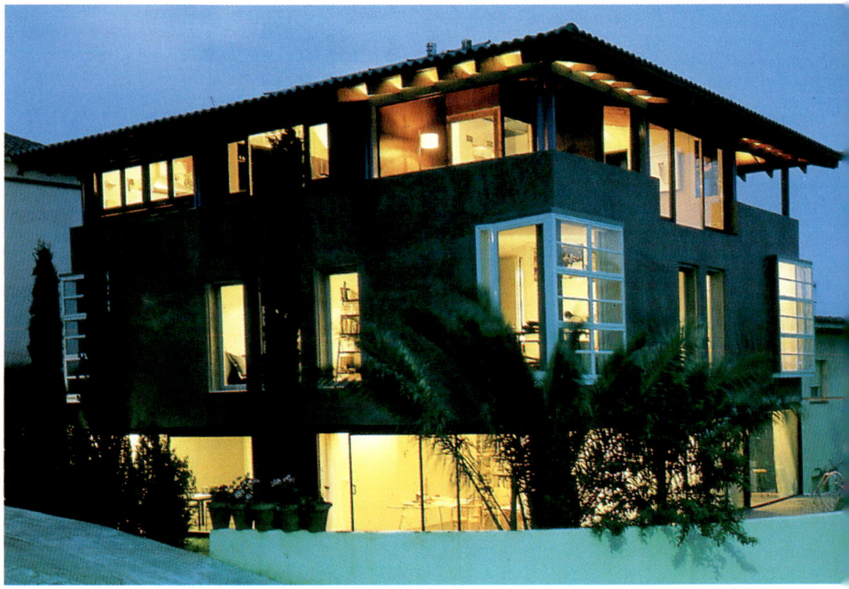

PLANTA BAJA

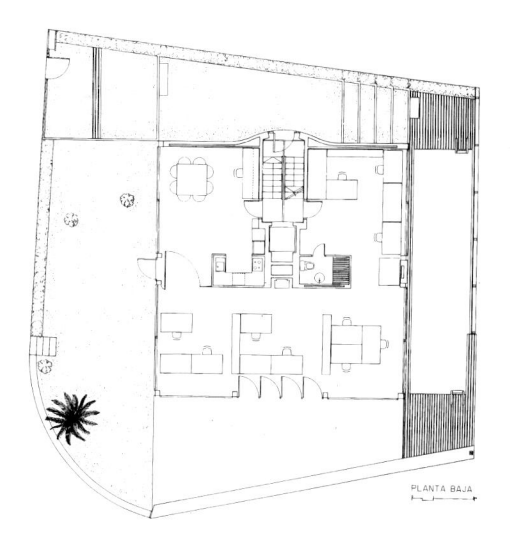

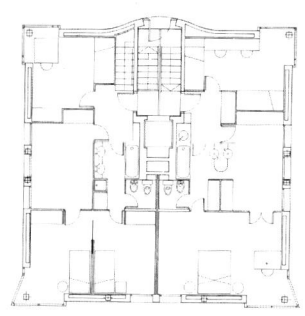

PLANTA PRIMERA DUPLEX

PLANTA SEGUNDA

where a band of rendered wall runs between the ground floor windows and the loggia beneath the great wooden eaves of the roof. The composition of the façade follows the classical scheme of division into three parts, symmetrical with respect to the central axis. This scheme is found in Medici villas, such as Poggio in Caiano, for example, and probably derives from mediaeval military architecture, with its two lateral towers defending the entrance to the castle. In the Casa Cases the historical reference is very understated, with the continuous loggia on the top floor and the window on the ground floor exempting the daytime zones of the two apartments from a symmetrical system of openings. In these zones the plan is in fact entirely free, modulated almost exclusively by furniture which, to avoid breaking the continuity of the space, never touches the ceiling.

Despite being a closed volume, the exterior of the Casa Cases projects out onto the surrounding landscape. On the ground floor, in fact, the windows give complete transparency and permeability from the swimming pool on one side through to the garden on the other. On the top floor, the loggia opens the house up to the panorama and creates a space that is at once exterior and interior. Even on the intermediate floor, which, as the night-time zone, is much more enclosed, there are individual windows in the corners which project out beyond the plane of the façade, as if seeking to capture more effectively the surrounding natural environment. The insertion in the landscape has been thought through in the most minute detail in terms of materials and colours. The roof of dark tile, the olive green Venetian rendering, the paving of fired slate and above all the powerful presence of wood in the roof structure visible from the garden: all of these evoke the tonalities of the pine groves on the surrounding hills, their dark green foliage contrasting with the reddish earth and the honey-coloured rock.

Fossar de la Pedrera

Monument to Lluís Companys, President of Catalonia 1934–1940 - Barcelona

With Marius Quintana, Pere Casajoana and Ignasi de Lecea

1984–1986

The Fossar de la Pedrera is located in a deep depression in the mountain of Montjuïc, site of an old stone quarry and next to the old cemetery of Barcelona. This quarry, which over the years had become a common grave, was selected as the burial place for all the victims of imprisonment and persecution. It is the final resting place, therefore, of many men and women who sacrificed their lives for Catalan independence. The site remained completely neglected until 1985, when the Urban Design Department of the city of Barcelona heeded the initiative of the 'Association of the Martyrs for Catalunya' to restructure and dignify the complex.

Access to the precinct is provided by one of the old paths of the adjacent cemetery. Visitors go through an intermediate zone which acts as a filter between the exterior and the more intimate and almost sacred space of the Fossar. This filter is formed by a series of pre-existing cypress trees and stone columns engraved with the names of the victims of the mass shootings of 1939.

From this entrance point, it is possible to overlook the entire burial space, framed by the rocky perimeter of the quarry which dramatises the character of the space. The monumental eastern side of the Fossar functions as an architectural backdrop and a viewing point over the continuous and homogenous surface of the collective grave. A stone wall supports two inclined planes which form the monumental axis of the complex. This axis, further stressed by the access stair-

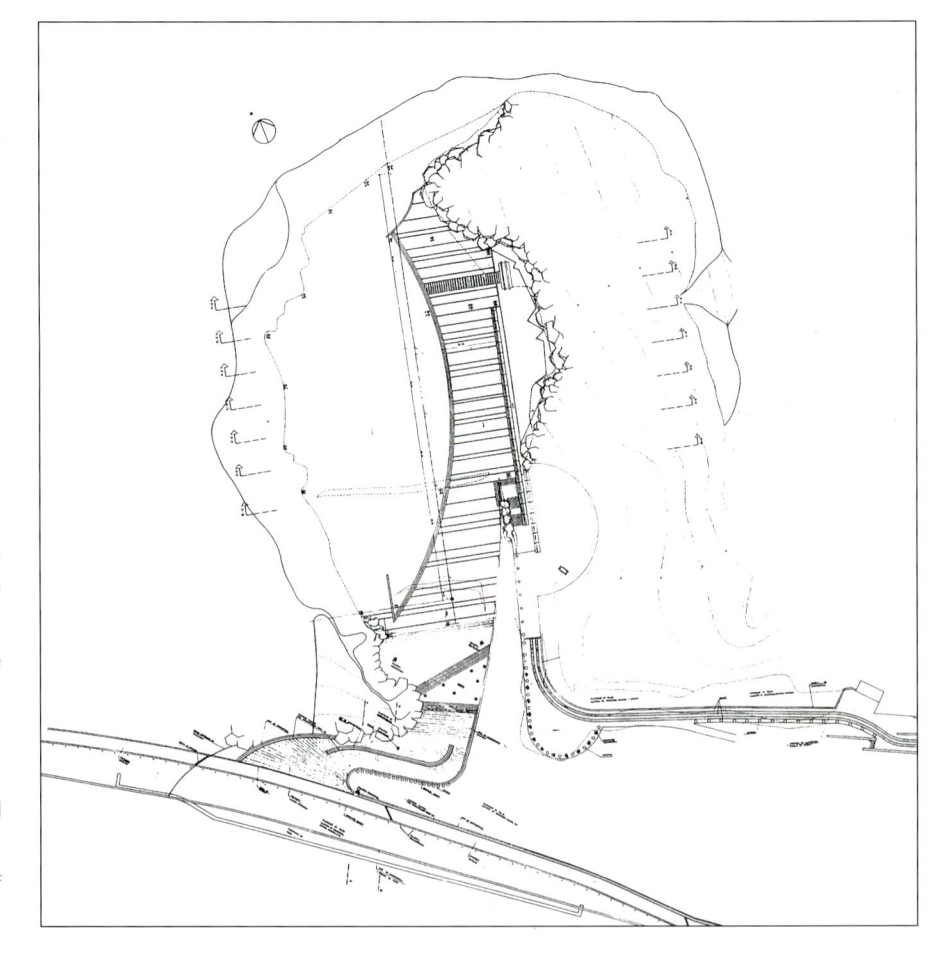

69 Fossar de la Pedrera 1984-1986

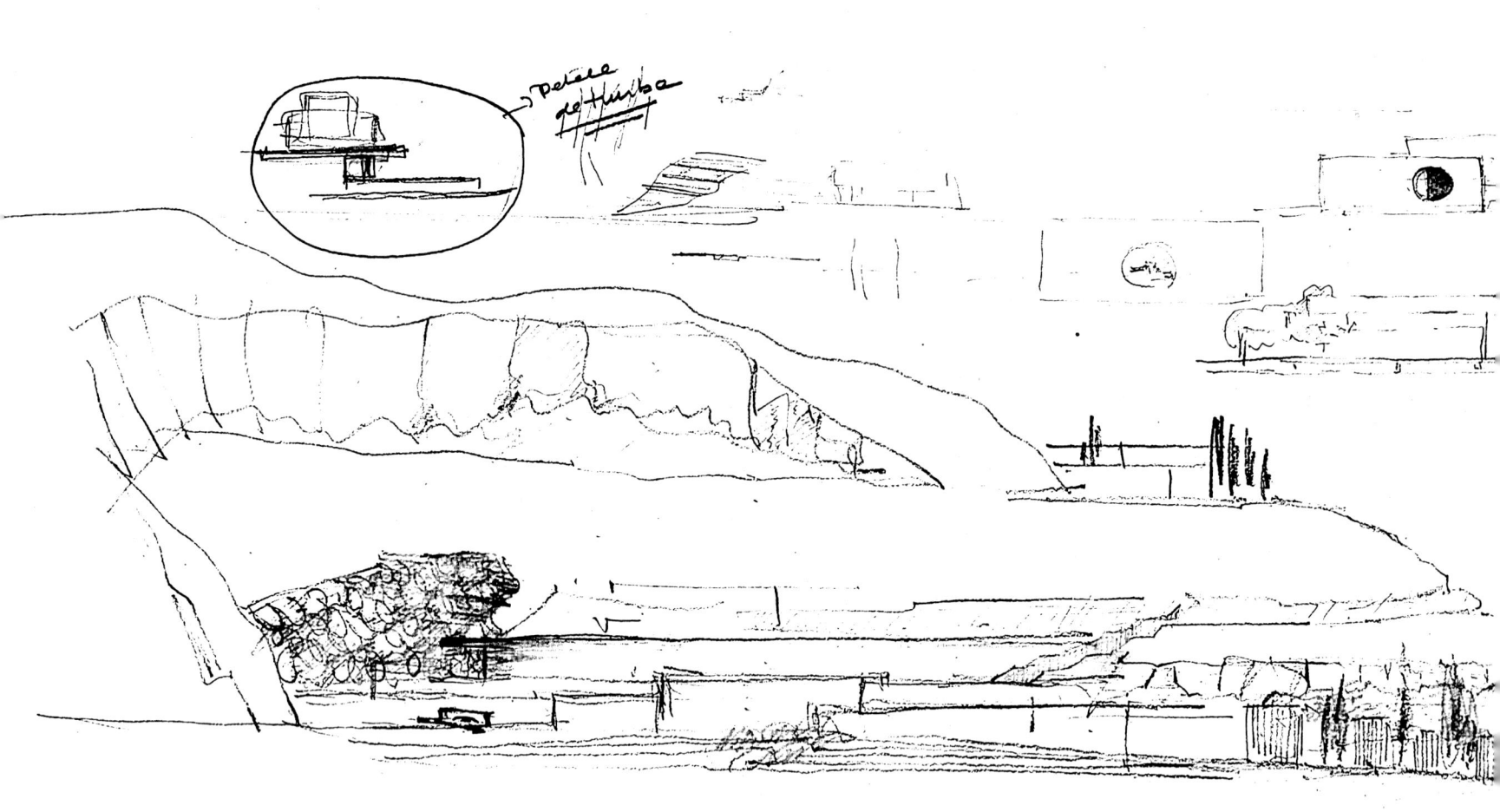

way, ultimately leads to the tomb of President Lluís Companys.

The mausoleum is surrounded by water except at the access point, which is a paved rectangle coming from the pergola. It is a very simple structure intended to lend dignity to the place, while at the same time avoiding presidential monumentalism within the essentially communitarian spirit of the complex. It consists of two concrete arches that rise from the water and are lightened by arched metal plates. The arches define a space in which the tomb lies beneath a marble gravestone. This space is subtly enclosed by a wide metal grate which does not block the view from the outside and also functions as a door. The modesty of the construction, however, is underlined by the quality of the surrounding area: the stone wall and the reflection of the water surface.

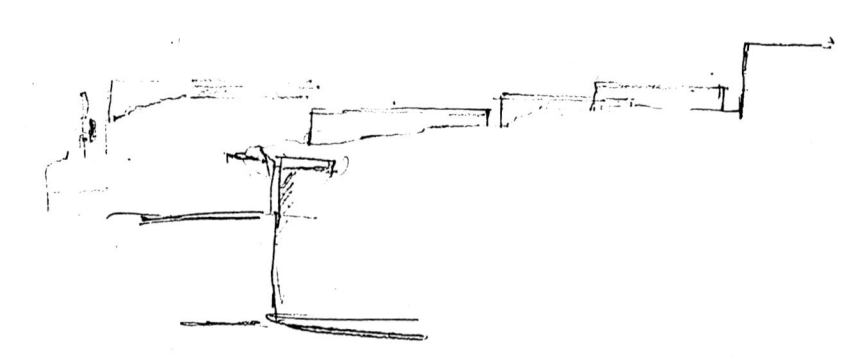

71 Fossar de la Pedrera 1984-1985

Reyes house

Cala Pregonda, Menorca; unbuilt

WITH MARIUS QUINTANA AND STUDENTS: JAUME PIÑOL, ALESSANDRA DINI, HUBERT VAN DER LINDEN AND MAURA MONENTE

1985

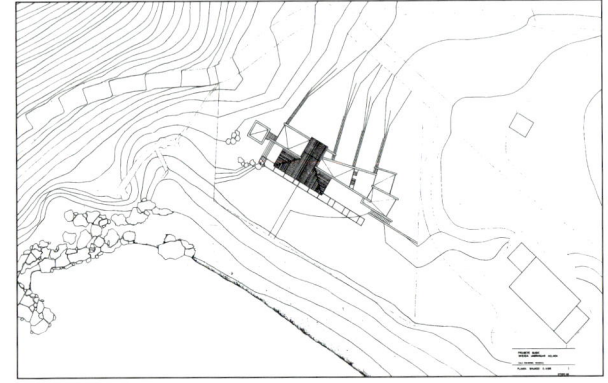

It was in one of the most captivating settings in the world that I was to experience the difficulty of carrying out an architectural intervention without inflicting damage on the gifts offered by nature. The Pregonada cove is an inlet on the northern coast of the island of Menorca. It is protected by planning legislation from the kind of tasteless development that has spoiled so much of our country's coastline. A Catalan businessman, enchanted by the place, bought a large plot of land with the intention of building a holiday home on it.

Determined not to violate the natural setting, we designed a house screened by the type of walls traditionally used to mark out land divisions all over the island. It was also to be tucked in behind the sand dune that marks the boundary between the beach and the countryside.

The house was never built, partly because the client was killed in a road accident, but above all because local people were strongly opposed to the idea of building there. Ultimately, in spite of all our efforts to make our intervention as sensitive as possible I believe they were absolutely right.

73 Reyes house 1995

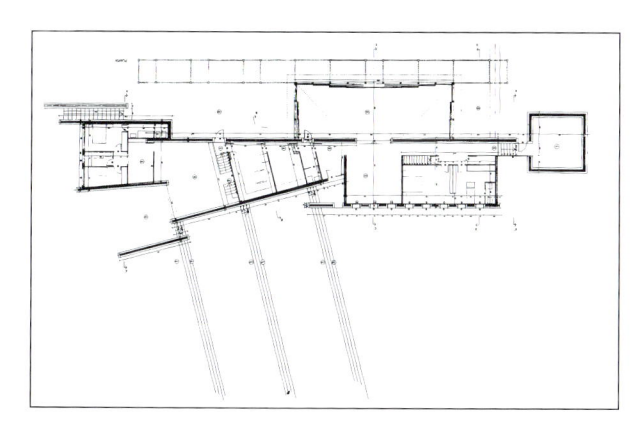

Bernad house

Remodelling of the interior - Barcelona; unbuilt

WITH MARIUS QUINTANA AND STUDENTS: JAUME PIÑOL, ALESSANDRA DINI, HUBERT VAN DER LINDEN AND MAURA MONENTE

1985

Some friends of mine asked me to remodel and slightly change the everyday aspect of the dwelling in which one of them had been born and had lived almost all of his life. The apartment is located in a building in the centre of Barcelona's *Eixample* and shares the typical structure of this part of the city – tall townhouses in continuous rows that form closed square blocks of considerable depth. One facade is on the street, while another overlooks the interior of the block.

The typical layout of these apartments has large rooms at either end, connected by a corridor (generally dark), off which the kitchen, bathroom and bedrooms are located. The project I proposed affected only the central part of the house. The idea was to bring daylight – sunshine – from the block's inner courtyard to the middle of the apartment by folding back and introducing vertical splits in the new walls which separated the kitchen from the corridor. These walls opened up like a funnel in the direction of the living room, the source of the daylight.

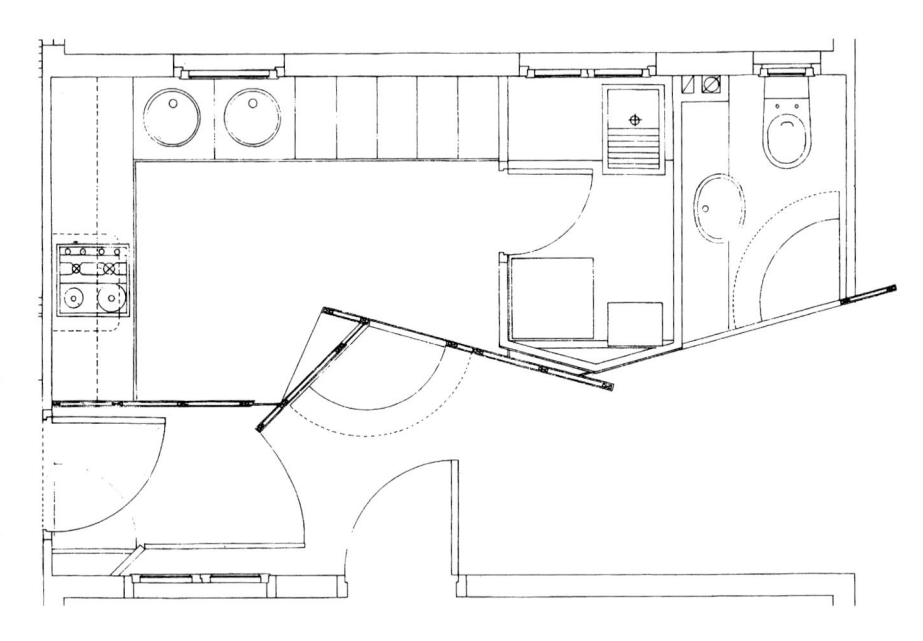

75 Bernad house 1985

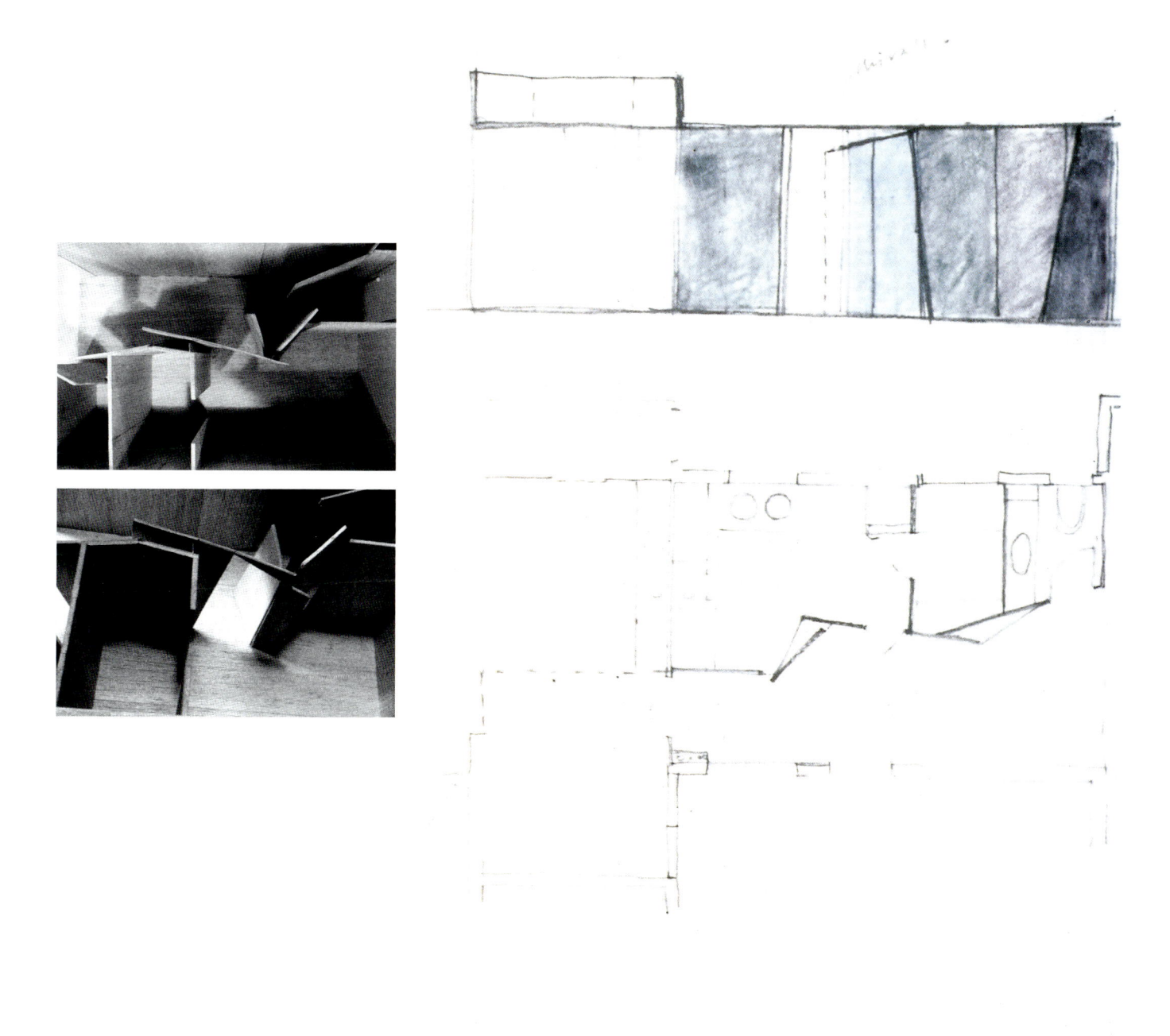

Eina, 20 anys d'avantguarda

Design of the survey exhibition on the EINA design school - Barcelona

FAD AWARD FOR EPHEMERAL ARCHITECTURE 1987 - WITH MARIUS QUINTANA AND XAVIER OLIVÉ

1987

Exhibitions are, by virtue of their condition as ephemeral architecture, a particularly fruitful terrain for certain forms of experimentation not always readily practicable in other, more stable fields of architecture. In the present case, the physical reality of the existing building was left unaltered. The interior space, by contrast, was reorganised in depth in order to accommodate the complex display materials making up the exhibition.

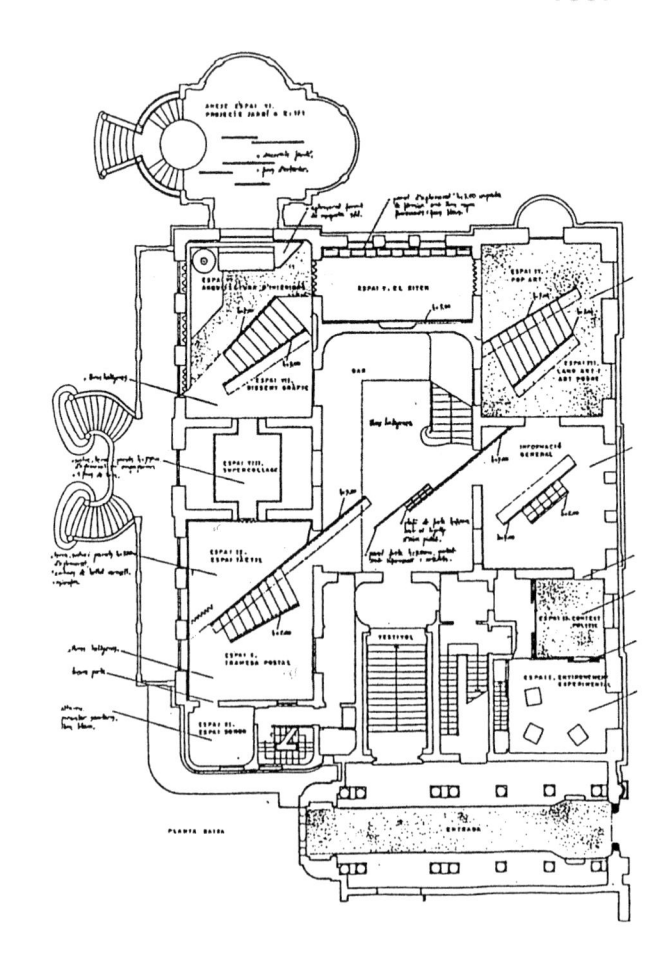

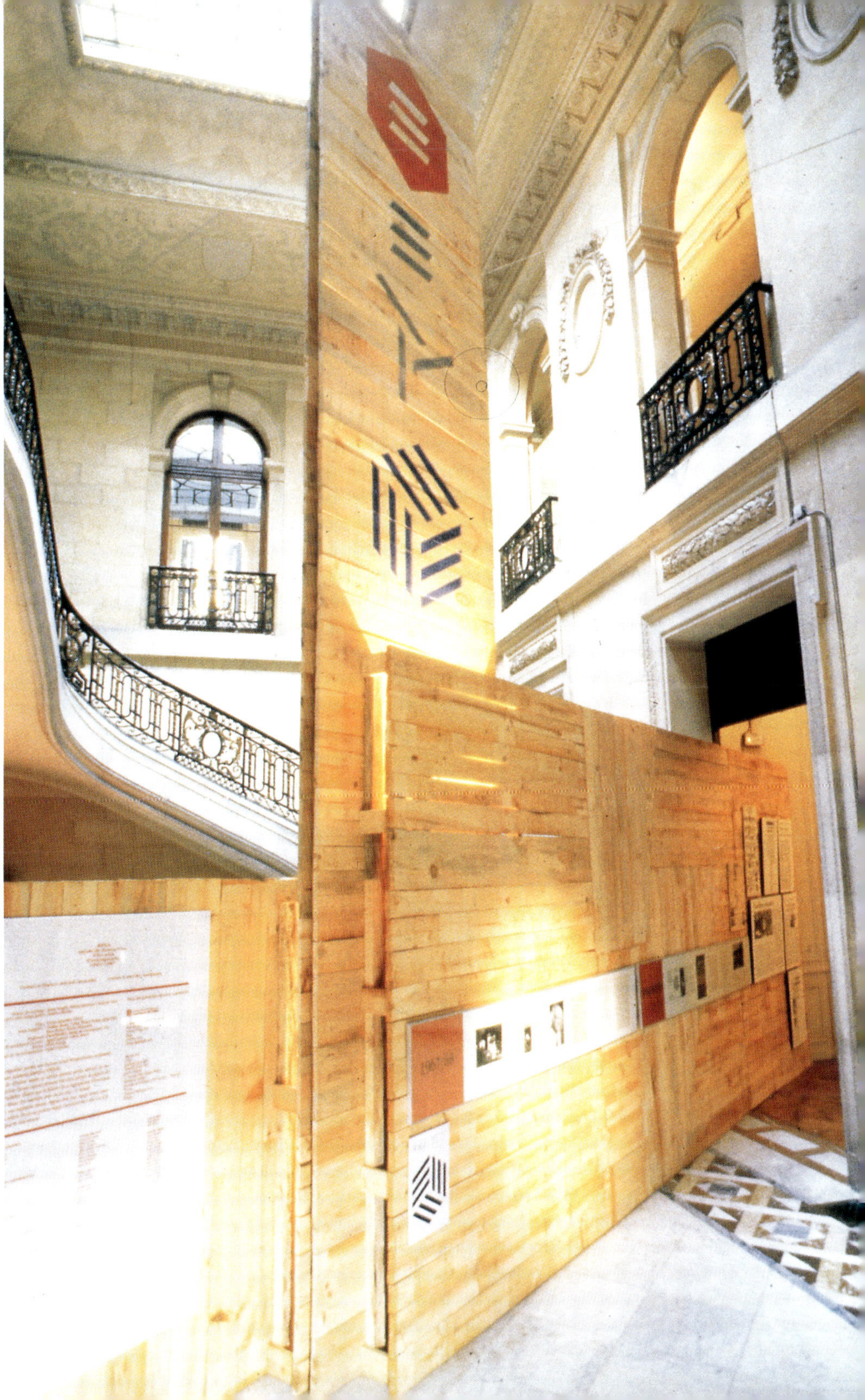

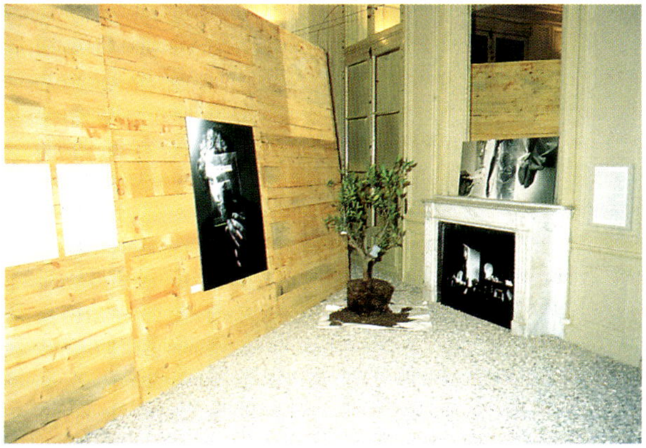

Barcelona Film Festival
1987–1990

The extensive repertoire of scenographic elements found in much contemporary culture represents a new way of communicating images of our surroundings: decontextualising, dramatising, ironising, staging, reinterpreting – these have been the fundamental narrative devices (until recently specific to cinema) that have endowed so many contemporary architectures and artworks with signification.

The Barcelona Film Festival, held between 1987 and 1990, opted to take the city as its real-life set. The city – the chosen theme of so many directors – was reinterpreted by artists and architects. They constructed, with the collaboration and direction of Beth Galí, ephemeral architectures designed not to be filmed but to be remembered – witty, amusing or touching tributes to the films and directors who form the wellspring of the Film Festival.

'Hollywood-Hollywood'
Barcelona Film Festival

FRANK O. GEHRY IN COLLABORATION WITH BETH GALÍ

1987

The enormous letter puzzle represents the image that Frank O. Gehry saw every day of his childhood: the great Hollywood sign on the hills above Los Angeles. The duplicated layout gives the piece a sculptural and urban dimension which the original does not possess. The bending of the letters and their composition in a more aleatory sequence also serves to give a new meaning to the whole, a world that is sinking, yet still maintains its nostalgia for a mythified past.

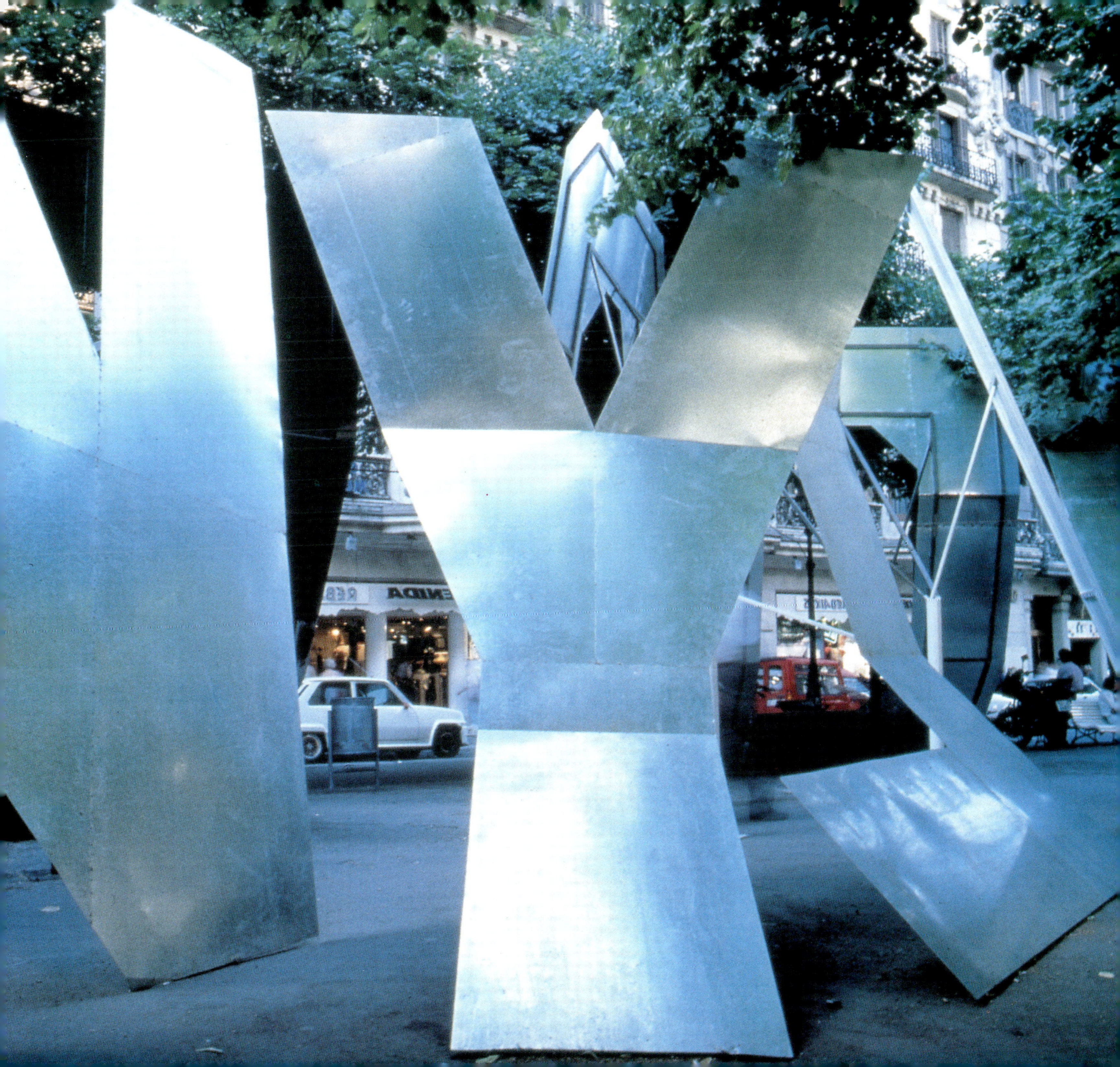

'La vie en rose'

Barcelona Film Festival

HANS HOLLEIN IN COLLABORATION WITH BETH GALÍ
1987

The staircase as a recurring image throughout a whole period of cinema history. It starts off pink as the setting for the musical fantasies of the bright, conformist Golden Age of Ginger Rogers and Fred Astaire, but ends up red and bloody like the famous Odessa Steps scene in *Eisenstein's Battleship Potemkin*. The staircase is a single form which takes on a whole series of meanings thanks to the communicative capacity of a great mythic period in film history.

'L'occhio del diavolo' (The devil's eye)
Barcelona Film Festival

GAE AULENTI IN COLLABORATION WITH BETH GALÍ
1988

Sensuality and eroticism in the cinema are dealt with in this fantasy space, with its orifice-like spy-holes in each of the 49 columns which make up the forest of phalluses.

Through each spy hole the occasional voyeur will find one of the 49 different images concealed inside the columns, recalling the revelation of those moments when the presence of Eros shatters the comfortable complacency of the 'decent-minded' citizen.

'Llum de lluna' (Moonlight)

Barcelona Film Festival

JOSEP M. CIVIT IN COLLABORATION WITH BETH GALÍ

1988

The idea here was to recreate the light of the full moon on nights when there was none. A powerful spotlight shines its blue brilliance the entire length of a block-long stretch of the Rambla de Catalunya. For a few moments the people walking along that stretch have the sensation of being in the midst of a dense undergrowth, under a full moon, with the song of night birds in their ears.

'Atrapados' (Rain again)

Barcelona Film Festival

DANI FREIXE IN COLLABORATION WITH BETH GALÍ AND JAUME CASTELLVÍ

1988

A high-heeled shoe on the ground, a lipstick and a head-scarf are the only occupants of a convertible smashed into a tree. The rain, the windscreen wipers and the still switched-on radio are the only dynamic elements in this montage, which refers us back, through absence, to so many mythic film moments constructed around the road in the rain.

'Ritmo loco' (Crazy rhythm)

Barcelona Film Festival

ANTONI LLENA IN COLLABORATION WITH BETH GALÍ

1989

This montage subtly represents the absence of the actors, reproducing on the floor of an improvised film-set the swiftly flowing movements of a fragment of 'Crazy Rhythm', drawn on the ground by Antoni Llena. The silent steps of Fred Astaire glide across the Rambla de Catalunya, establishing a dialogue between the symbolic footprints of the great dancer, then recently deceased, and the reproduction of the same sequence on the two video monitors positioned alongside. If the cinema has no past tense, and is for that reason the stuff of myth, then the dance sequence is a manifestation of immortality.

Bercy Park

Competition to design the Bercy warehouse site - Paris

WITH MARIUS QUINTANA, FRANÇOIS NORDEMAN AND ALAIN AYGALINC

1987

The project for the site of the old Bercy wine cellars and warehouses transformed the demands of the location into the starting points for the design of the future park. The space occupied by the old warehouses was a narrow void surrounded by major traffic infrastructure and further confined by the main entrance to the Ministry of Finance building and by public transport facilities. These very limitations could, however, also act as a support and a stimulus for the new project.

The objectives of the programme were:
1. To maintain the existing mass of trees;
2. To protect the site by taking advantage of its geography;
3. To integrate the precinct into the urban and transport system of the city of Paris.

The project was articulated around the site's fundamental feature – a depression in the terrain with respect to the surrounding traffic routes. The park space is organised by the interchange between the three superimposed planes. The first layer consists of the existing level, where an exceptional mass of trees has grown up over time marking out the internal streets. The second is formed by the elevated walkways laid out on top of the walls and by the porticoes running perpendicular to the Seine and connected to one another by lightweight footbridges. This is an aerial plane that traverses the space at treetop height. The third layer, finally, is constituted by the raised ground of the embankments where the park makes contact with the circulation routes. The latter is a plane constructed above the rapid transit routes that connects with the terraces of the Omnisport pavilion situated at one end of the park.

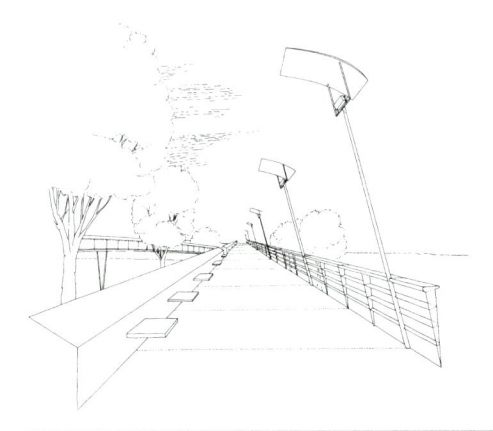

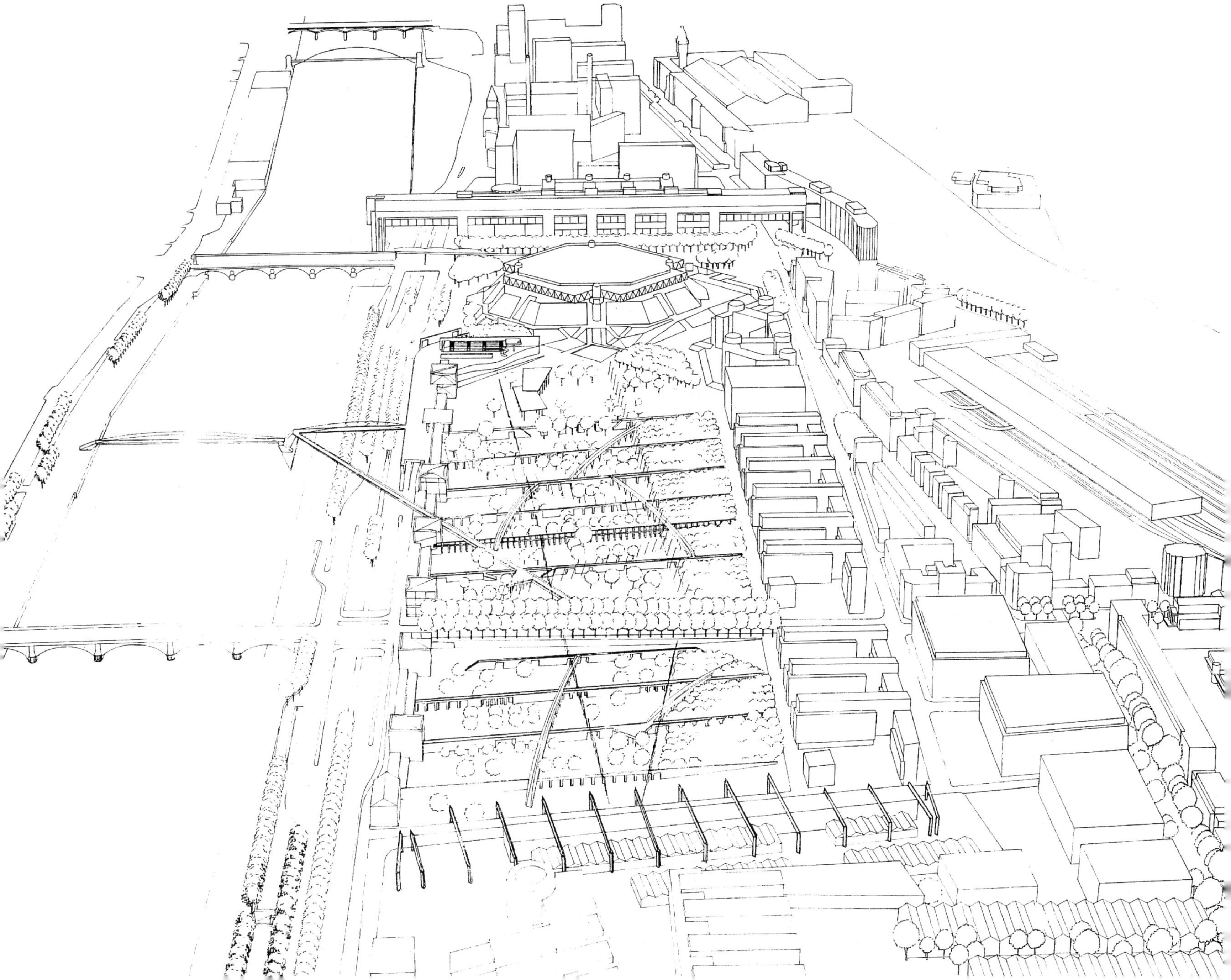

Discotheque in Poble Espanyol

Project to convert the church in Poble Espanyol into a music bar
Barcelona; unbuilt

WITH MARIUS QUINTANA, ALFREDO VIDAL AND STUDENTS: CRISTINA MARAGALL, ALESSANDRA DINI AND HUBERT VAN DER LINDEN

1988

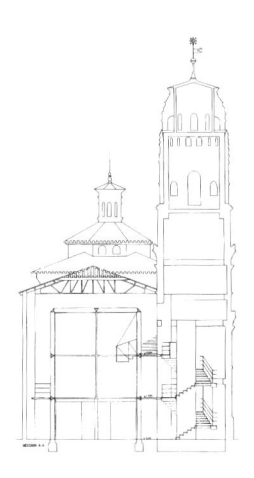

It was decided in 1927, as part of a series of interventions then being carried out in preparation for Barcelona's 1929 International Exhibition, to construct a Poble Espanyol – a Spanish Town featuring typical architecture from each of the regions of Spain. The main promoters of the project were the architects Falguera and Raventós and the artists Utrillo, Plandiure and Nogués. The Poble Espanyol was badly damaged in the course of the Spanish Civil War and subsequently experienced a whole series of trials and tribulations. Barcelona City Council decided in 1983 to restore it as a space in which the popular traditions and crafts of Spain could be presented, and as a leisure facility offering food and drink from different parts of the country.

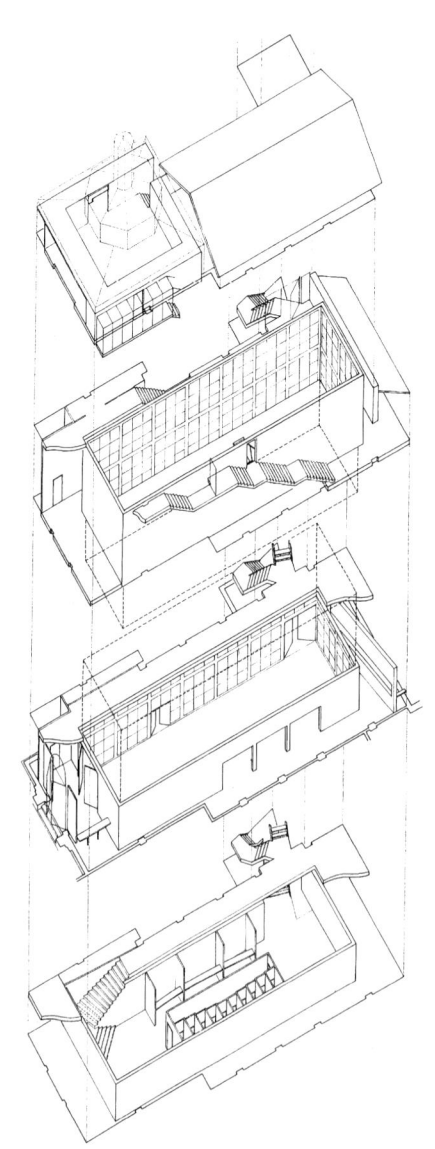

One of the new projects was the conversion of the church in the Poble Espanyol into a music bar. The building, like many others in the complex, is a collage, in this case of two well-known Spanish churches. The main facade is a

copy of the church of Alcañiz in Teruel, while the rear facade and the bell tower are derived from Utebo church in Saragossa. We liked the idea of transforming a space originally conceived for the celebration of religious rites into a secular leisure facility.

On closer consideration, we detected several similarities between the earlier religious services and the building's new function as a temple of the night. In both cases there is a concentration of people who come to show their devotion to a particular act. The space itself invites friendly communication, because everyone is embraced by the same welcoming atmosphere. There are other similarities too.

Although the building was in a state of considerable dilapidation, the interior retained the interest of the great empty space. We thus proposed to build a great translucent box occupying the whole of the interior, which measures 6 m by 21 m x 9 m in height and is faintly illuminated all around. We introduced circulation galleries in the spaces left over between the walls of the church to act as a cushion and to accommodate the other services (additional bars, toilets, DJ booth, etc.). The single diaphanous space was infringed on solely by a small viewing gallery at the highest level of the box and by the large bar on the ground floor.

87 Discotheque in Poble Espanyol 1988

Park at the southern end of the Rovira Tunnel
Barcelona

WITH MARIUS QUINTANA AND STUDENTS: ALESSANDRA DINI, HUBERT VAN DER LINDEN AND JAUME PIÑOL
1989-1991

The present park is situated in the upper part of the southern end of the Rovira Tunnel and was constructed in response to local demand. It is worth recalling that in 1985, Barcelona City Council demolished one of the viaducts of the Ronda del Guinardó expressway leading to the Rovira Tunnel in order to extend either end of the tunnel by a further 40 m, with the aim of laying out a landscaped space on top of the new stretches. This landscaped space has been conceived as a connection between the upper part of the tunnel entrance and its lower level, serving as a recreation space while at the same time constituting the landscaped framework around the Rovira Tunnel.

The difficult topography called for a system of paths making use of the gentler slopes to afford a gradual and easy ascent. Superimposed on this path system is a sequence of steps and pedestrian bridges providing more rapid links between the different points of the landscaped space. Situated at a point of inflection between the two slopes, inside a sand enclosure, is a sculpture representing a half-submerged submarine by the Catalan sculptor Riera i Aragó. As in the Parc del Migdia, the paths are raised above the terrain, with the result that they seem to float in air. Exposed concrete is used for the structure of the pedestrian bridge, the borders of the paths and the steps sunk into the ground and wood for the handrails and floor of the bridge. Elsewhere, the ground covering consists simply of grass and vegetation and beaten earth.

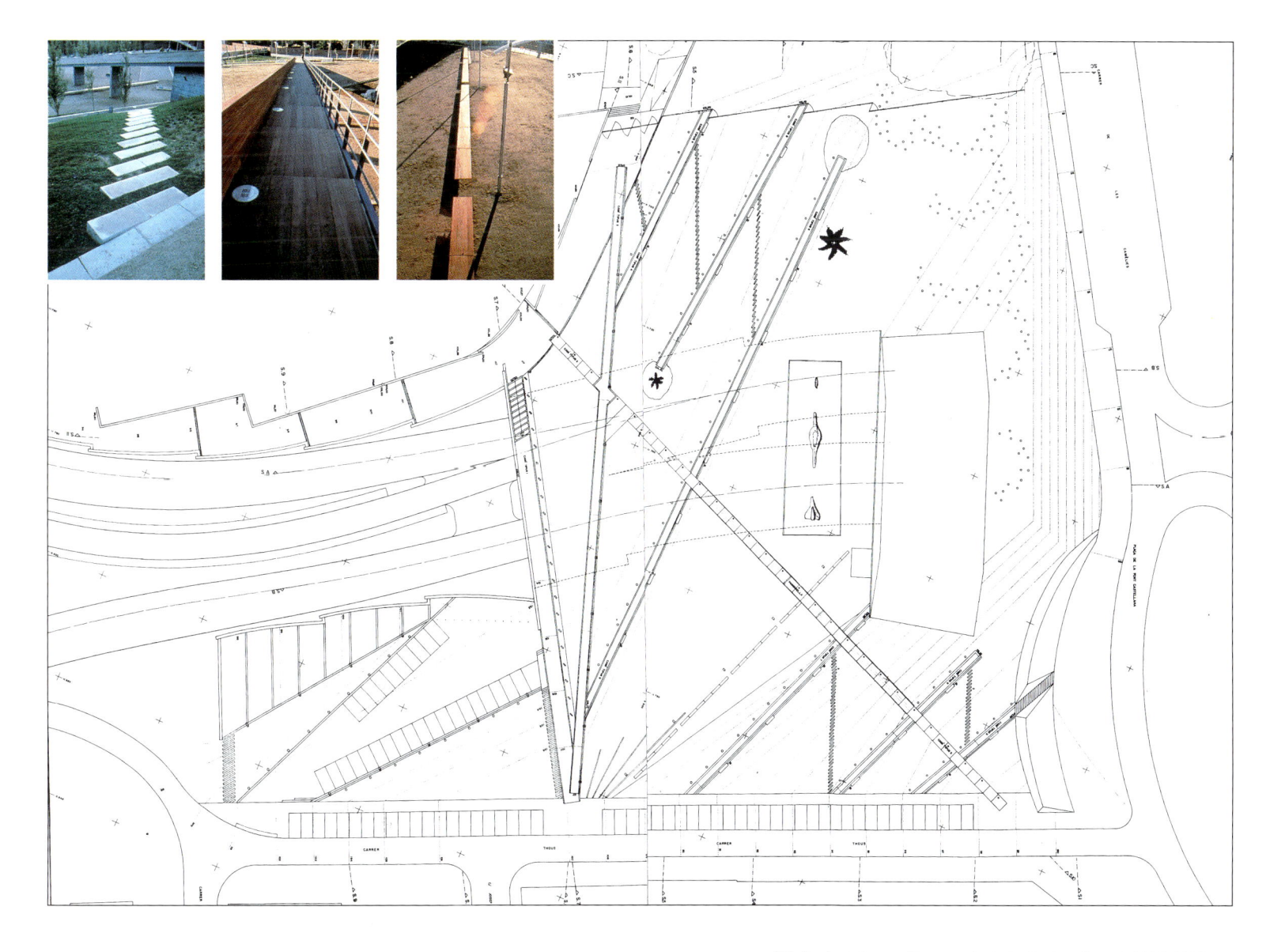

89 Park at the southern end of the Rovira Tunnel 1989-1991

Antwerpen – stad aan de stroom

Competition to remodel the harbour area in Antwerp - Antwerp

WITH MARIUS QUINTANA AND STUDENTS: ALESSANDRA DINI, HUBERT VAN DER LINDEN, JAUME PIÑOL AND WILLEM HEIN SCHENK

1990

The main concern at metropolitan level was to free the city from heavy traffic. To do this, we proposed completing the highway belt that runs around the city, so that through traffic could find an easy alternative route. It is, in fact, impossible to ever have a happy or even just peaceful coexistence between heavy traffic and pedestrians. A major highway inevitably creates a barrier which pedestrians cross with difficulty.

Bearing in mind the three areas of intervention, the first general concept was to extend the city to the north and south, leaving the entire riverfront as a public space. There is an area of intense construction to the south, which could be developed as a forest of high rises. Visually, these would work as a bookend to the city skyline. To the North, the partial filling of the Bonaparte Dock and the continuation of the street pattern into the Islet are meant to create a strong interwoven connection between the historic centre of Antwerp and this new area. The Islet would be progressively filled with construction for commercial and service use, as well as for housing. The mixture of uses, here as well as in the South, would ensure continuous activity during all hours of the day and night.

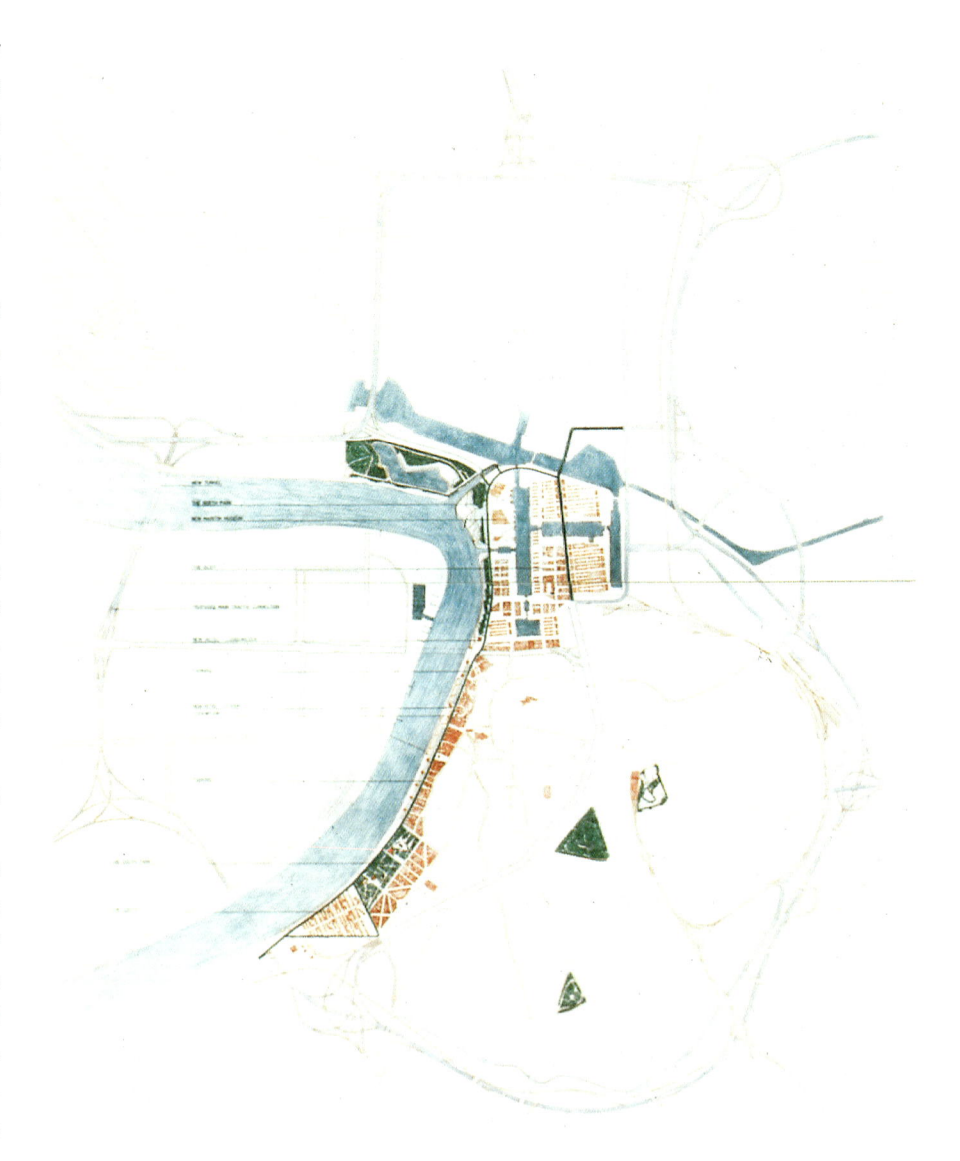

We proposed parks along the river, to both the north and south. The northern park would extend to the old dry docks, where we proposed to relocate the Maritime Museum. The southern park would offer a kind of cultural promenade through the various museums already present nearby. The clearing of the area was presented as a schematic move to stress the importance of extending the greenery to the water. This could be achieved less drastically by 'surgically' removing only those buildings that are clearly dilapidated or that can be easily relocated. This operation could even be done over time, within the general framework of the area's treatment as a park.

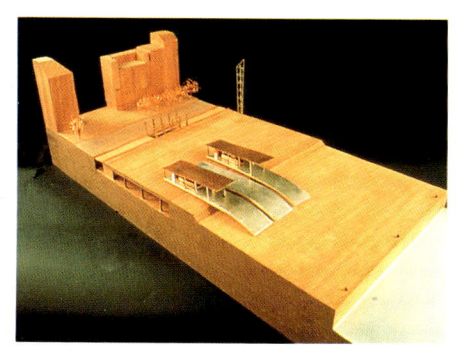

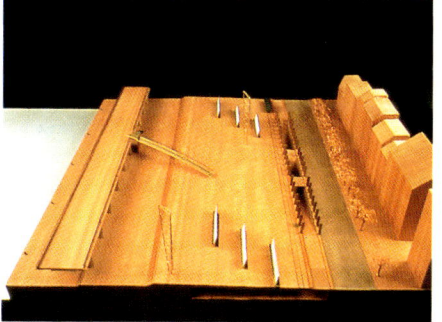

These two green masses frame the central and most important part of the project: the quay, which is presented here as a vast open space. I would like to dwell on this point for a moment to attempt to communicate the rich stratification of meanings that such open space has always had for us, becoming the connecting thread and *leitmotiv* of all subsequent choices. Culturally and historically, we are conditioned to think that intervention means addition: the mark for instance that we make with a pencil on a blank sheet of paper. Perhaps we can question this assumption and realise that the blank paper left around our mark is just as important, just as much a part of the intervention as the mark itself. It is, in fact, only thanks to the contrast between the black and the white that we can even read the mark. I maintain that clearing a space along the entire riverfront is a basic operation that will enable us to rediscover the city, to feel it, while at the same time allowing it to recover its lost relationship with the river, by setting it against a space of comparable scale. The project has been painfully stripped down until its essence is bare and every move, however minimal, acquires real significance. Once the integrity of the quay has been restored, we will create a type of section that offers a solution to the technical problems of the quay, with the least possible means.

Against this backdrop, we find some elements that can be read as set designs. The old can live with the new. The existing terrace, an important object in the memory of the city, is kept and flanked by new elements, like ramps and stairs that multiply the possible patterns of movement. We also find small bars, light towers, windbreaks, etc. In a place where architects lower their voices, where design becomes essential, where they opt for openness over clutter, simplicity over complication and lightness over weight, people will finally be able to find and create their own space, and the city as a whole will be able to appropriate and recover that basic part of itself which was lost.

Jover – Sala house

Private house in Port de la Selva - Girona

WITH MARIUS QUINTANA AND STUDENTS: HUBERT VAN DER LINDEN, JAUME PIÑOL AND METCHHILD STUHLMACHER

1990–1992

Port de la Selva is a little town on the Costa Brava, on the shore of the bay of the same name. It is located on the north side of the Cap de Creus promontory, where the Pyrenees come down to the sea. The bay opens to the sea to the north, exposing it to the strong *tramontana* and mistral winds. The nucleus of the town lies on the eastern side of the bay and faces west. This westward orientation is unique amongst the towns and villages of the Costa Brava, and brings a special light and colour to the landscape. The bay is overlooked and guarded by the monastery of Sant Pere de Roda, whose ruins crown the mountain on the west side of the bay, bearing witness to the monastic culture that existed in many parts of the Pyrenees in the 12th century. They are also a focus of visual interest from Port de la Selva.

The plot on which the house stands is located on the boundary between a small development of private houses and the centre of the town, in the midst of a grove of young Mediterranean pines. The terrain has a 40-degree slope and

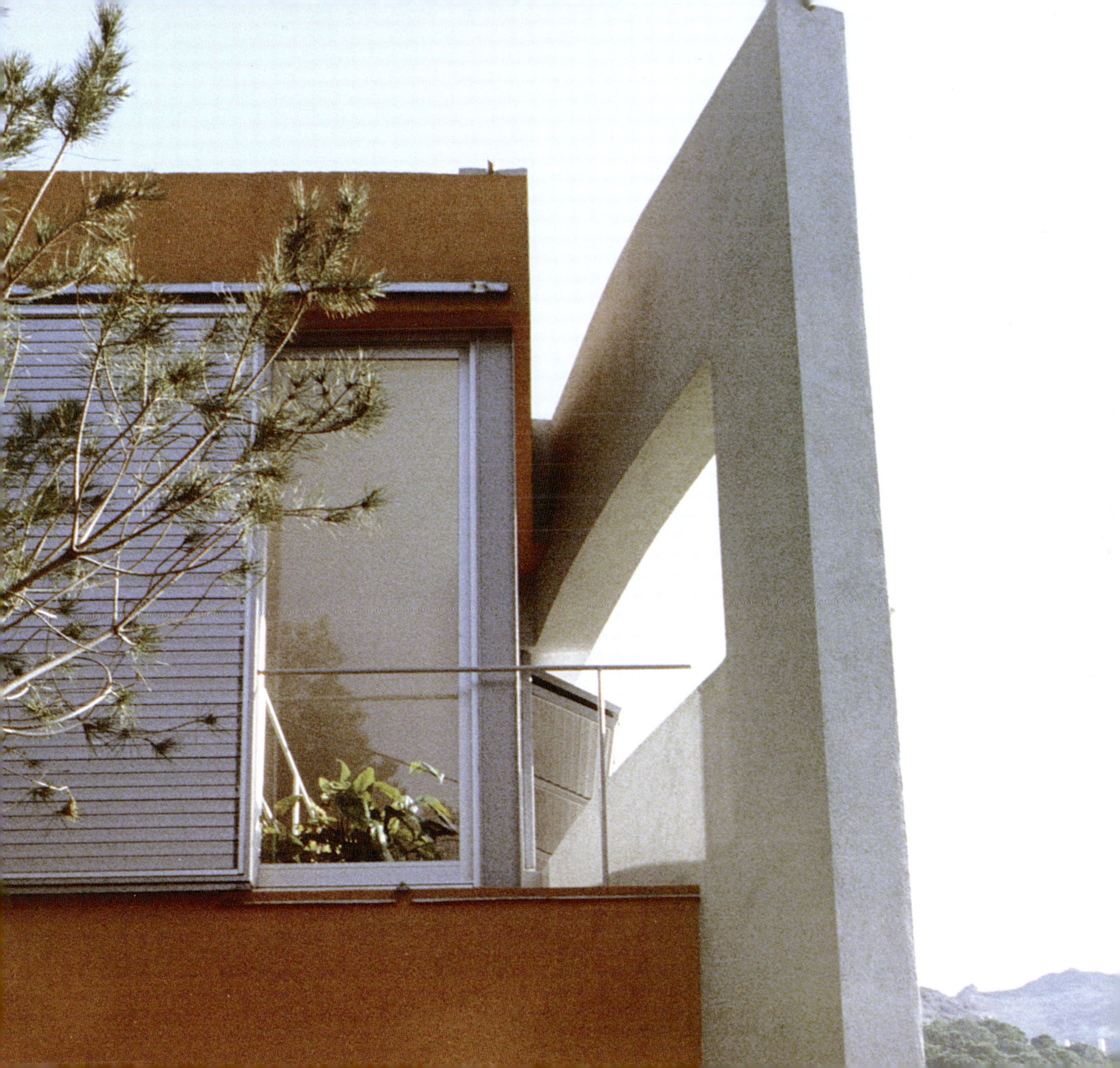

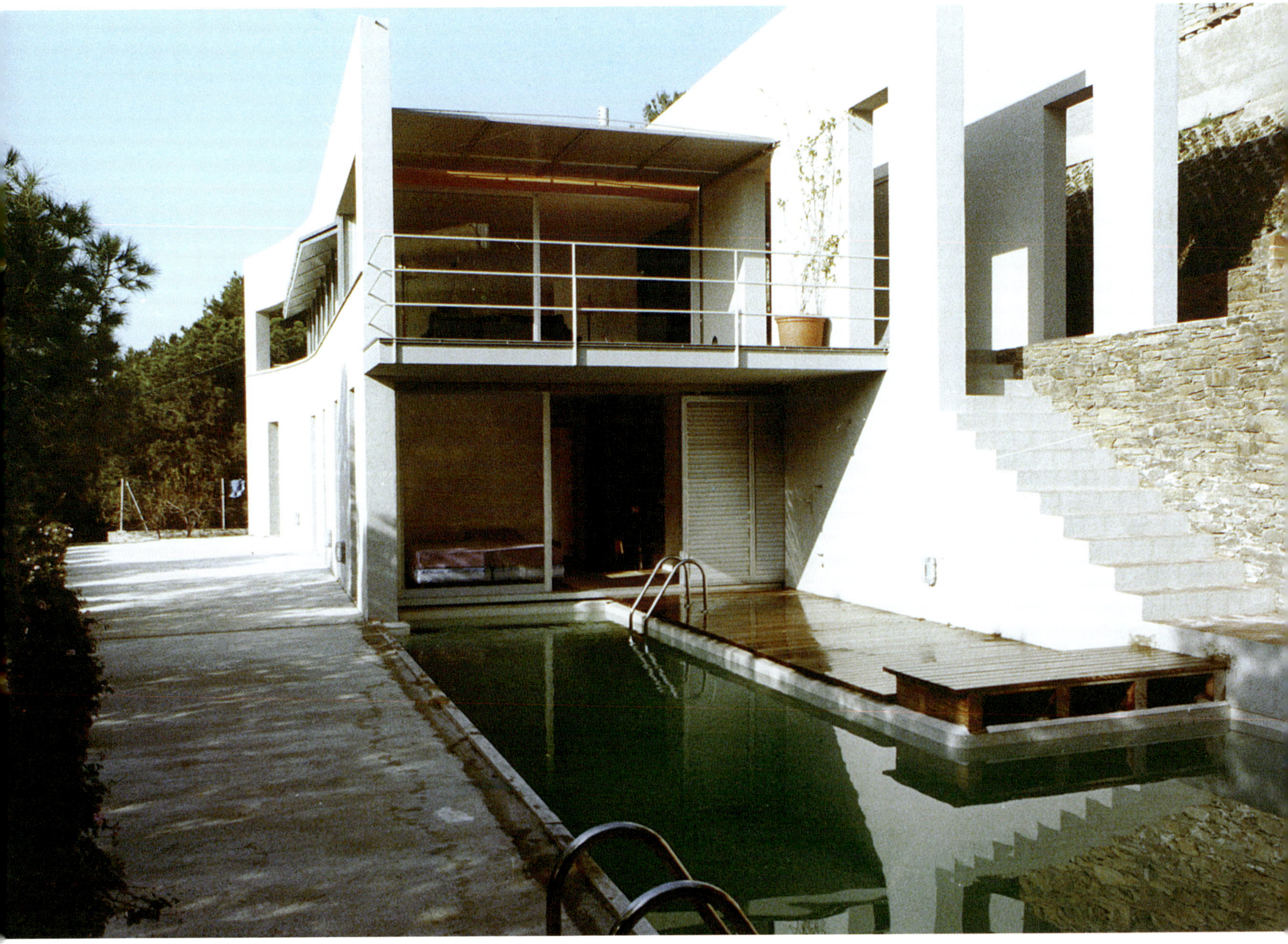

the accesses to the house are from a street running along the highest part of the site and from the public steps on the north side. The house is a second home for a family of six. The living room, dining room and kitchen are located in the upper part, where they enjoy the best views of the bay and Sant Pere de Roda. The bedrooms and swimming pool are in the lower part. The platform – which affords parking and entrance to the house – is the only constructed element at street level, since local planning regulations do not allow new buildings to project up beyond the level of the street.

Three walls running parallel to the curves of the topography order the terrain and create the spaces of the house. The interior rooms are minimal in area and each has a corresponding exterior space that adds to its size and establishes a direct relationship between interior and exterior. The walls, with their continuations, accompany this transition from inside to out. This relationship is exemplified by the swimming pool, which is considered an element of the house rather than the garden – an exterior facility related directly to the bedrooms, especially that of the parents.

Migdia Park and Sot del Migdia

Park and open-air auditorium - Barcelona

WITH STUDENTS: JAUME BENAVENT AND XAVIER ARRIOLA AND ENGINEER: JAUME LLONGUERES

1988–1992

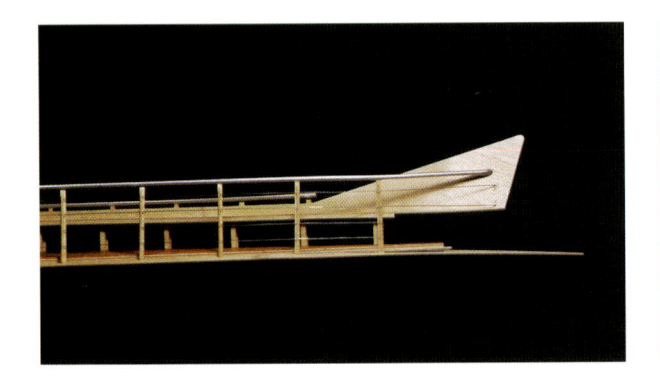

The Parc del Migdia belongs to the section of Montjuïc mountain that was left undeveloped when J.C. Nicolas Forestier laid out the park around the buildings constructed for the Barcelona Universal Exposition of 1929. Consequently, it was the last remaining sector to be incorporated into the overall development of the mountain. The new park covers an area of some 52 hectares and is sited on the southern slope of the mountain. Its position is delimited by a series of consolidated, existing elements, such as the Castle of Montjuïc, the Southwest Cemetery, the Fossar de la Pedrera, the port area and the Olympic Ring.

The Olympic project also entailed the displacement of a series of existing installations, including the Botanical Garden and the municipal vivarium, and activities like the concerts and festive events now held in the new Olympic zone. The road system also had to be upgraded and additional parking facilities provided. These new requirements prompted a reconsideration of the former uses of the mountain. There were proposals for the incorporation of a new Botanical

97 Migdia Park and Sot del Migdia 1998-1992

Garden, an open-air auditorium with an alternative function as a car park and the new Migdia Park, and for road and parking elements relating to the Olympic project.

The park project was approached as an extension of the laying out of Montjuïc as a park with a full range of facilities, while rejecting the insertion of new constructions and emphasising its character as a natural landscape. It thus continues the woodland character of the mountain, while simultaneously addressing considerations intrinsic to a park-garden. As far as vegetation was concerned, the idea was to complete Forestier's earlier intervention using native plant species and to acclimatise various Mediterranean trees. The extensive use of industrial and recycled materials in the treatment of certain sections of paving facilitated the rapid execution of the project and reduced costs.

As far as its final image was concerned, the project also focused on the area's role in the configuration of the northern façade of the Southwest Cemetery as a visual framework that could be seen from the Olympic installations. It also considered its significance as an element in the mountainscape, which would be definitively integrated into the city by the completion of the new interventions. The geometry of the system of paths constitutes the only signifying element of the park: like some grand calligraphic gesture, the paths zigzag across the inclined plane of the terrain towards the cemetery.

There is a series of strategically situated balconies that act as observation points. They correspond with the angles formed by the intersection of the various paths and afford views of the Olympic Ring, the pit of the Sot del Migdia, the Fossar de la Pedrera and the old castle in the harbour area. The principal access to the park is via the Sot del Migdia, which takes the form of a great pedestrian avenue – a spacious 'Rambla' or promenade leading to the upper part of the park, which is delimited by the cemetery.

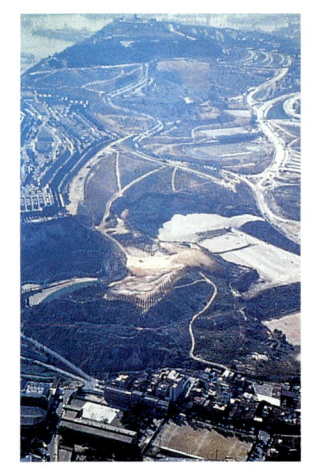

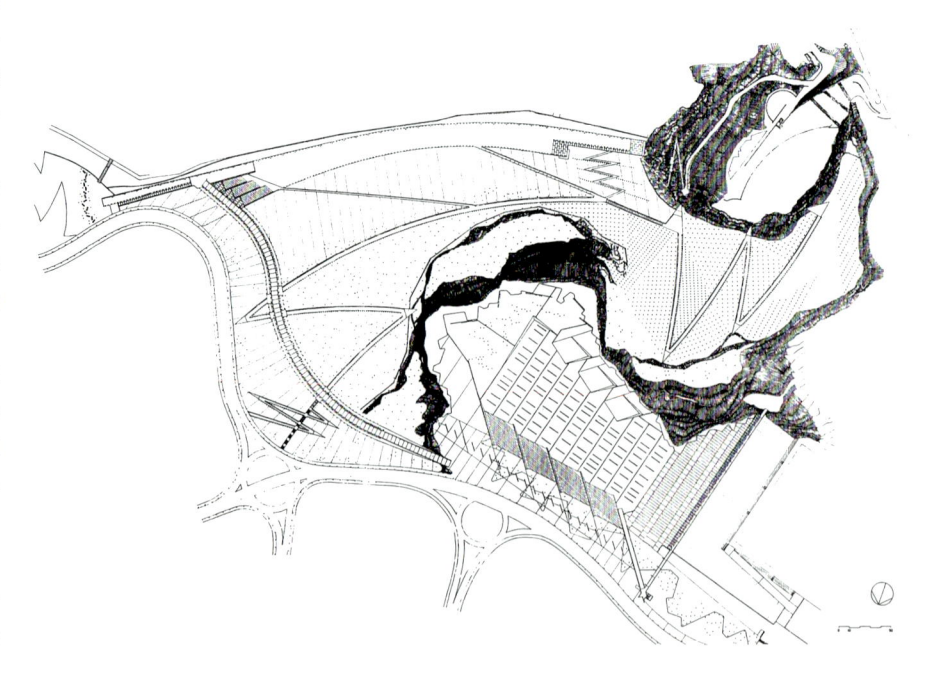

99 Migdia Park and Sot del Migdia 1988-1992

Migdia Park and Sot del Migdia 1998-1992 100

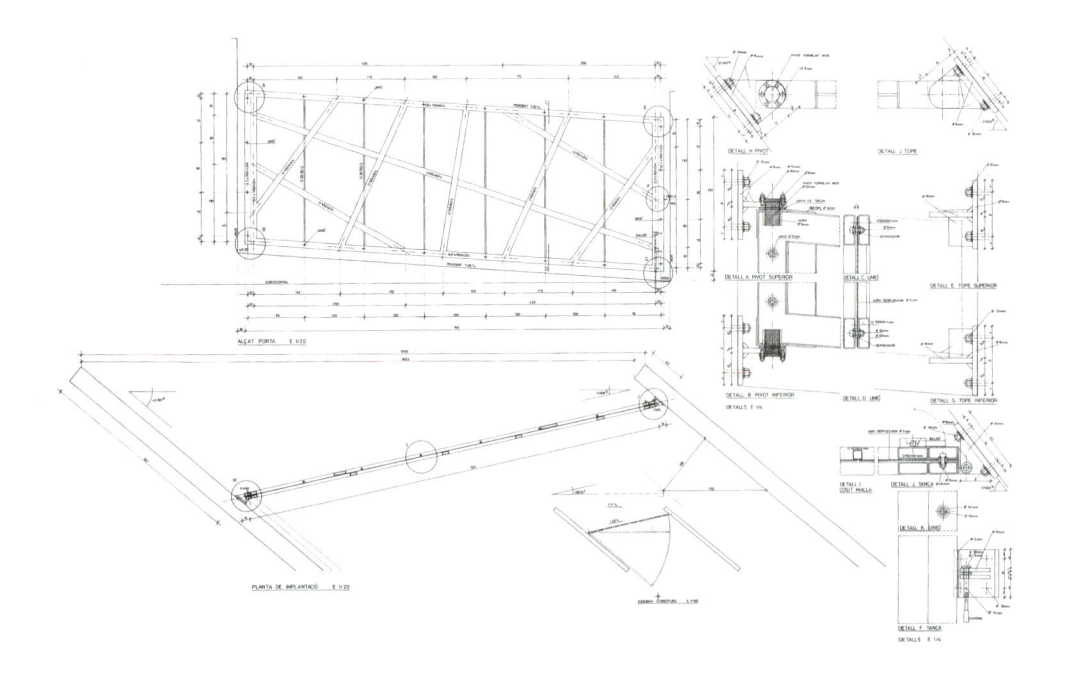

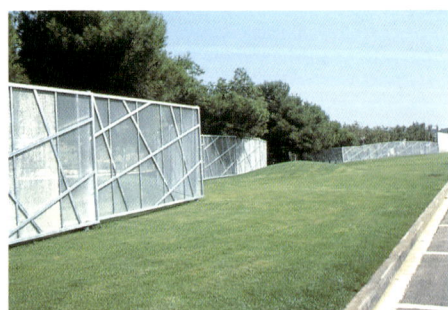

101 Migdia Park and Sot del Migdia 1998-1992

Façade and new access to the southwest cemetery

Barcelona

With students: Jaume Benavent and Xavier Arriola

1991–1992

This section of the Cementiri del Sud-Oest had grown extremely dilapidated in the previous few years. Consequently, the proposal to improve it set out to restore the order and linearity of the blocks of funerary niches as originally conceived on the cemetery's construction in 1890, while reinstating the old tradition of planting a cypress for each niche. A succession of partitions, constructed using metal meshes that allow the passage of light, was installed at the 'heads' of the blocks of niches, creating a continuous sequence of crowning elements that recomposes the cascading walls of the old Cemetery.

The treatment of the façade entailed the introduction of four elevations comprising a total of 65 modules, with a total length of 325 m. The 5 x 5 m modular screens consist of a frame of three tubular steel struts supporting a very dense stainless steel mesh to create a screening effect. An extensive plantation of cypress and pine trees was interposed between these partitions, with the idea of creating over time a uniquely spectacular effect with a verdant mass of cypresses along the cemetery's seaward façade.

The location of the new access was decided on the basis of its proximity to the main entrance to the Parc del Migdia. Situated in a gap in the Cemetery's boundary wall, the new access gate is 3 m wide and 8 m high. Its slight forward inclination is designed to accentuate the interruption of the enclosing wall, while at the same time symbolising the delicate equilibrium of life – the fragile separation between life and death. The interior slab set against an end wall of a block of niches reaffirms the singularity of the operation.

From the exterior, a carpet of bluish sandstone leads in over the grass to the interior. The proximity of the accesses to the cemetery and the Parc del Migdia itself made it necessary to remodel the square on which the two entrances are situated.

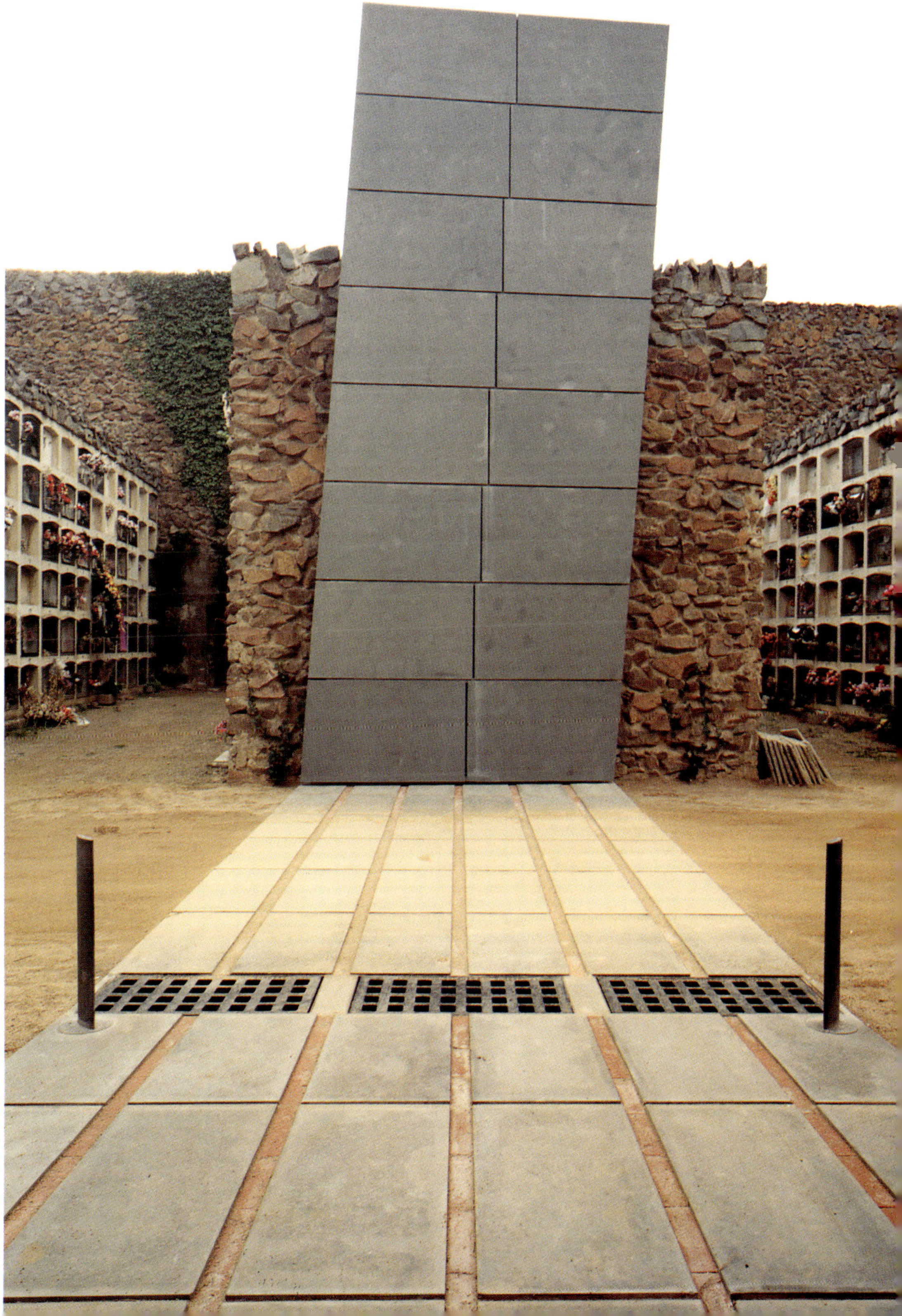

New accesses to the mountain of Montjuïc
Barcelona

WITH PERE LLIMONA, XAVIER RUIZ-VALLÉS AND STUDENTS: JAUME BENAVENT AND XAVIER ARRIOLA
AND ENGINEER: JAVIER RUI-WAMBA

1991–1992

The pedestrian bridges over the Avinguda de Rius i Taulet are something of a structural innovation in our country. Constructed in high-strength concrete (700 H), they cover a span of 30 m with an almost imperceptible structure. The choice of a minimal structure was effectively imposed by a site in which the new architecture of the footbridges would have to coexist with the historical architecture constructed for the 1929 International Exhibition.

The pedestrian bridges form part of the general project to provide access to the mountain of Montjuïc undertaken in preparation for the 1992 Olympic Games. The accessibility plan also included the introduction of 14 escalators to carry people to and from the Olympic facilities on Montjuïc. They cover a total height of 60 m.

In the first section of this general access system, the two footbridges span the frequently heavy traffic of the Rius i Taulet Avenue, and a considerable difference in level, to bring visitors directly to the foot of the escalators. Corten steel and glass complement the hardness of the concrete.

105 New accesses to the mountain of Montjuic 1991-1992

Habitationes misteriosas (Mysterious rooms)

Competition for the new headquarters of La General savings bank - Granada

WITH STUDENTS: ALESSANDRA DINI, JAVIER BRUNELLO, RAMON CANALS, MARGARET KOOLE, ROLAND KUHN, KATHLEEN LINDSTROM, AROLA TOUS AND JUAN PABLO SAUCEDO

1992

It was not easy to decide how to group together the programme required for the offices of the client – a major Spanish savings bank – in a very tall vertical building. City redevelopment plans indicated that the space to be occupied by the office building was to be surrounded in the not too distant future by enclaves of single-family houses. This small 'garden city' zone suggested to us that the vacant space should be conceived as an extension of the urban fabric to be generated by the garden city. That meant it would be formed by a pattern of low-rise buildings with garden courtyards – typical of Granada and many other Andalusian towns. The low density essential to the establishment of such a system of houses and gardens would be disturbed only by a slender tower inserted into its centre like a needle. Without this vertical element, the height of all of the buildings in the office zone would invariably increase, resulting in a significant imbalance in urban planing terms between the component parts. The tower is located some distance from the historic centre of Granada and seems to mark the city's boundary. It serves as a point of reference while remaining respectful of its context. Its various functions constitute the organisational structure of the building, which flows downwards from on high. A perimeter wall closes off the space, with openings for access to the walkways that cross laterally from the point providing descent via ramps to the landscaped buildings. The ramps enter the buildings.

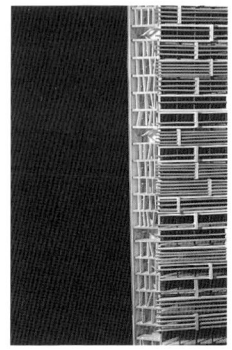

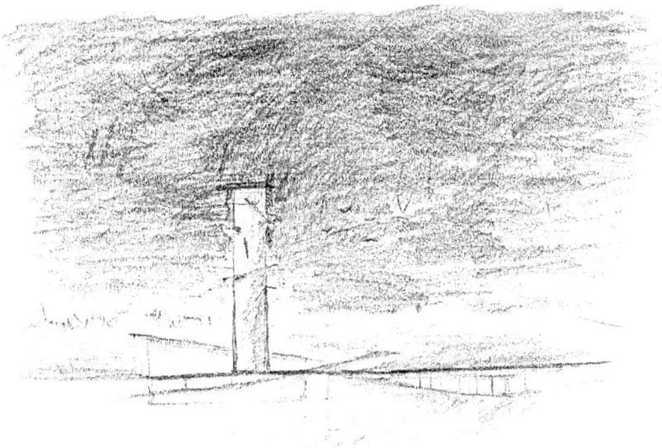

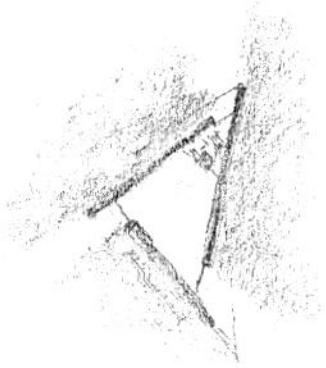

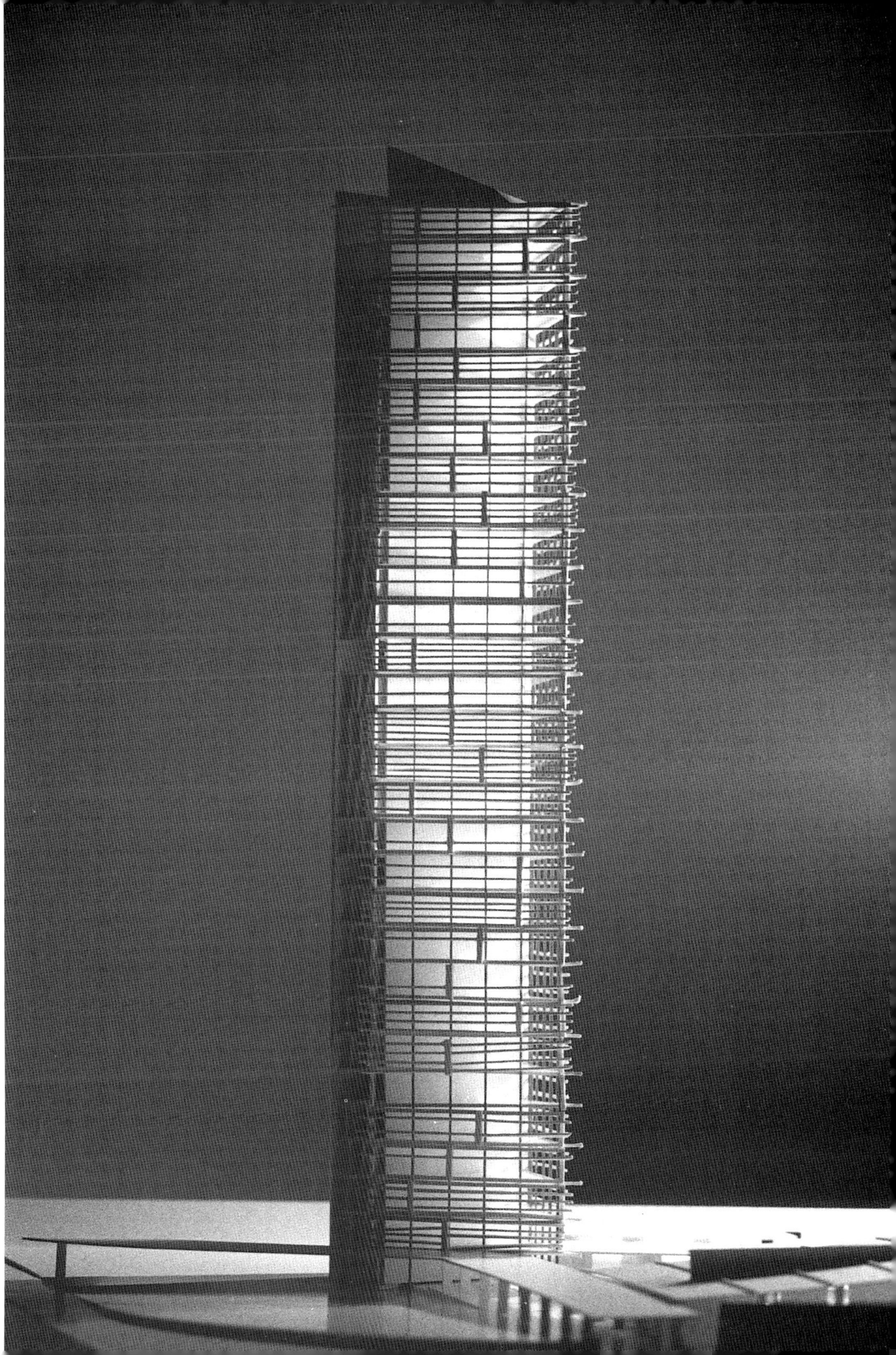

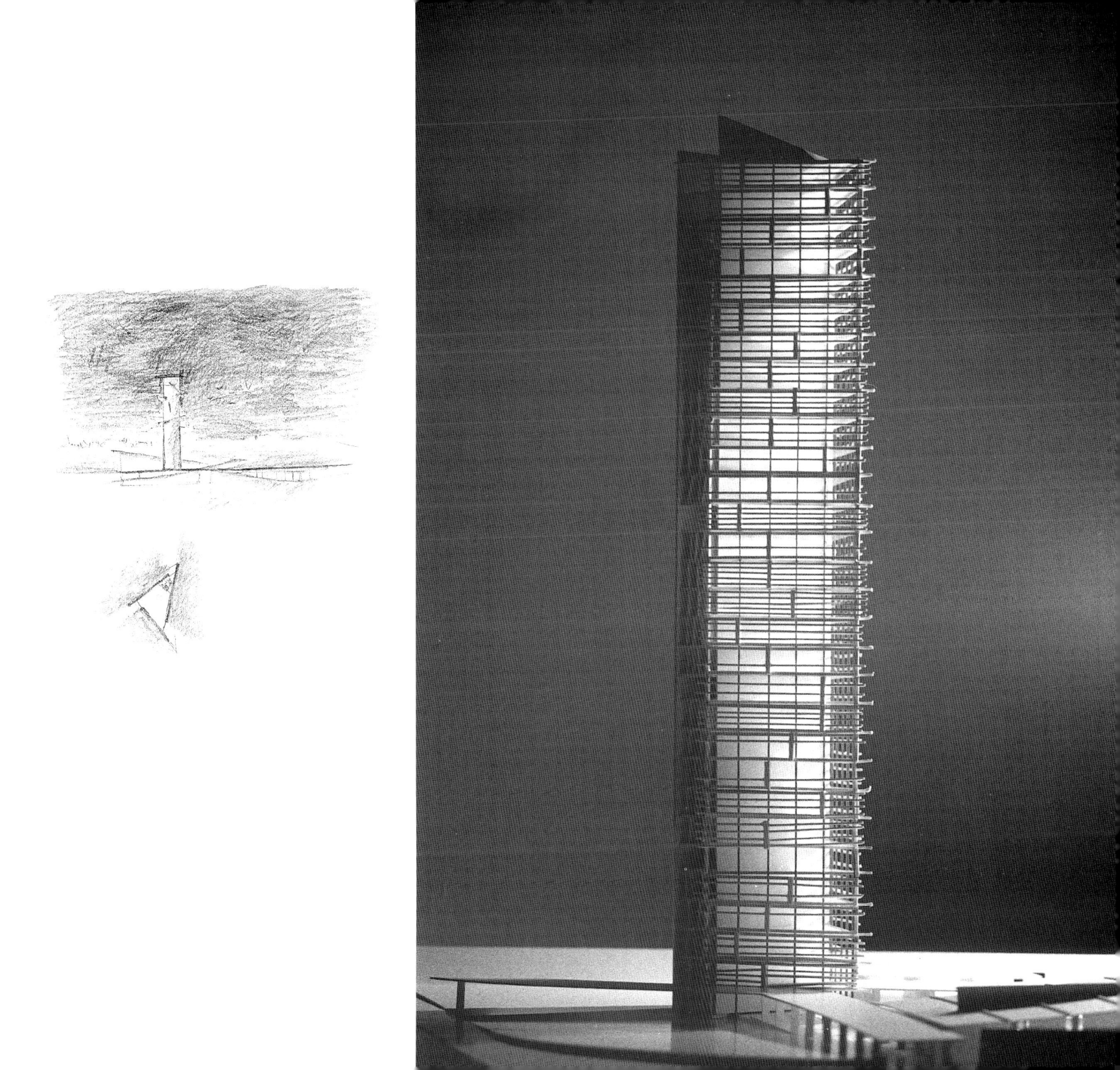

LEMA HABITACIONES MISTERIOSAS

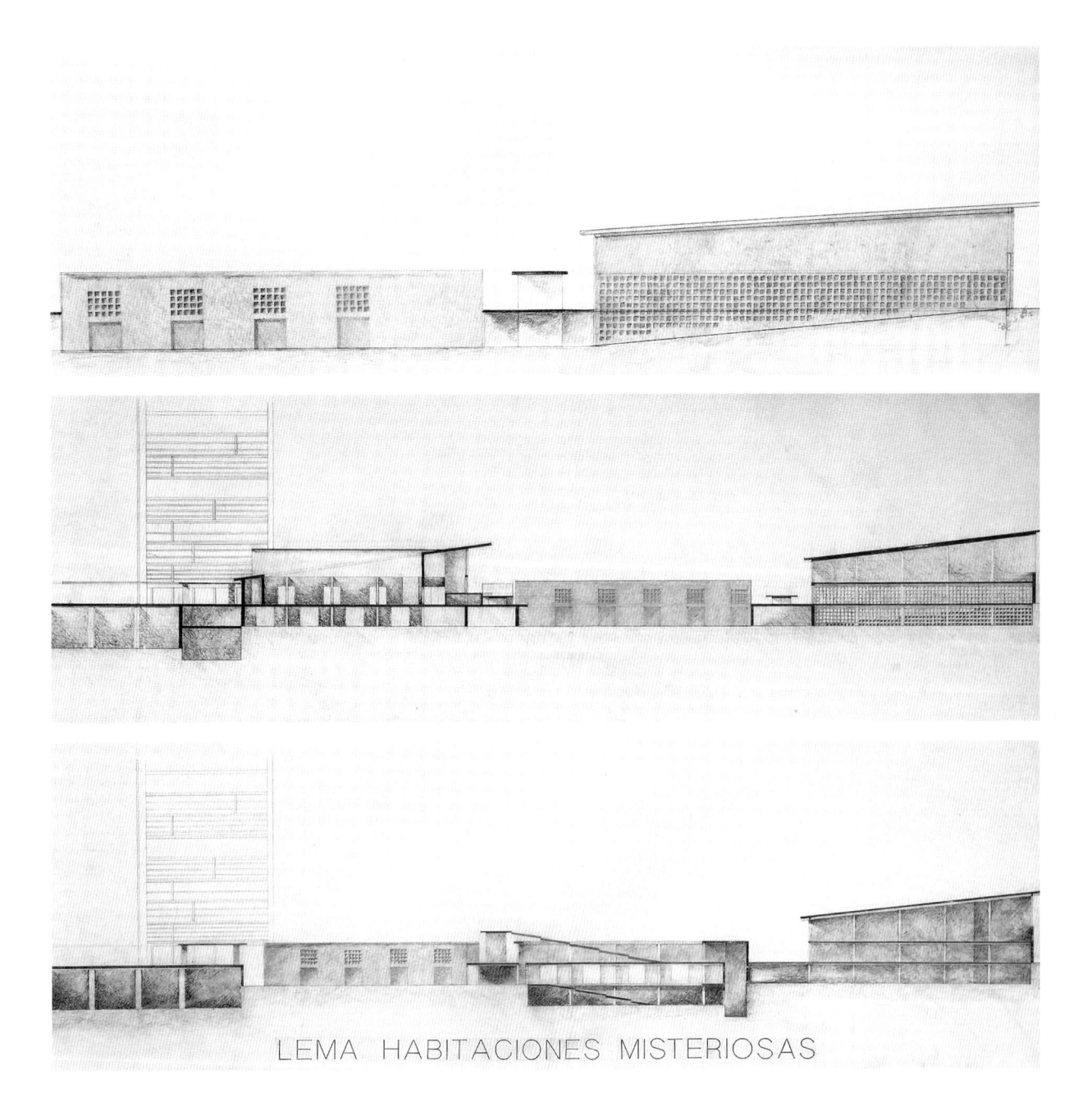

109 Habitaciones misteriosas 1992

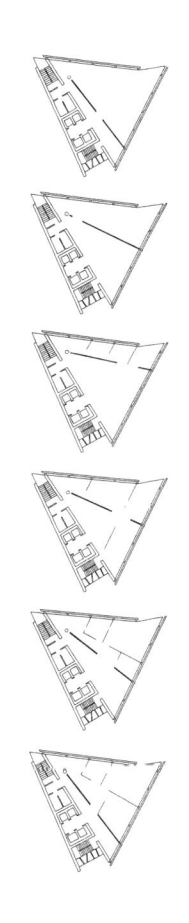

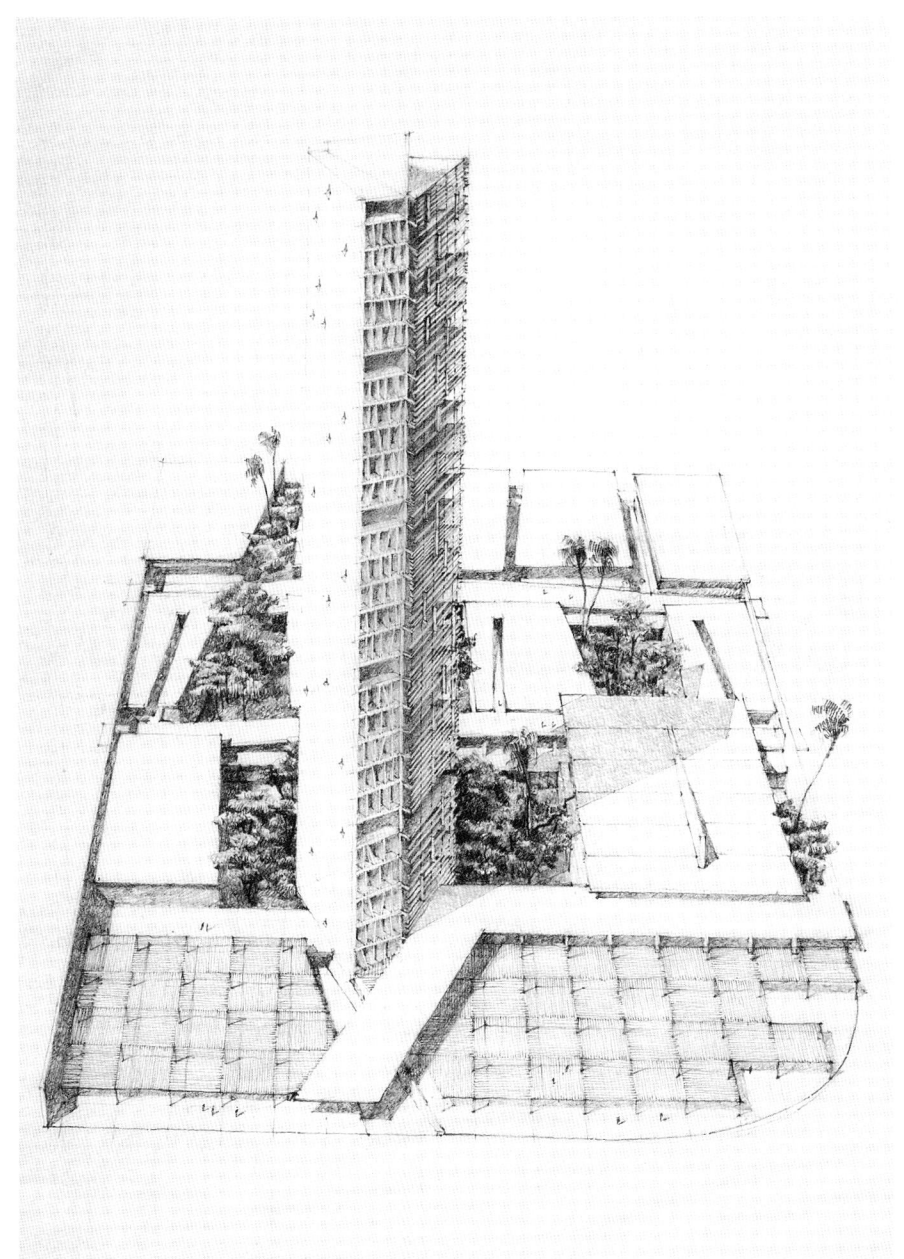

Spreebogen

Competition for the new Bundesrat, the Chancellery and the Bundestag - Berlin

WITH MOISÉS GALLEGO AND STUDENTS: JAUME BENAVENT AND ALESSANDRA DINI

1992

The enormous symbolic value of the project and the vastness of the site called for landmark buildings which, together with the Reichstag, would be capable of setting the image of the new Germany, without erasing the traces of history. It seemed important to respect the void created by the war, placing the most emblematic buildings – the Bundesrat, the Chancellery and the core of the Bundestag – as singular edifices in a park area. What's more, the location of the less symbolic activities of the Bundestag at one level below grade allows the three buildings to come to the surface, appearing only in their most emblematic functions.

The rest of the programme is concentrated close to the perimeter of the site, where it can effect the transition from the tight city grid to the openness of the ceremonial spaces. The Bundestag is shaped around the idea of marking the cross-axis of Platz der Republik with a building that responds to the monumentality of the square without sacrificing the human scale or diminishing the importance of the Reichstag. A lightly sloping platform – serving as both public space and built landscape – gently rises towards the building and goes through and beyond it, simultaneously extending the square and roof of two storeys of administrative offices for Committees (55,683 m^2) and Parliamentary Groups (41,072 m^2). The offices are in direct contact with the park and receive light by way of planted patios and along the three sides of the perimeter.

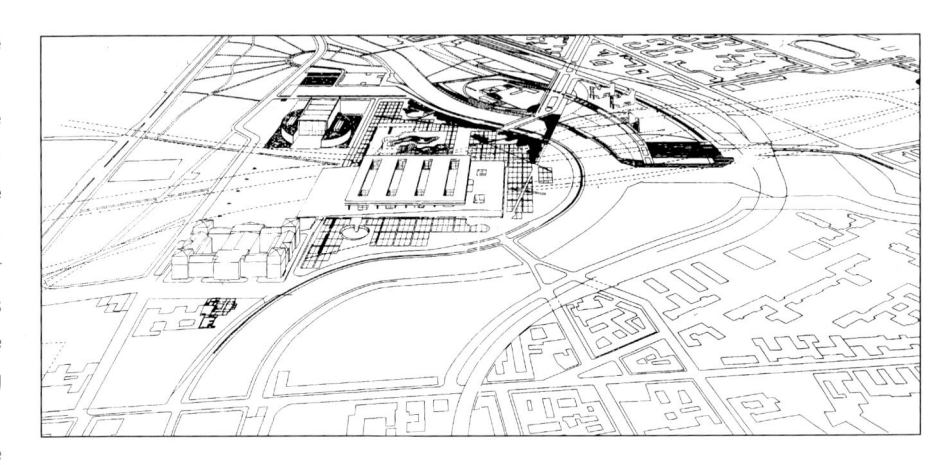

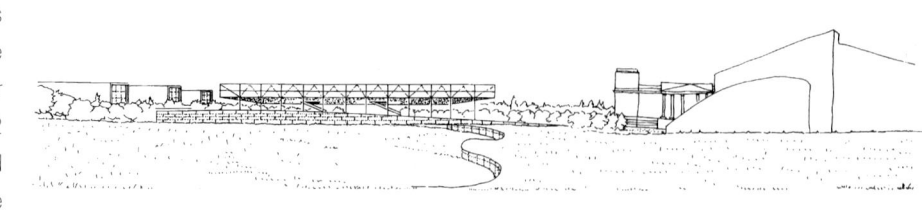

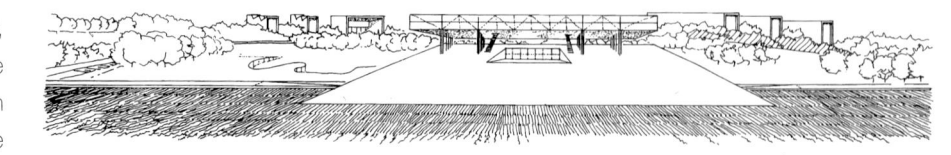

Hovering over the intermediate public space is a slender, two-storey slab containing the most important part of the Bundestag: the offices of the Members of Parliament, with their corresponding administrative services (85,084 m^2). The

extremely planar proportions of this building – one hundred and seventy-two metres long by eight metres high – and its almost two-dimensional appearance, mean that it never competes with the Reichstag, while its complete permeability means it is never perceived as oppressive or forbidding. Along the Platz der Republik and perpendicular to the main building, a further level below grade houses the social and recreational parts of the programme (6,880 m²) as well as the exhibition *Questions on German History* (4,800 m²) and the space for visitors (6,852 m²). The building is hidden from view from the square but is revealed on the side adjoining the park by the manipulation of the landscape. It forms a visual limit to the park, yet manages to avoid being perceived as an obstacle from the square.

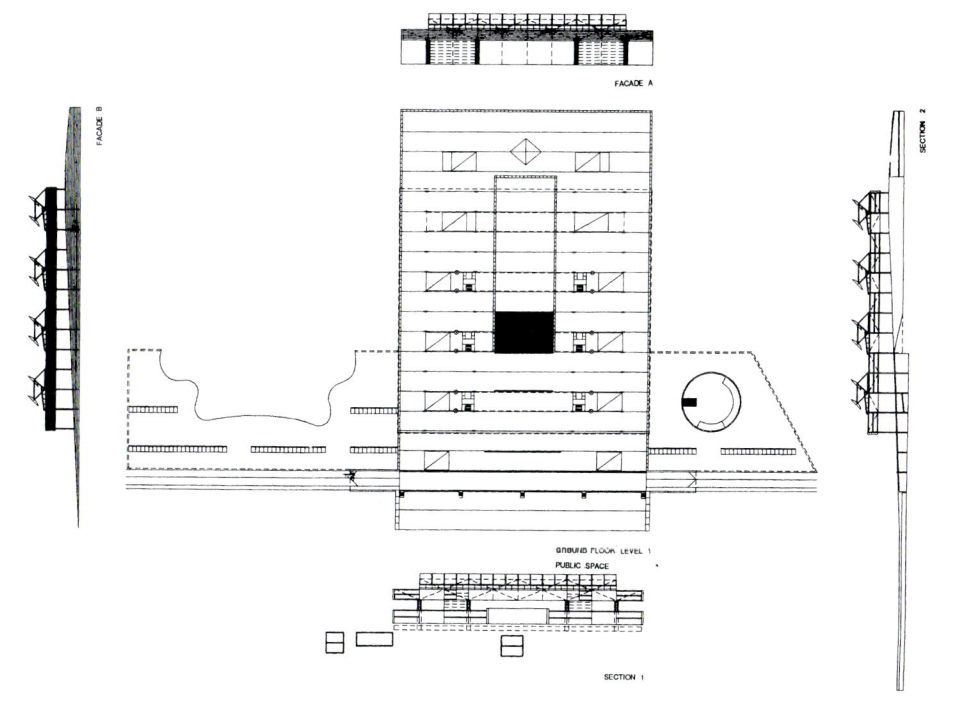

Since the Bundestag deserves to be an integral part of Platz der Republik, it seemed valid to alter slightly the course of the tunnels designed to pass under the best part of the site. The structure of the building is intended to straddle the tunnels, with two rows of pillars between them. To complete the Platz der Republik on the western side, the Federal Council building directly confronts the Reichstag, as a reflection of the balance between the two chambers of Parliament. This is thought of as a self-contained form articulated in three volumes, with the plenary chamber in the centre. Whereas the Bundestag is characterised by a lightness and transparency which allow it to respond to both the formal space of the Platz der Republik and to the park, the Bundesrat emerges as a piece of architecture which, although on the same axis as the Reichstag, eludes any direct frontal engagement with it.

In terms of the division of powers, it seemed logical to separate the Executive from the Legislative branch of Government. Viewing the entire site as a vast park, with the viaduct as its visual limit, the Chancellery is located on the other side of the river, with its main building oriented towards the Parliament. The visual, rather than physical, accessibility of the Chancellery establishes a direct and immediate relationship with the Parliament, whereas the ceremonial length of the drive leading up to it dignifies the approach and seems more appropriate for a part of the Government that is less intimately connected with the people. As a blind box with only one façade, the building opens up towards the river, forming a single grand vestibule flanked by wings of offices. The Chancellor's offices hang in the middle like a lintel above the entrance.

On the other side of Alt Moabit Street, the Chancellor's residence in the old Customs house is directly connected with the Federal Chancellery by the existing underpass. Taking advantage of the planned park to the east of Moabiter Werber, this guarantees the Chancellery a certain privacy and a buffer zone between it and the city.

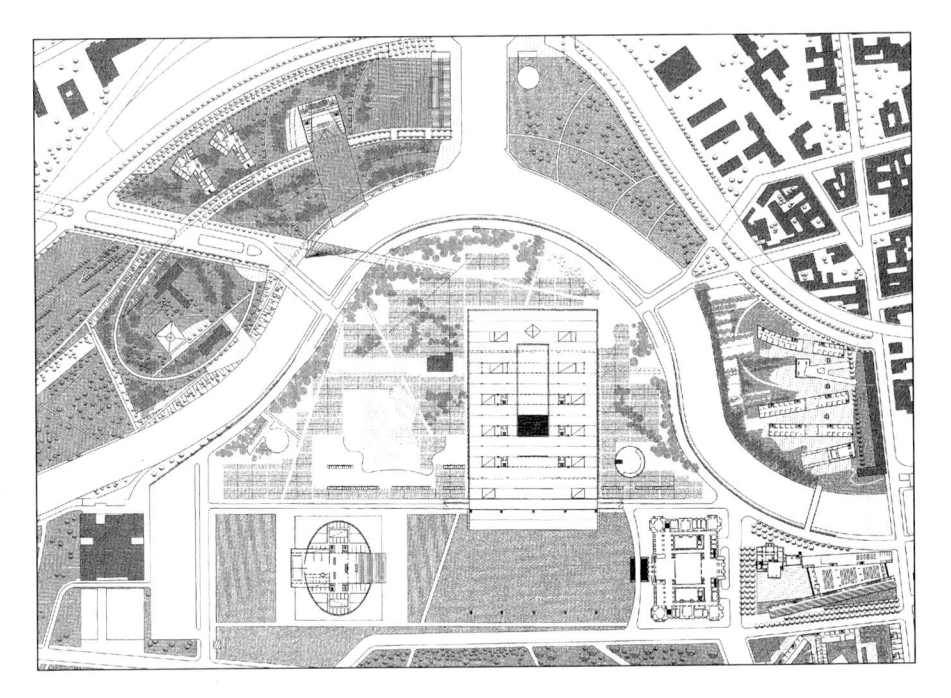

To the east of the Reichstag lies the transition point between the Spreebogen district and the city, as the viaduct to the north and the Tiergarten to the south prevent any further direct contact with the urban fabric. A series of narrow rectangular buildings attempts to break up the system of large city blocks typical of Berlin. They are placed irregularly along the east-west axis to filter views through to the Spreebogen area, and most of all to avoid creating new barriers in such a historically sensitive part of the city, where the memory of the Wall still weighs heavy. These buildings accommodate the functions most closely related with the outside world – the Federal Press Conference suite, the Press Club and the Documentation Centre – which, in their role as provider or recipient of information, act as a link between Parliament and people. A public library was also proposed to conclude the sequence on the side of Pariser Platz, effectively completing the square and creating a point of cultural attraction.

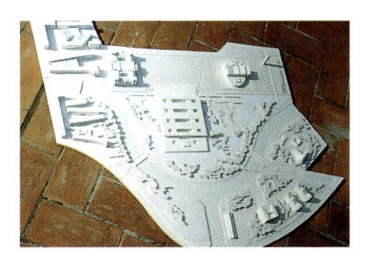

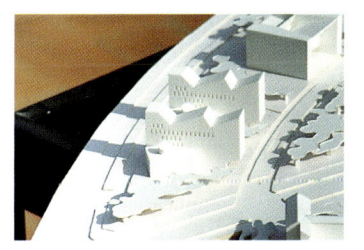

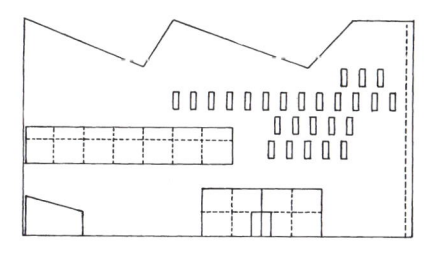

FACADE B

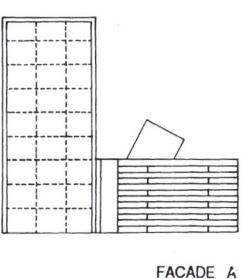

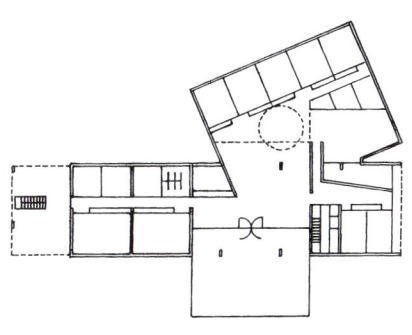

FACADE A

GROUND FLOOR LEVEL

Una nube sobre Berlin (A cloud over Berlin)

Competition to lay out two parks at Potsdamer Platz - Berlin

With students: Jaume Benavent, Armin Schäfer, Alex Giménez, Jeroen Luttikhuis, Arola Tous, Andrea Tous and Susana Guillermo

1995

In the course of this century, Berlin has suffered one of the most tortured development processes in history. Its historic centre was totally destroyed by war. What was once a compact and well-structured nucleus is today a distressing void, inhabited only by modern dinosaurs sustained by long, disjointed extremities that vainly seek the cohesion and comfort of urban structures that are no longer there. The reconstruction of our cities should not neglect their early history, but neither should it ignore their more recent past. It is the public zones – urban spaces for communal use – that take on the key role in urban cohesion and restructuring. Streets, squares, avenues, parks and all those other, designed public spaces make up a grid responsible for restoring to the city a proper understanding of its structure.

It was with this idea in mind that the current project directed its reorganising efforts, taking into account the symbolic role that the new communal spaces should exercise. The implanting of such spaces appeared to us to be especially promising because of their exceptional location in the city. The presence of East and West in Berlin will continue in our memories and it will be hard for the city to cast off this distinguishing quality. A project remote from this reality would be divorced from half a century of the city's history. And the worst thing that could happen to this city of such dramatically varied fortunes would be to sacrifice its unique feel by getting carried away by an ambitious commitment to renewal. This indescribable, emotive capacity – gradually cultivated by the city's wounds – has come with the passage of time to constitute its greatest virtue in relation to other European cities.

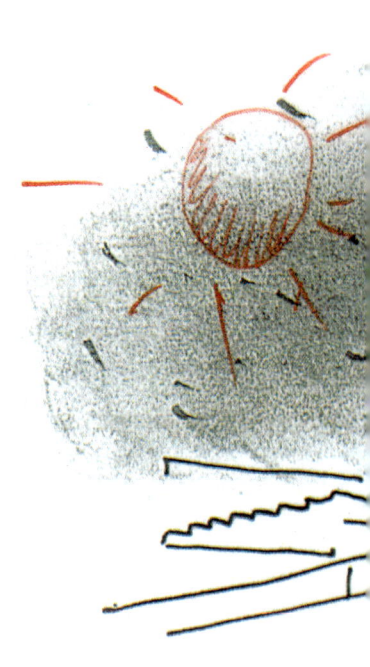

115 Una nube sobre Berlin 1995

The project for Potsdamer Avenue comprised four geometrical planes – the transverse section, longitudinal section, west elevation and east elevation. These are all specific solutions derived from general concepts. We attempted to make these general concepts felt, without their being literally perceived in the final appearance.

a. Transverse section: connective capacity

The excessive distance between the façades of the buildings that bound the space of Potsdamer Avenue acts as a barrier, causing breakdowns in the connection between the two sides. The transverse section asks to be understood as a desire subtly to reflect the gesture performed by so many thousands of visitors over the years to get to a higher level in order to see the other side. In this case, getting up higher enables us to find life. We are talking about the accumulation of spaces for leisure use, but also for reflection. Spaces with life, but also tranquil spaces.

The upward movement from the street to the west of the highest point in the direction of the opposite façade is effected by means of a series of stepped planes. These produce a very gentle, almost imperceptible ascent to the longitudinal promenade at a height of 1.70 m above the side streets. A variety of small pavilions for bars and restaurants are located along the latter. There is a linkage, in other words, with communal recreational activities, which will ensure the full utilisation of the space. From this raised promenade a sequence of steps and ramps descend to the East side.

b. Longitudinal section: linearity

The total length of 500 m with a regular section made it difficult to adapt to a constantly changing context. The city's own inflections meant each space had to be considered in relation to them. We opted to concentrate the singular points at the nodes of urban inflection, in such a way that the designed space would relate to each of the different parts of the neighbourhood. The singular points along the course of the Avenue are concentrated at the moments of greatest urban tension: the meeting with the river and with Potsdamer Platz. In other words, at the beginning and the end of the Avenue. From the Potsdamer Platz end, a sheet of water diverts pedestrian traffic to the sides in order to arrive laterally, in the baroque manner, at the central space. The singular quality of the place is re-affirmed by an installation by the artist Hans Haacke, which contributes to the memory of the new neighbourhood. At the opposite end, the play of the bridge and the footbridge serves to singularise the encounter with the river and at the same time marks out the gateway between East and West, in addition to its immediate function of connecting the new district with Gleisdreiek.

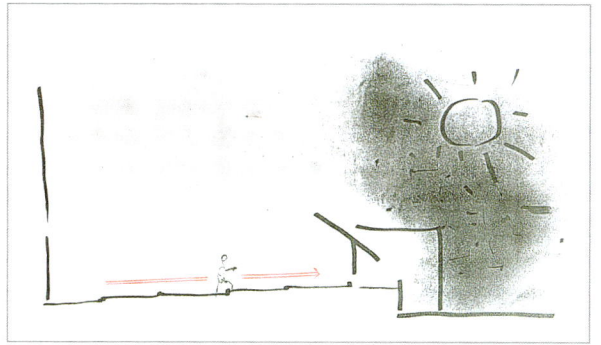

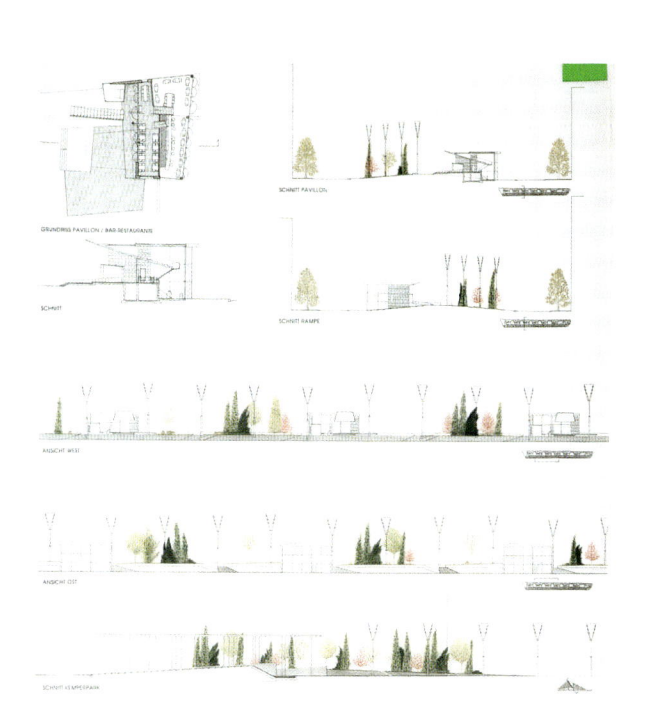

c. West elevation: open permeability

The introduction of a linear element of considerable width dividing a residential neighbourhood can give rise to problems of permeability in that element and hence of connection between the two sides. The slope of the terrain makes a kind of reverential bow to the opposite side, amounting to a gesture of attraction in its direction. Urban spaces need to be lived by the citizens. If they are not, they are liable to become agents of degradation and division within the neighbourhood.

The slightly sloping surface in the foreground, consisting of a longitudinal ramp-stairway, gently accompanies the visitor to the upper promenade under the trees. The stepped plane accommodates the activity generated by the bars and restaurants. Like luminous panels, the lights at night announce the presence of life and hence accessibility. The stepped surface is entirely transitable, wide, open to the upper promenade from which numerous ramps and flights of steps lead to the eastern façade.

d. East elevation: secret permeability

Berlin is a romantic city. This site ought to pay tribute to its most precious quality – to create small, secret, fragmented spaces where a respect for privacy should be the primary objective. This is the aim of the east elevation: to break the wall, to find routes of escape for re-encounters with others and tranquil spaces.

The elevated promenade, in counterpoint to the great open space of the stepped surface, is fragmented into landscaped subspaces in the style of the hanging gardens and balconies over the east street. From these, ramps and stairs at frequent intervals lead down to this street, ensuring effective connection between the two.

The small architectural elements for bars and restaurants are located half way between the raised promenade and the street, so that the street is inhabited and animated by these and their open-air terraces in summer. The East façade is thus composed of an alternating sequence of glazed, luminous buildings, hanging gardens and frequent accesses to the open space of the West.

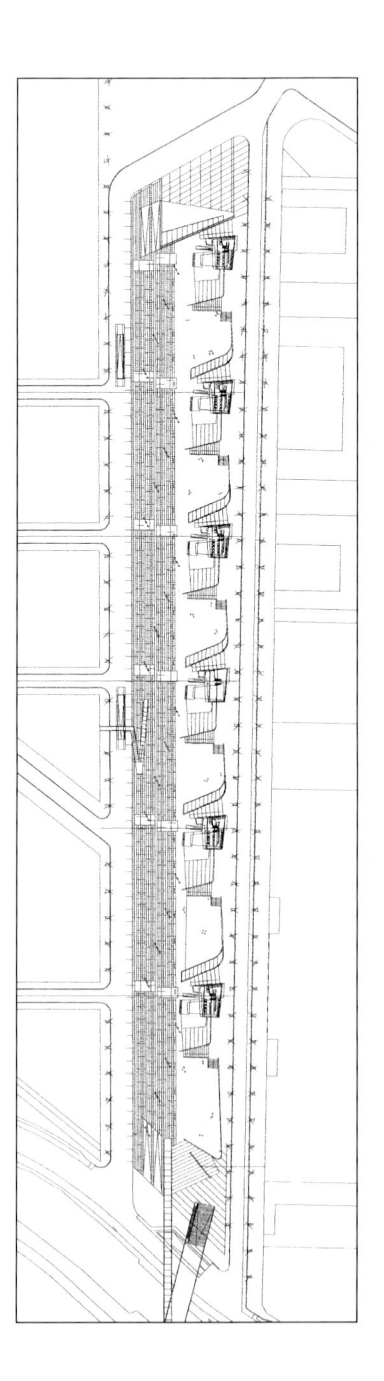

Kemper Park

Kemper Park has an intermediate scale: too large to be considered as merely a square, but too small to be regarded as a city park. The aim, then, was to arrive at the most appropriate scale, in terms of both dimensions and use. The park's twin faces – towards the Tiergarten and towards the Sony building – prompted us to think of a dual interpretation of its space: one sector in direct relation to the park and the other, more urban sector connecting with the neighbourhood. However, in its situation and its triangular form, Kemper Park simultaneously exercises a tension of centrality that the project could hardly ignore.

The project can be interpreted as a natural extension of the setting, allowing its own limits to speak for themselves: a pair of large, sloping planes form two landscaped zones as a continuation of the Tiergarten and the landscaped area of the housing. In front of the Sony building, the paved square is the external continuation of the building's roofed public space. Its central character is reflected by the way the entire space revolves around the *Mitjó* sculpture by Antoni Tàpies, situated beneath the central canopy. The pieces making up the space are thus transformed into the monumental base for the Tàpies sculpture.

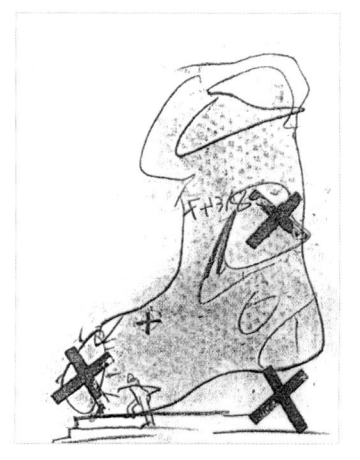

'Mitjó', A. Tàpies

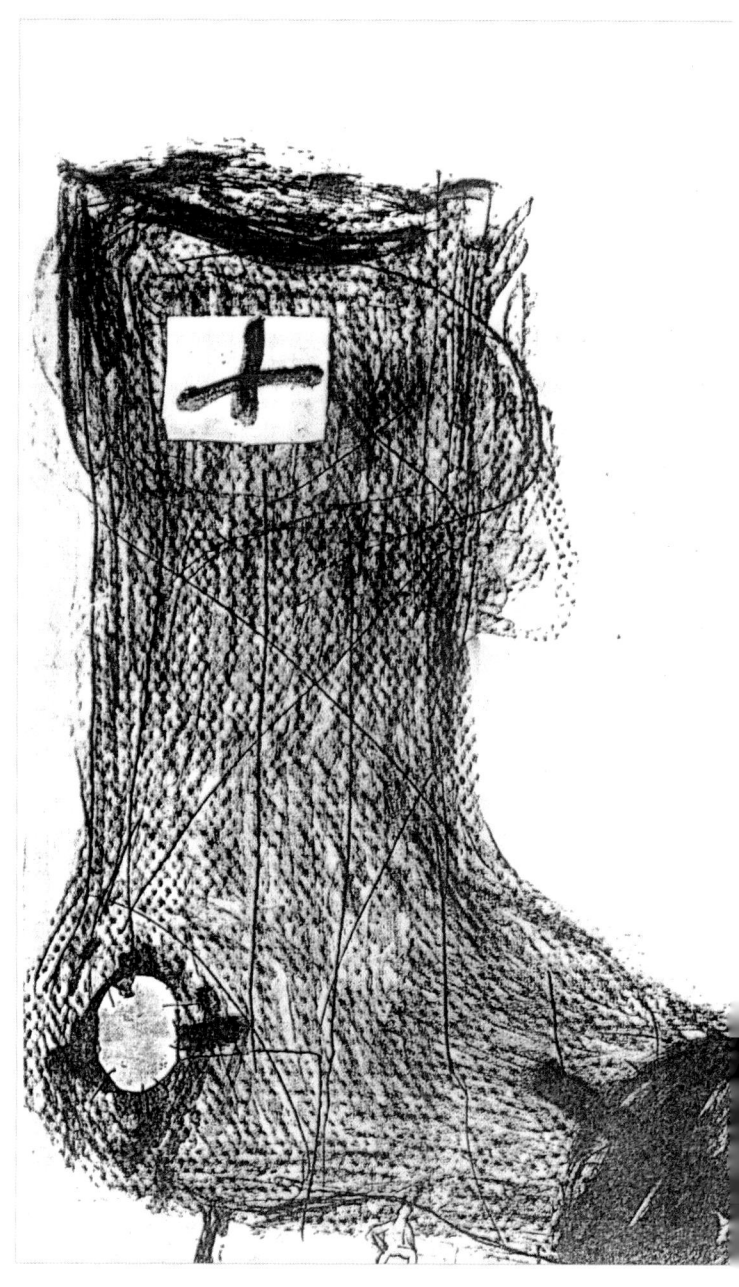

Zafra Parc

Project for the new front of the harbour of Huelva - Huelva

With students: Jaume Benavent, Alex Giménez, Clemens Nuijens, Vicenç Mulet, Anna Birgisdottir, Arola Tous and Andrea Tous

1994

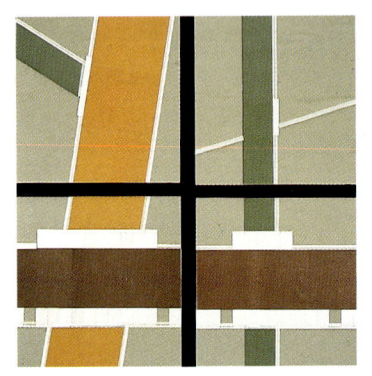

If we analyse the evolution of Europe's port cities, we find that a similar phenomenon has taken place at most of them in terms of the displacement of the mercantile and industrial harbour zones and the corresponding loss of the urban role originally possessed by the docks. The importance of maritime transport generated large areas of waterfront occupied by infrastructures relating to the activities of the port. Another, even greater tendency was for such cities to grow up with their backs to the harbour and hence to the sea or river. Maritime and river transport and traditional fishing activities have evolved over time, shifting the old facilities that had generated mercantile wealth to sites less closely linked to urban structures. The latter relate instead to industrial zones located at varying distances from the actual cities, freeing up large areas of land close to the historic urban centre for other uses.

This has been the recent case of Barcelona, where the gradual displacement of the commercial and industrial port to zones specifically dedicated to industrial activity has given rise to considerable expectations by making available land for building and by promoting new residential development all along the coastline. Above all, however, it has meant the definitive recovery of the seafront and the transformation of the old commercial docks into a marina and public recre-

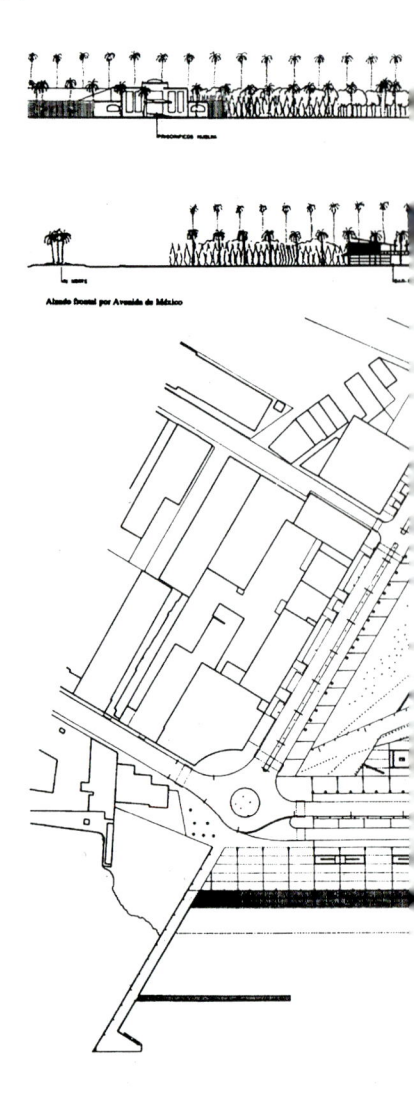

121 Zafra Parc 1994

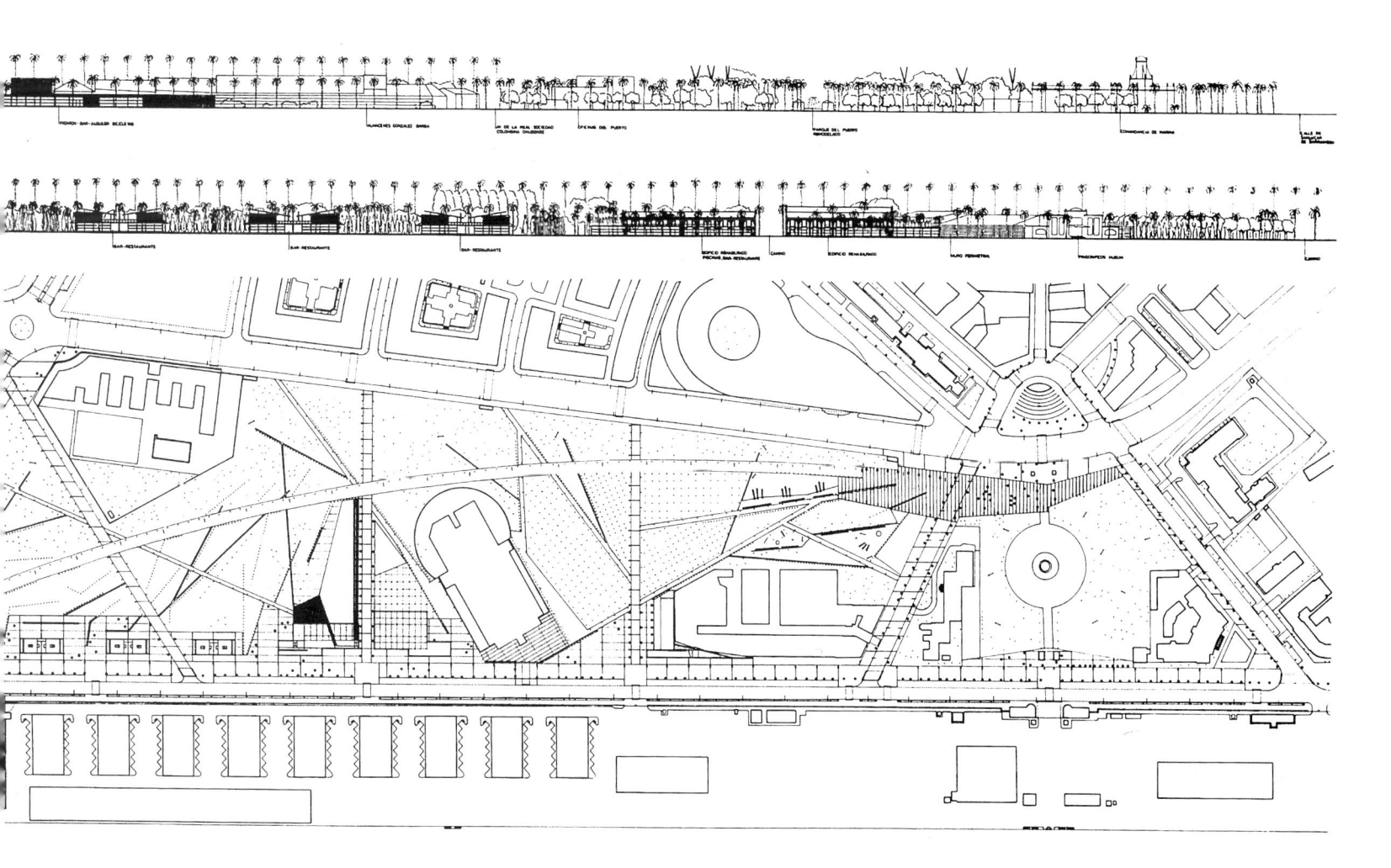

ational facility. The city that once lived with its back to the sea has turned around and made its seafront its principal façade.

It would be strange if the city of Huelva were not to follow the same dynamic in the not too distant future. The Zafra redevelopment plan, prompted by the demolition of the old Zafra y Pescaderías station, is a first indication of the expectations that exist towards the sector's transformation. The objective of the plan is to encourage the city's historical tendency to develop in the direction of the river Odiel. Our project adopted a similar orientation.

The starting point was the park's division into two clearly differentiated zones by a paved avenue flanked with palm trees. This cuts across the park diagonally from the Plaza Doce de Octubre, on which one of the main entrances is located, to its northern edge, where the other main entrance is situated, near the platform over the river Odiel. This major axis is bounded to the east by a natural grove of *Pinus pinea*, similar to the pinewoods in the vicinity of Punta Umbria, and to the west by a strip of landscaping with regular plantations of *Populus italica*, oranges, olives and other indigenous trees. Within the hierarchy of the internal circulation routes, this axis, together with the two transverse avenues, constitutes the basic pedestrian structure of the park. The main axis is paved with coloured asphalt agglomerate, while the two transverse avenues are paved with pipeclay. In addition to the basic structure, there is also a system of paths and walks that communicate the different sectors of the park, surfaced with sandy soil to distinguish them from the other pedestrian routes.

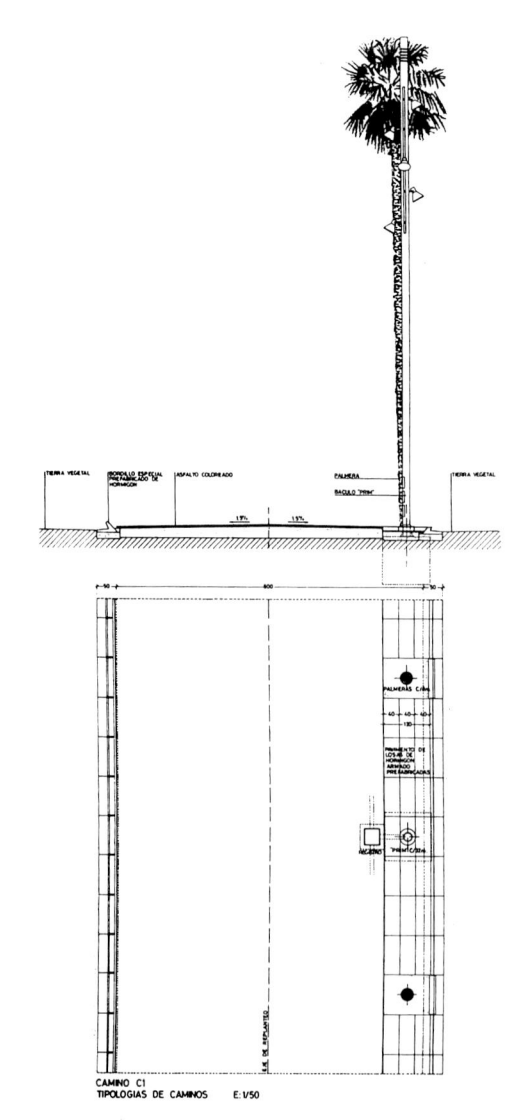

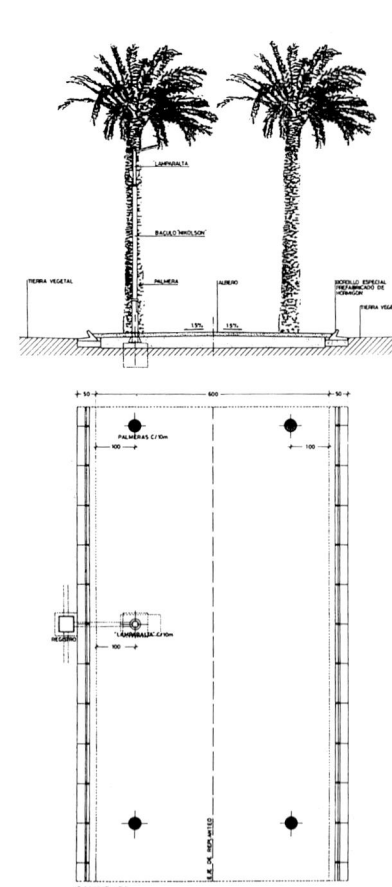

The zone in which the bars, restaurants and leisure areas are situated along the Avenida de Méjico, is paved with large-sized slabs of precast concrete, clay or natural stone. The vegetation is organised according to ease of maintenance and consists for the most part of indigenous bushes and trees. The design, distribution and selection of plant species in a large park should take account of economic considerations if subsequent maintenance is not to prove problematic. For this reason, the project avoided the excessive use of small parterres of shrubs or grass. Where there are lawns, they are always large enough to be mowed mechanically. The row of California fan palms marks out the slightly curving avenue connecting the two ends of the park. It also delimits the natural wood situated between the avenue and the street that bounds the new Zafra residential development. The phoenix palms, meanwhile, are laid out on either side of the transverse avenues. The walls of cypresses follow the line of the footpaths in the direction of the wood, but they also form semi-enclosed precincts reminiscent of spacious salons and the more intimate, secluded Arab garden. The cypresses are intensified at the two main accesses – from the Plaza Doce de Octubre and the roundabout near the new marina – so that entrance is effected gradually, with the park revealing more of itself as the visitor penetrates further inside. Between the curving avenue and the zone of intensive use along the Avenida de Méjico, there are gardens with regular plantations of fruit trees, olives and poplars that seek to organise the geometry of the existing buildings by camouflaging them within the general order/disorder provoked by their continuing presence.

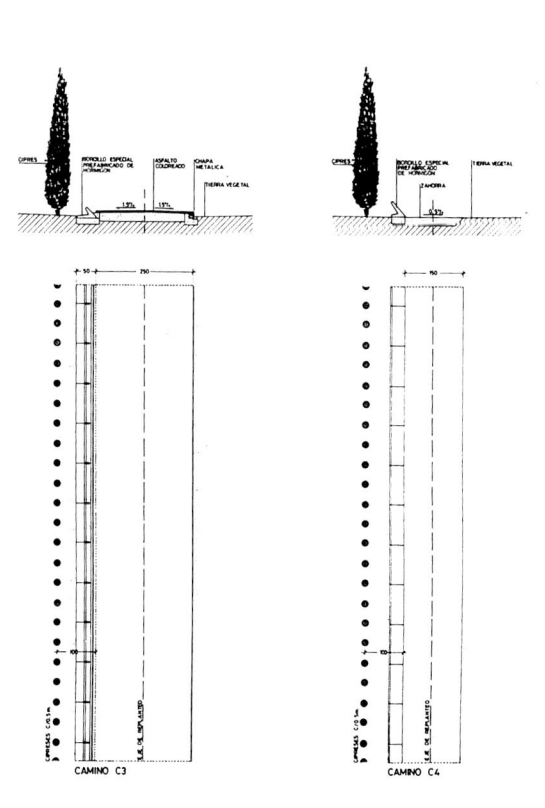

Respect for subtle irreverence towards tradition

It is impossible to evaluate any work of art without taking into account the relationship it establishes with tradition – the most remote and the most immediate. Any realistic assessment, however, would also need to consider the work's relationship with other works of its time. The creations of an individual artist, be they painter, poet or architect, are possessed of value not only in their own right but in their relationship with history – with the works from the canon present within them and with their peers.

The tradition frequently appears in the architecture of Beth Galí in altered form, in one of its fundamental aspects – that implied by the rejection of the classical principles of architecture. These principles are not exclusively those relating to the use of Graeco-Roman morphology and syntax. Above all, they concern the transcendental character of classicism as manifested in its will to universality and continuity, and in its courtly and aristocratic nature.

The architecture of the Modern Movement never renounced this transcendental quality of classicism, and although it rejected its formal language in favour of abstraction, it retained the universal, eternal and courtly character of classical architecture. Loos, Wright, Perret, Mies are all proofs of this, as is the greater part of the architecture produced since the Second World War.

Galí's architecture, like that of several of her peers, has avoided such a link with classicism from its first beginnings, turning instead to many of the resources of the visual arts – not only painting but those of other, less conventional art forms like graffiti, *arte povera*, land art, conceptual art, minimal art and film. These artistic realms, remote from the classical character I have referred to above, endow her architecture with a rare anti-rhetorical quality – frequently encountered in the art of recent years – and a subtle appeal to the sensual dimension of architecture.

This link with the art of her generation has enabled Beth Galí to focus on grace rather than the solidity of traditional architecture, fragility rather than strength, the ephemeral rather than durability and a subtle irony rather than the courtly mode. This irony incorporates a sense of humour that is rarely found in traditional architecture and is close to the joyfully anarchic manifestations of Dadaism. These reveal themselves in Beth Galí's work in a freedom of composition, an apparently spontaneous use of materials and a paradoxical and playful show of respect for and subtle irreverence towards tradition.

It is often the case that when an artist's work is evaluated, a lot of attention is devoted to the most original and most personal aspects, the ones that manifest themselves as intrinsic to the formal expression. However, if we look with an unprejudiced eye at this supposed originality, we become aware of the subtle relationship that always exists with other works of the past, more or less remote and with a greater or lesser degree of fidelity. This relationship has to be free, although it may not always be conscious; it is an interpretation of the past which, thanks to reflection, is brought up to date, liberated from the dead weight of history and presents itself as non-temporal.

The presence of tradition in Beth Galí's work is clear and inevitable; what is less so, or at least less evident, is the question of which tradition it is linked to, and in what way. To a recent tradition, of course, and one not exclusively architectural, but also artistic, painterly, sculptural and conceptual. Might she have had Kurt Schwitters' Merzbau in some corner of her memory when she designed her bookcase unit or the staging of the Second Barcelona Film Festival? Could it be that the design of the exhibition *EINA 20 anys d'Avantguarda* had some connection with the sculptures of Carl André and Marcel Duchamp? Or that the Fossar de la Pedrera contains references to Walter de Maria and Robert Smithson? Or that the library in Joan Miró Park makes reference to Mies van der Rohe's German Pavilion? Or Sot del Migdia Park to Donald Judd and Tony Smith?

The architecture of Beth Galí clearly taps into the language of the wide range of art practices that have come to the fore over the last thirty years. It translates this language into an architectonic idiom that extends from the strictly architectural discipline itself to that of landscape architecture, taking in assemblage and environment art along the way. These are all art forms created in a three-dimensional space with the object of immersing spectators in a range of conceptual and sensory stimuli in order to involve them directly and intimately. They affect the sensory and intellectual faculties and actively intervene in the perception of time and space.

Hence the anti-classicism and anti-rhetoric of Beth Galí's architecture. In place of the arrogance and potency of Modern architecture, she offers us the humility, fragility and irony of a new architecture which, finding itself in a new avant-garde, affirms the high tradition, rejuvenated and renewed. It is aware that art neither progresses nor perfects itself. It is simply that the material of art changes and is transformed, just as the aesthetic experience and the very concept of architecture are transformed.

Antoni Marí

Corberò a la Tecla Sala

Design of the exhibition of the work of the sculptor Xavier Corberò - Barcelona

FINALIST FAD AWARD FOR EPHEMERAL ARCHITECTURE 1994 - WITH STUDENT: ANNA BIRGISDOTTIR

1994

Designing the presentation of art works is often reduced to the creation of an appropriate setting in which the works themselves are necessarily expected to be the main protagonists. Consequently, in exhibitions of paintings it is the vertical plane – the wall – that constitutes the support for the picture, and as such the prospective framework in which the installation project directly intervenes. In the case of sculpture, by contrast, the supporting plane is the horizontal and so it is here that the design of the project must be concentrated.

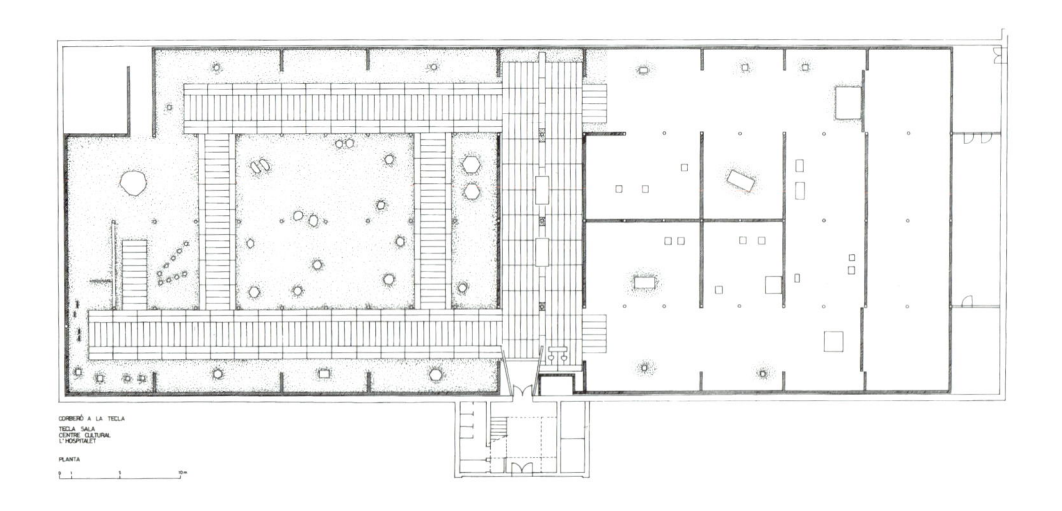

This was one of the starting points for the staging of the exhibition of sculpture by Xavier Corberó in the Tecla Sala cultural centre in L'Hospitalet. Very often the specific difficulties of the venue and the solution of these provide the discursive thread in relation to which the project selects a certain course of action. In the case of the Xavier Corberó exhibition, one of the difficulties that the project addressed from the outset was that of finding a way of ensuring that the spectator would not be placed too close to the sculptures themselves, in view of the physical instability of the works and the associated risk of accident. The project focused its attention on selecting the materials for the repaving of the floor of the Tecla Sala, which was in a very poor condition. It was decided to rest the sculptures on a continuous expanse of white marble sand, which at the same time served to dissuade the public from walking across it and hence coming too close to the works on show.

The itineraries were organised in terms of the chronological sequence of the pieces, guided by a floor of stained wood of the kind habitually employed for coffering, laid out on the sand like a continuous floating carpet. The venue's original lighting was rotated to focus on the ceiling, producing an indirect illumination of the space as a whole, with a new lighting system focusing on the individual pieces of sculpture. Only in the central square, occupied by a group composed of chess pieces, was the light directed down onto the ground. The reflection of the great square of light off the white sand projected a halo of warm light onto the ceiling, contrasting with the existing fluorescent lighting.

Monument

Exhibition on the Mayors of Barcelona. Construction of the monument to Mayor Pich i Pon - Barcelona

WITH ORIOL BOHIGAS

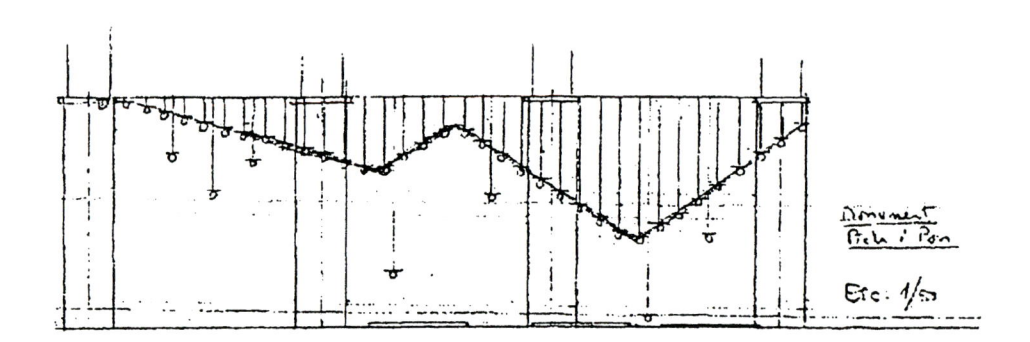

1995

The history of Barcelona's Universal Exhibition of 1929 began in 1913, when Joan Pich i Pon – electrical entrepreneur, leader of the Radical Party, prime-mover in the early Lerrouxist workers' movement, mayor of Barcelona and, finally, right-winger and assiduous churchgoer – suggested a modest exhibition of electrical goods. The idea gradually took shape with the support and direct intervention of Francesc Cambó, who commissioned the municipal architect Josep Amargós – one of his most trusted confidants – to draw up the first projects for laying out Montjuïc. These were to form the basis for the present road layout.

The Electrical Industries Exhibition was never held, but neither Cambó nor Pich i Pon gave up their project. The International Exhibition was finally inaugurated in 1929 with the enthusiastic backing of the dominant bourgeoisie and Cambó's stratagems to win over the city council, following numerous delays occasioned by the Great War. Josep Puig i Cadafalch, the old Modernist master and a leading member of the Lliga Catalana, was appointed chief architect.

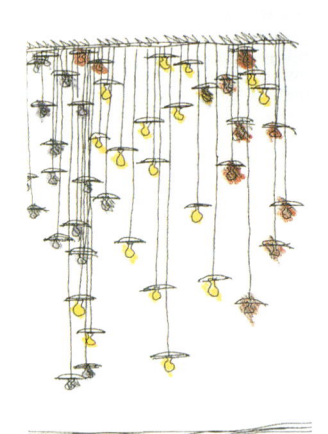

131 Monument 1995

Indumentària

Women's clothes shop - Barcelona

WITH STUDENTS: JAUME BENAVENT, CLEMENS NUIJENS AND JAUME PIÑOL

1994

'A space for dressing' – this was the subtitle suggested by the owner of the shop, which sells women's fashions. It sums up the attribute that the best explains the project. A shop that is simultaneously a dressing room – a comfortable one, where you can sit and relax with a cup of coffee while looking at clothes.

Situated in the historic heart of Barcelona, in a section of the old city centre that has not yet been invaded by renovation fever, INDUMENTÀRIA undoubtedly represented a commercial risk as a fashion outlet. At the same time, however, it was a new element, a new contribution, and hence a stimulus to the rehabilitation of this part of the city.

The project set out to transform the dark and dilapidated old walls into luminous, translucent surfaces in order to create a sense of space and light in the heart of Barcelona's Gothic Quarter.

133 Indumentària 1994

Remodelling of the historic centre of 's-Hertogenbosch

's-Hertogenbosch

WITH STUDENTS: JAUME BENAVENT, ALESSANDRA DINI, JAUME PIÑOL, ALEX GIMÉNEZ, ARMIN SCHÄFER, ANNA BIRGISDOTTIR, AND WITH RIEN VAN ROSMALEN, HARRIE VERHALLEN - MUNICIPIALITY OF 'S HERTOGENBOSCH

1993–1998

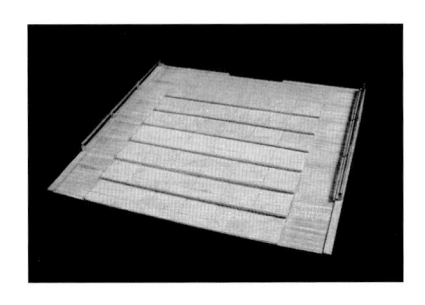

The project to remodel the historic centre of 's-Hertogenbosch proposed a construction system compatible with the differentiated character to be established in the streets and squares of the old town centre. The master plan approved by the Municipal Council categorised the streets according to a set of basic criteria regarding their width, significance and position within the town's structure. The project thus opted for a construction system that allows urban space to be designed in terms of these categories, while preserving the architectural constants which, by ensuring continuity, make the historic town centre recognisable. These constants, which we might call the 'skeleton' of the urban space, are the constituent elements of the general construction system. This system invariably consists of a band of extremely hard-wearing natural stone, the colour of which varies according to its location, set into the streets and squares like a carpet. Laid out on this band are all the elements which go to make up the urban space – ramps for pedestrians and vehicles, kerbs, litter bins, streetlights, traffic signals and so on. Within this skeleton structure, the materials change according to the category and perceived value of the street, ranging from granite to softer materials like wood and grass. The possibilities are infinite. The horizontal plane formed by the streets is an ordered one, with no unnecessary objects, where people

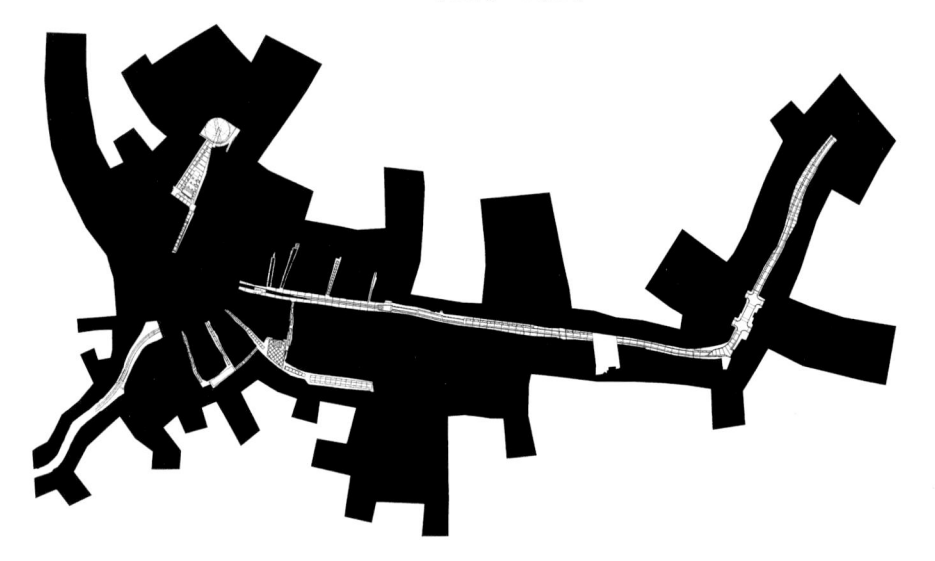

Kerkplein

can genuinely sense the empty space of the town.

These tranquil, ordered surfaces are only modified at particular points, like stressed syllables in a sentence. This has the effect of restoring meaning to the urban space. In the case of Kerkstraat, the specific point is Kerkplein. This square – on which several little streets converge – has lost its identity over the years, becoming little more than a bend in Kerkstraat. The project set out to orient the space towards the church by introducing a new flight of steps in front of it, transforming a mere bend in the street into a space with a character of its own. In the case of Karrenstraat and Dode Nieuwstraat the specific point is the junction of the two streets. Here the paving accentuates the unaligned meeting of the streets to form a square.

The problem of urban space in many towns and cities is the gradual appearance of small objects with certain specialised functions. The street furniture has been thought out here in terms of the same criterion of versatility as the rest of the project. In other words, a given object can be set down in different ways and serve different uses.

Kerkplein

137 Remodelling of the historic centre of 's-Hertogenbosch 1993-1998

Hinthamerstraat

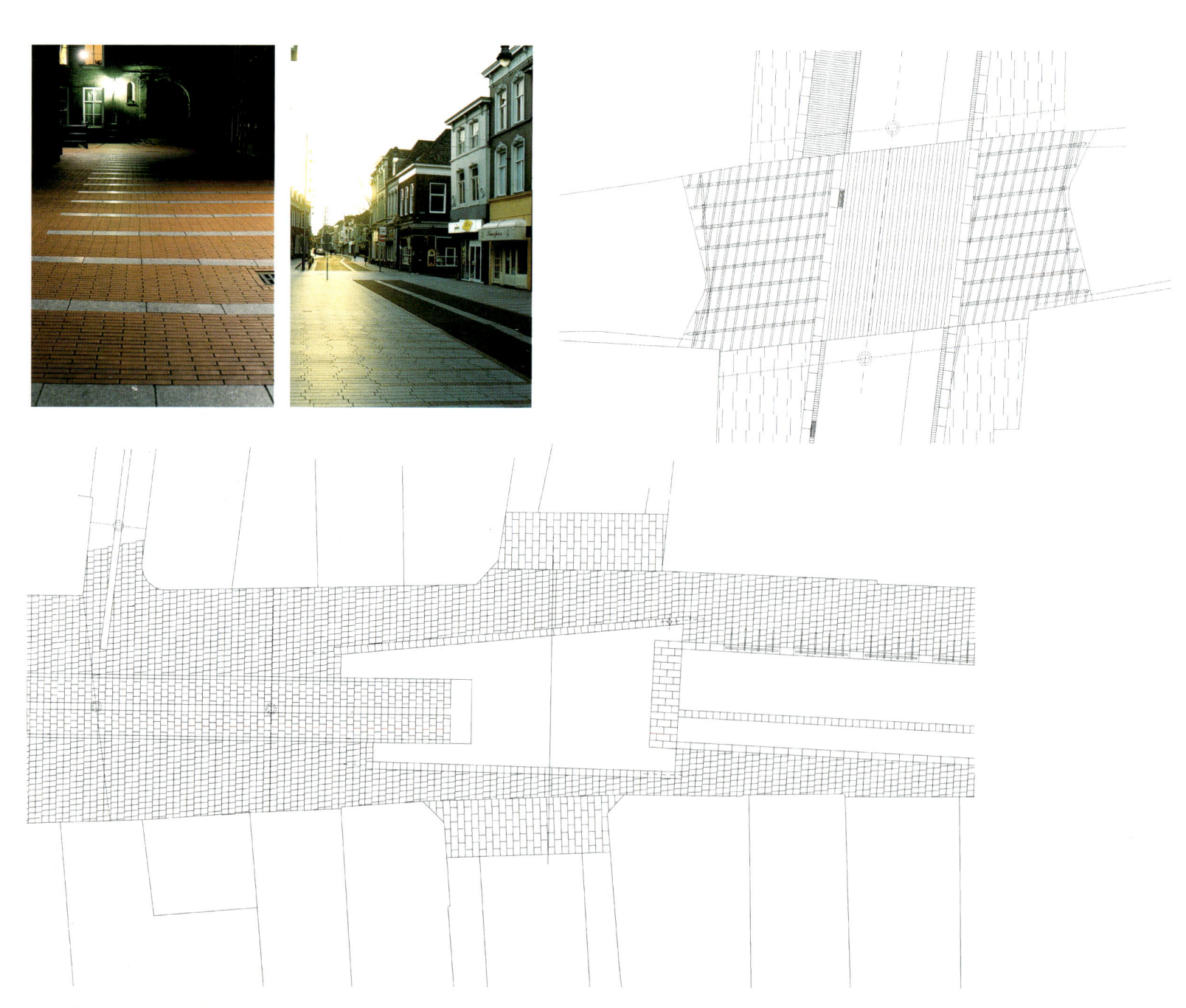

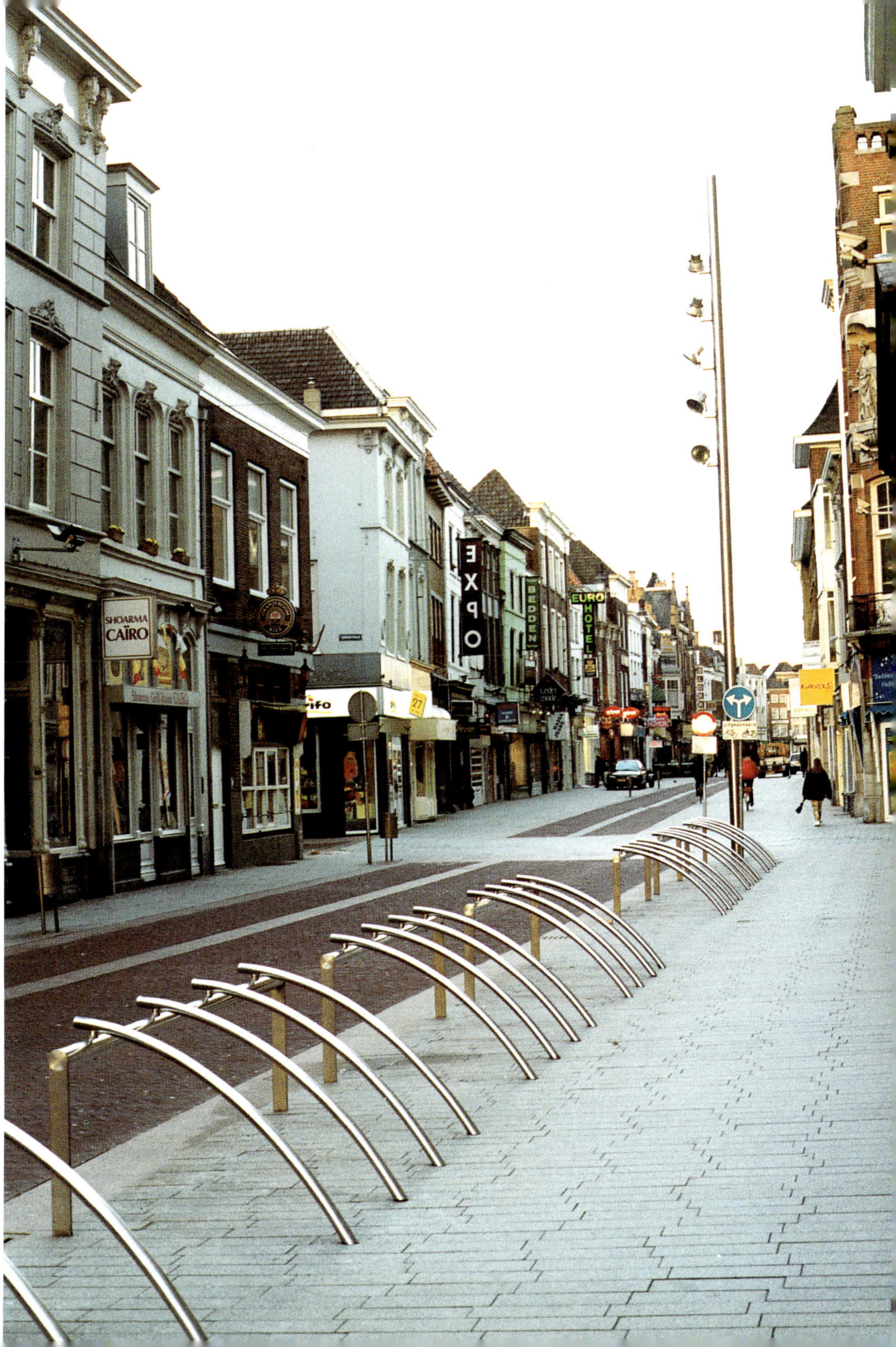
SHOARMA
CAÏRO
EXPO
BEDDEN
EURO
HOTEL

Vughterstraat

Jacobsplein

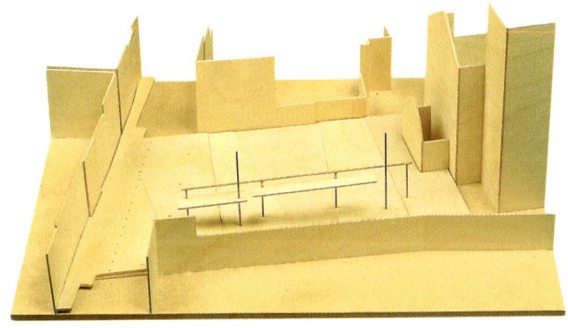

Vughterstraat

I would like to thank M.C.J.M. van Rosmalen, J.C. Dona, W.A.M van der Made and the mayor of 's-Hertogenbosch for the confidence they have placed in me at all times. Without their collaboration it would have been impossible to carry out the projects and the works constructed to date in their town.

Beth Galí

Beth Galí, the importance of a Spanish architect to the city of 's-Hertogenbosch

Five years ago, the centre of 's-Hertogenbosch - the focal point of city life for centuries - was in need of a facelift. We decided to put ourselves in the hands of the Catalan architect Beth Galí. What prompted this adventure?

Public spaces are one of a municipal authority's primary responsibilities. Something for which we are rightly called to account. It is up to the authority to make sure public spaces are safe, clean and attractive. But there's more besides. In our approach to the centre of 's-Hertogenbosch, we pursued a clear cultural ambition that viewed these spaces as publicly owned artistic assets, which are open to discussion as such. The city as a forum for and subject of debate concerning issues of beauty and ugliness, the tension between history and renewal and the balance of costs and benefits. The only thing not open to discussion was the insistence on quality.

We visited and conversed with a variety of artists and architects in order to give professional shape to this ambition. We decided to award the commission to Beth Galí as she had demonstrated in Barcelona her ability to handle sensitively a historically important environment. There has been, and continues to be, a lively discussion about her actual designs. One of the traits I most admire in this architect is her willingness to engage in such debates with the municipal authority, civil service, local residents and contractors. More than that, she actually insists that all of these parties form part of her design team.

Now that the principal streets of the city centre have been redesigned and finished, the public spaces of 's-Hertogenbosch have been transformed into a work of art - one that merges in a contemporary way with the historical centre and lends it an exciting added value. Not art for art's sake, but applied art that provides space and forms the setting for every aspect of urban life: events, [[optochten]], markets, shopping and so on. It forms a stylish background for the dynamism of our city. Not a Spanish import, but open spaces designed here in 's-Hertogenbosch.

We embarked on this adventure and it has proved a tremendous success. Happily, it is not all over yet. Public spaces within and beyond the city walls remain for me an architectural and administrative challenge of the first order.

Beth Galí has sparked off the process with her designs. She has set the tone. And in so doing, Beth has become a friend of 's-Hertogenbosch for life.

Dr A.G.J.M. Rombouts
Burgomaster

Park bike

Bicycle stand - Manufactured by Santa & Cole

With Jaume Benavent
1994

The ever-increasing number of small items of street furniture appearing in our streets ought to be a cause of concern to everyone with an interest in improving our public spaces. These strange occupants of our pavements include the rickety structures of bent metal that serve to accumulate bicycles.

My frequent and always enjoyable visits to the Netherlands have taught me to love moving around the city on what is the Dutch vehicle par excellence. The bicycle is without a doubt one of our species' most intelligent inventions. Bicycles are great, but what about the awful contraptions we use to stop them being stolen?

The object I proposed for 's-Hertogenbosch is deliberately more impertinent and authoritarian than the ridiculous bits of twisted iron we bump into so often in the street. It is an object that will customarily be used for its intended function while also serving actively as an ordering element in the public space.

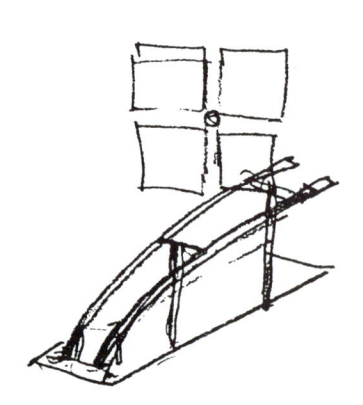

145 Park bike 1994

Stoa Building

Shopping complex - 's-Hertogenbosch

WITH STUDENTS: JAUME BENAVENT, ALEX GIMÉNEZ, JAUME PIÑOL, ALESSANDRA DINI, ARMIN SCHÄFER AND T + T DESIGN, MULTI VASTGOED BV

1993-1998

The siting of a new building in a historic town like 's-Hertogenbosch requires very careful attention. The historic centre has achieved a balance between today's living city, expressed through its commercial activity, and the historic city, apparent in the conservation of its traditional vernacular architecture.

It is worth noting a particular aspect of the city's urban layout that makes it particularly unique. This is the network of subterranean canals – originally designed to carry away domestic waste – which, connected together in a system of watercourses, constitutes a remarkable series of underground routes, passing through the interior courtyards of the houses in the medieval town.

The new building responds to the specific condition of forming a transition point between the smaller, fragmented fabric of 's-Hertogenbosch's medieval and 18th-century core and the larger block-like structures built in the 1960s and 70s. The building was conceived as a piece with a very urban character and a strong identity, capable of responding to the scale of the open space and the existing high-rise residential development. Given its situation, this is an emblematic building for the town, yet one that is also respectful towards it.

The first section to greet the pedestrian approaching from the marketplace is precisely aligned with the final building on Marktstraat and is set flush with the other buildings flanking Loeffplein. This is a compact volume, with a flat roof – like its neighbours – consisting of large skylights illuminating the upper floor from above, with semi-opaque façades. The second section is the central element – its interior com-

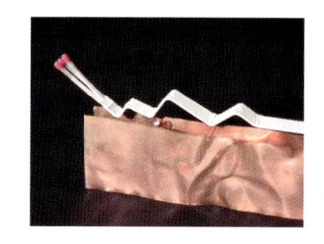

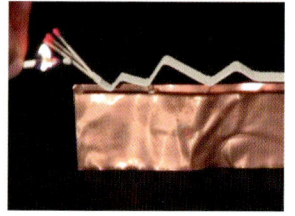

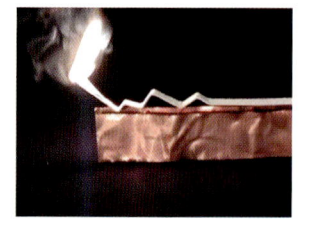

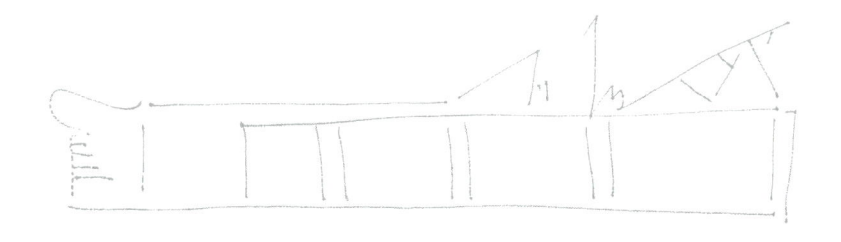

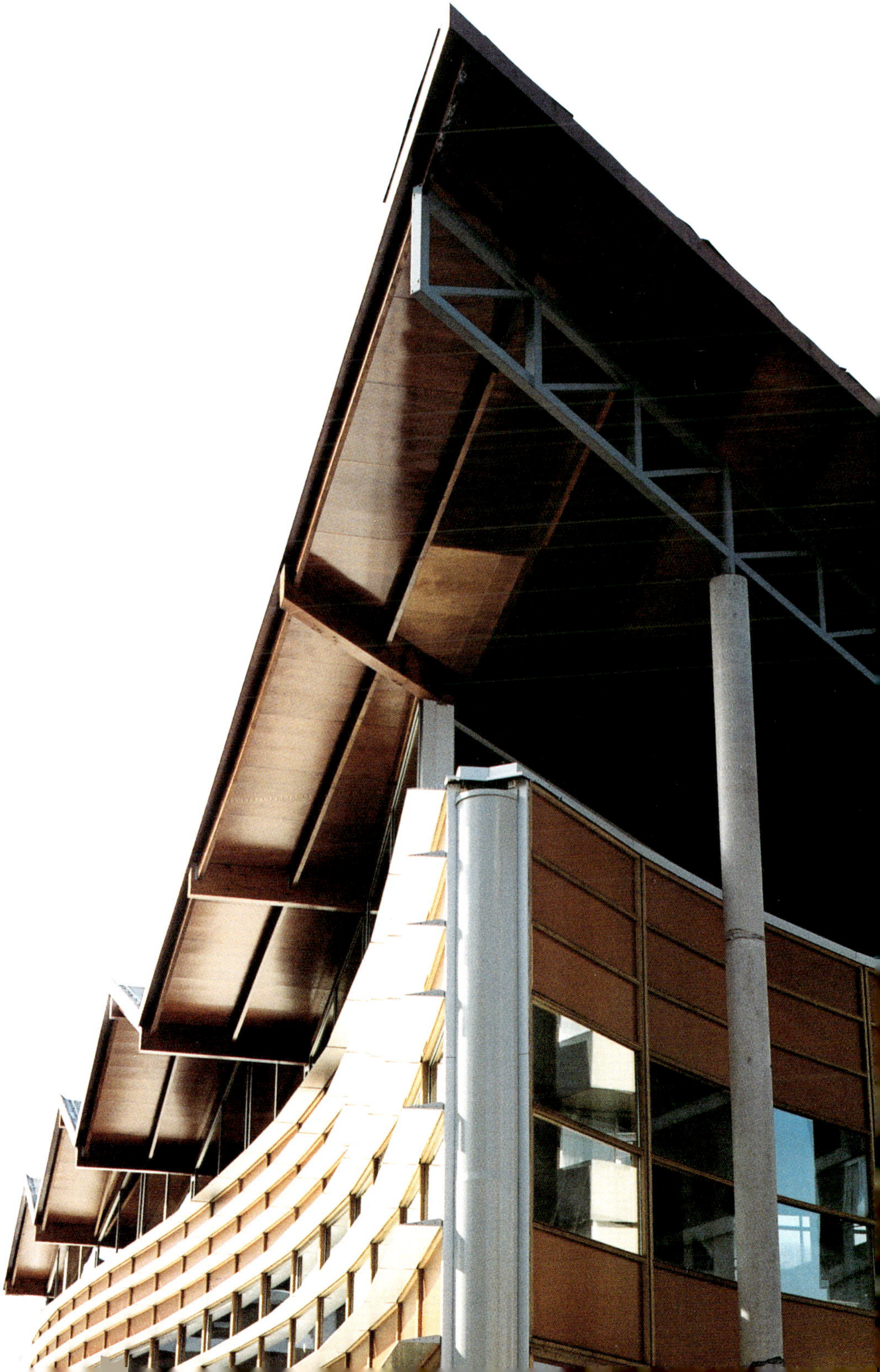

posed of a great double-height hall with overhead light entering through the cupola formed by two inclined glass planes and illuminating the circular tambour which designates and delimits the large central space. The essential feature of this section is its permeability, which facilitates the building's transverse connection from Loeffplein through to the area to the rear of its central point. From this point on, the building curves subtly to present its face to the Arena building. The gaze of the passer-by slides over the curving façade, leading on fluidly into the interior of the Arena. This is the final section of the Stoa building. As we move forward, Loeffplein becomes narrower, but the frontage of the shops at the same time becomes increasingly transparent, so that when night falls, the brightly illuminated final section of the building can be seen from the marketplace, from where it has the appearance of a lit match.

The rear façade of this section is set back slightly as if retreating under the pressure of the historic hospital building. This leaves the projection of a series of double-pitch roofs, which mark a return to the smaller scale of the historic city.

The portico running the entire length of the main façade, like a covered street, emphasises the passage from the marketplace to the Arena, as well as being an element that offers shelter from the elements. This creates a microclimate that is equally pleasant in winter and summer.

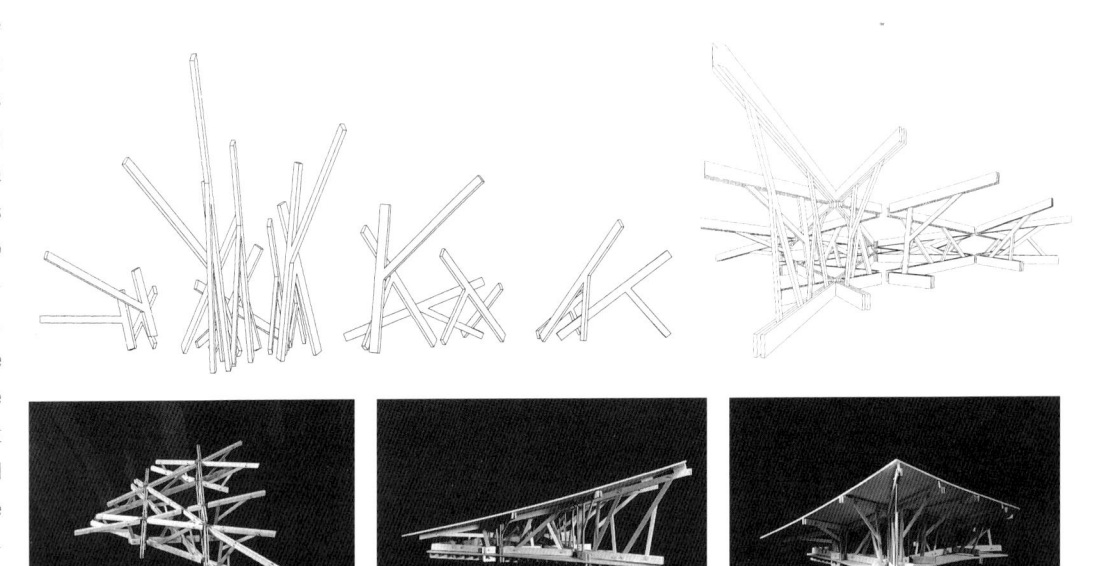

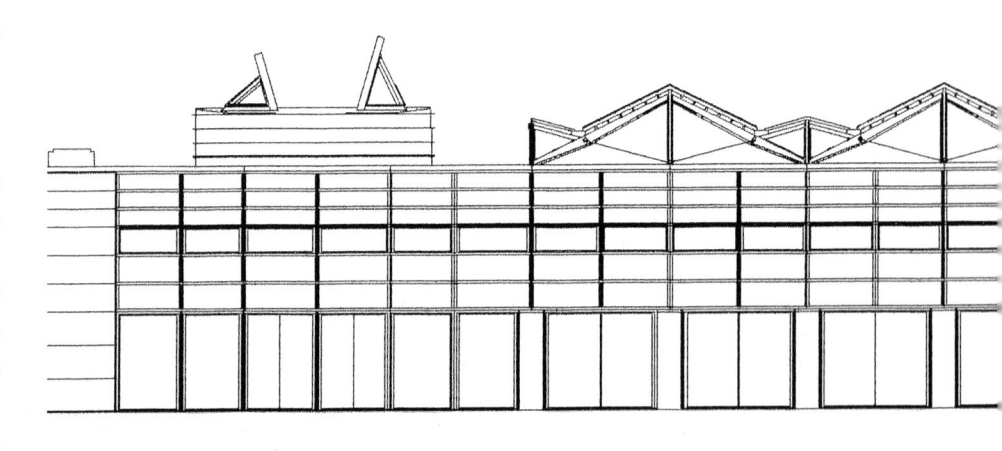

The building itself has been designed as a connecting bridge between the two commercial areas – the one that has grown up around the marketplace and the future area in the interior of the Arena – while constituting a commercial complex in its own right. It is a very long building, which runs the risk of becoming a deterrent to the pedestrian walking towards the Arena. In order to avoid producing an excessive distance and a sense of monotony between these two areas, three unique spaces have been designed, which serve to make the route more attractive. These are on a grand scale, full height, with one at each end and one in the centre of the building. The remainder of the building takes the form of a great container in which the various shops and offices are laid out according to the stipulated requirements, exploiting the intrinsic flexibility of the space.

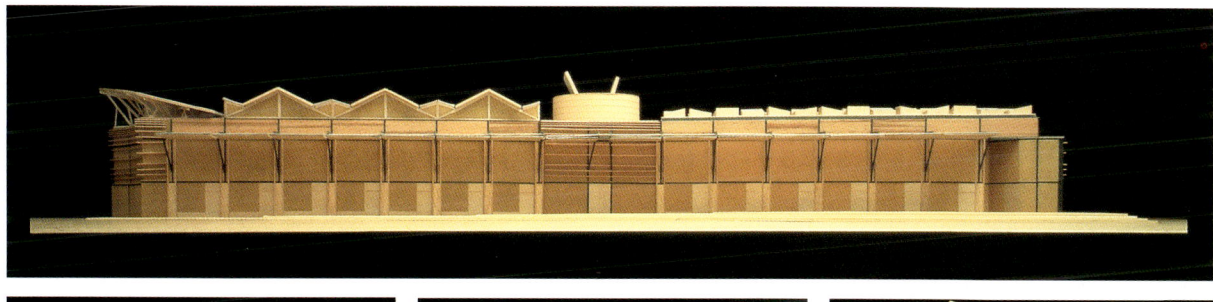

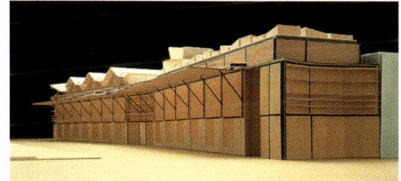

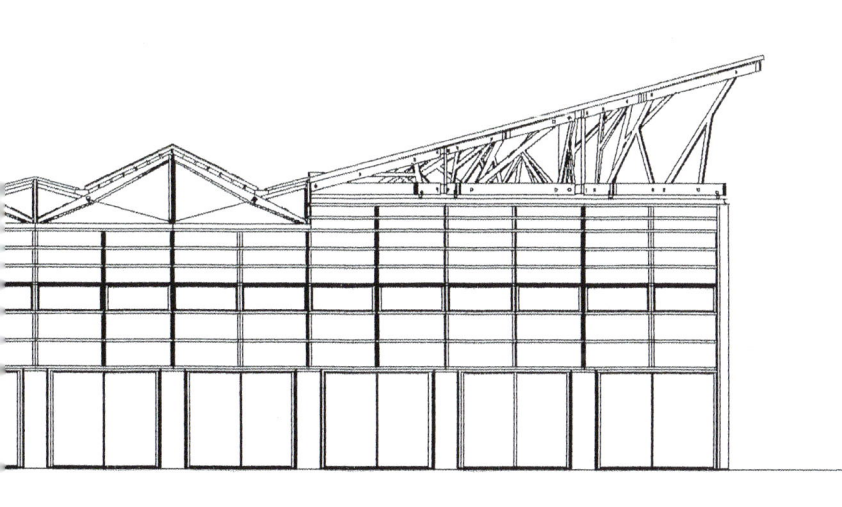

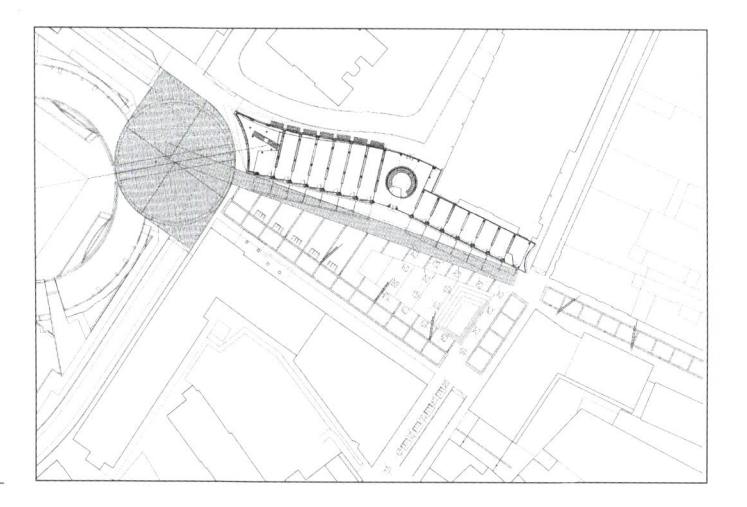

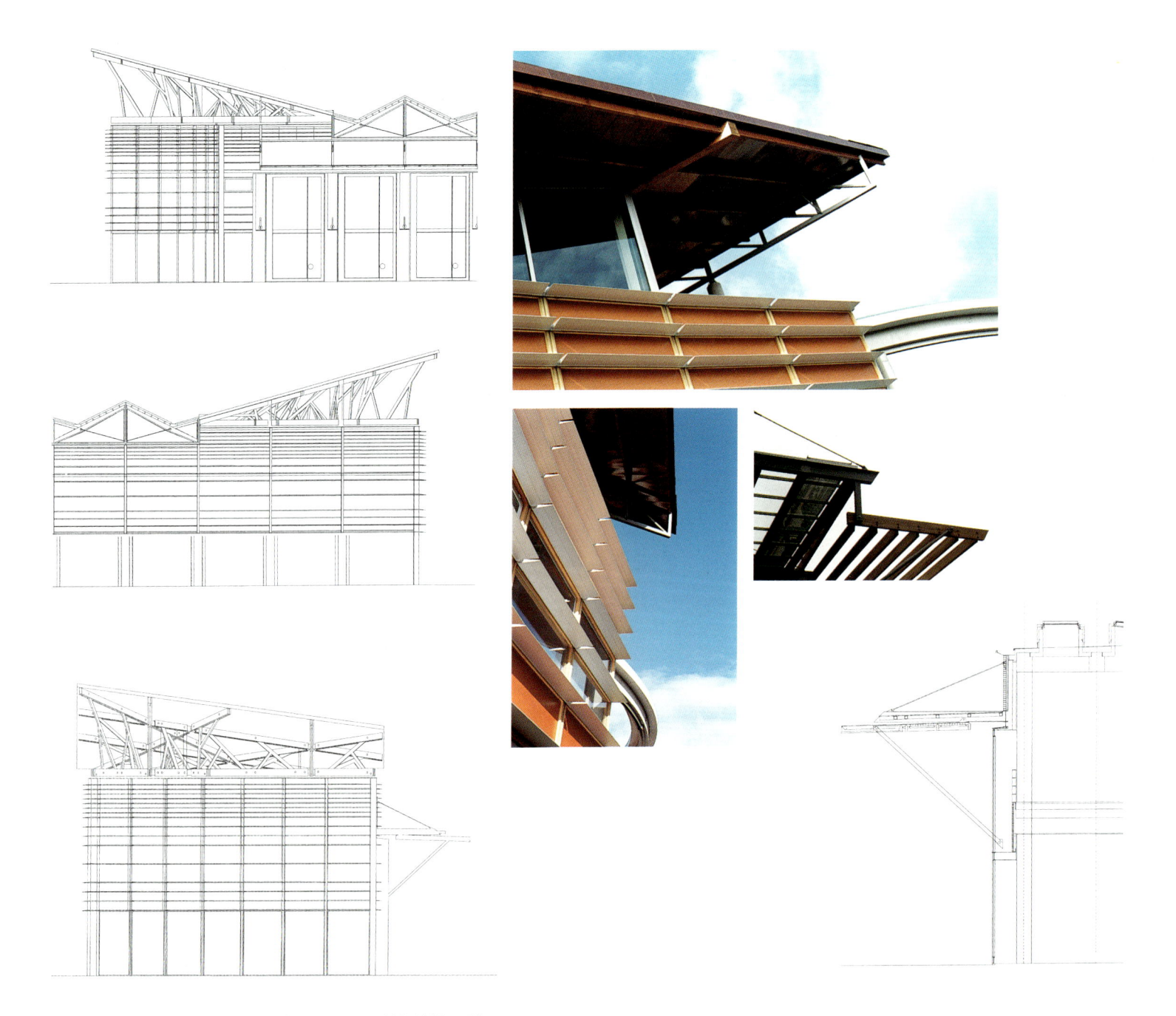

Stoa Building 1993-1998   150

151 Stoa Building 1993-1998

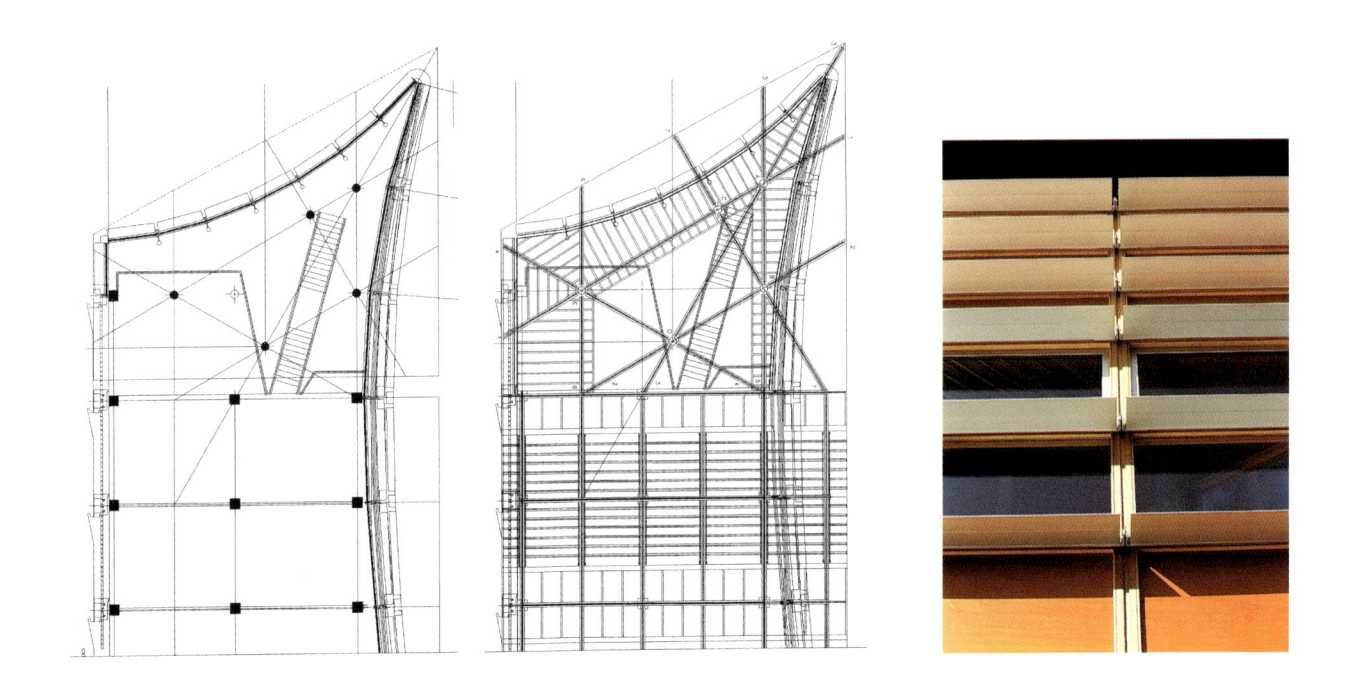

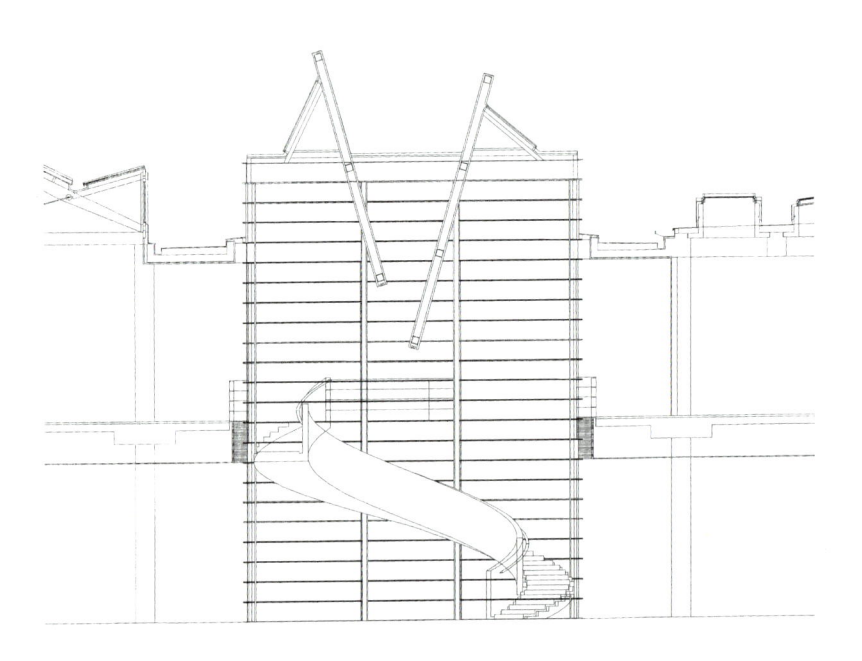

Stoa Building 1993-1998 152

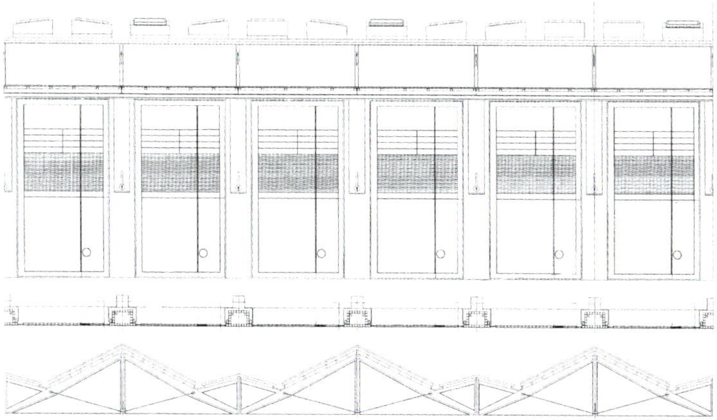

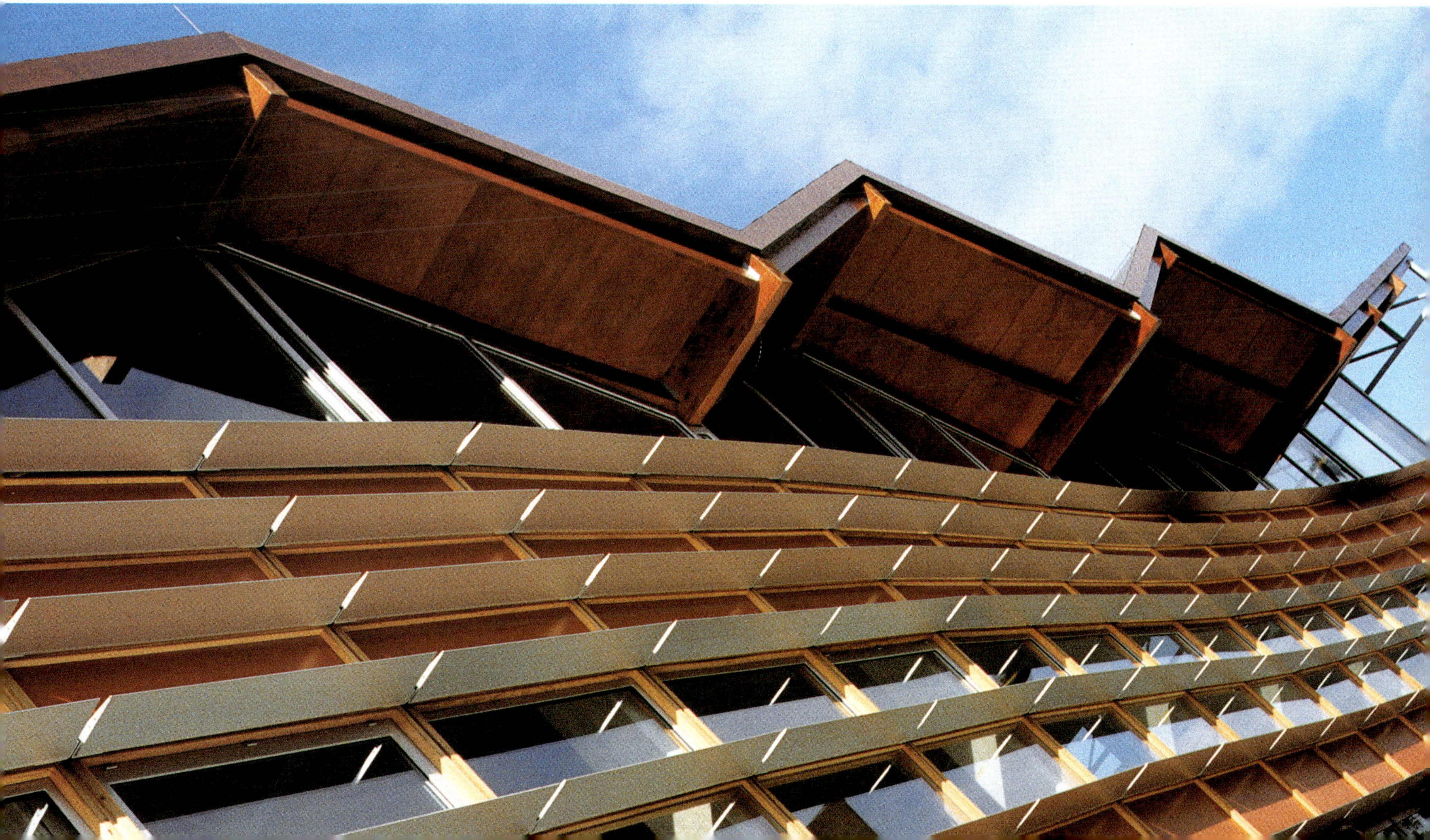

Remodelling of the historical centre of Roermond

Roermond

WITH STUDENTS: JAUME BENAVENT, ALEX GIMÉNEZ, INGER GROENEVELD AND VALENTINA ROJAS-HAUSER

1995-1998

In previous centuries, the approach to public space in almost every city in the world consisted of the positioning of specifically codified elements on a well-paved base. The siting of pieces of sculpture, for instance, with a view to a centrality or to certain axes was seen as resolving all the problems of urban space: its monumentality, its identity and its representative status in the city.

Since that time, the codes and the symbols have changed. Nowadays, architects have to look to the architecture itself for this same identity and representative status, but with different codes and symbols. Kloosterwandplein has evidently been designed in this latter sense – in other words, looking to the architecture of the urban space as such to define its identity. Situated in a thoroughly contemporary urban context, this is a square that the surrounding modern architecture does nothing to assist in terms of enhancing the quality of the space. In other words, we are not dealing here with a space situated in the historic centre of Roermond, where the existing environmental elements call for special treatment. It is one instead where the urban fabric is required to provide cohesion and to organise the incoherent setting typical of the modern city.

The final decision to site the bicycle park beneath the theatre's entrance podium was not taken until the project was already at a very advanced stage. The most serious problem was not the conversion of access points into holes leading down into the basement but to make them small, enclosed volumes that could be monitored from both inside and outside. Residual spaces in the city can easily become degraded. A hole in the middle of the city is just such a residual space. Consequently, security was one of the primary reasons for closing off the accesses to the basement level.

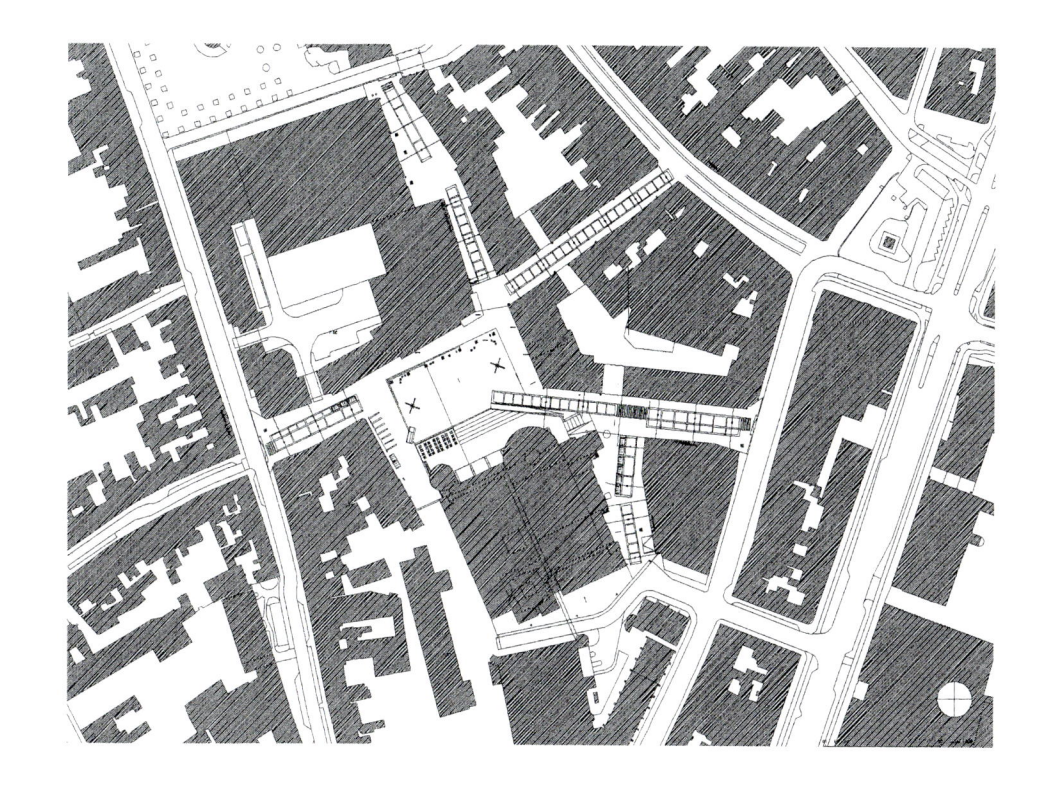

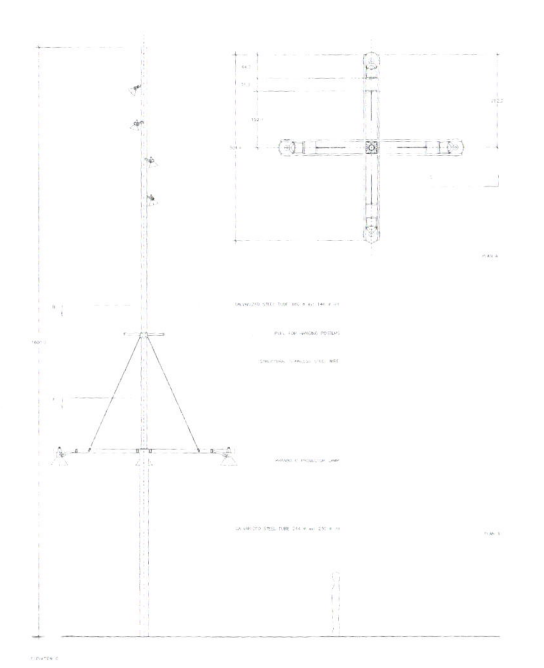

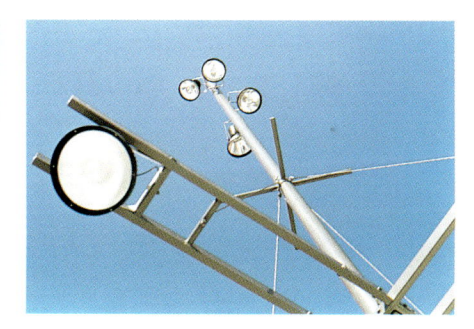

The relationship between the theatre, restaurant and square was viewed in the project context as a succession of different urban spaces, from the entirely open space of the square to the entirely closed one of the theatre. The project proposed an intermediate space between the podium and the square, including the insertion of an access ramp to the bicycle park in the basement. The space between the access ramp and the restaurant was conceived with the idea of offering the city a range of urban spaces and hence the possibility of widely differing uses. In this way, the podium can serve as a large terrace, the atmosphere of which varies according to our specific position.

Urban spaces of Piet Smith plan
Rotterdam

With students: Jaume Benavent, Alex Giménez, Willemijn Somers, Arola Tous, Susana Guillermo and Inma Merino

1996

The initial conception of the project had to take account of the fact that this space is destined to become a suburban district of Rotterdam, with its own autonomous character, in which the car will be an important element. Consequently, ordering the presence of motor vehicles constituted one of the primary problems underlying the design of the various public spaces. The second problem was to create an area that would be endowed with a significance in its own right; in other words, to give it a distinct and recognisable individual identity. The third problem related to the quality of the public space's construction as an architectural base and its durability in response to intensive wear and use.

The problem of the large-scale car parks featured in the Piet Smit Plan derives from their dual role as spaces for parking motor vehicles and as public squares in the service of the community once the vehicles have gone. The proposal for the parking zones included a slight cambering of the surface, so that when there are only a few cars, this space effectively becomes independent of the rest, forming a kind of public square for pedestrian use. The presence of trees and lighting arcs combine to create a space with its own particular significance. The lighting arcs rise into the air where they emerge from the wood, bestowing a more urban character – that of a public square – on the empty parking space.

Until the neighbourhood is fully integrated in the city, it needs to possess an identity of its own. This is one of the problems typically confronted by new neighbourhoods that are relatively distant from the city centre. By providing them with elements of signification, they can be identified with everything the neighbourhood represents for the city as a

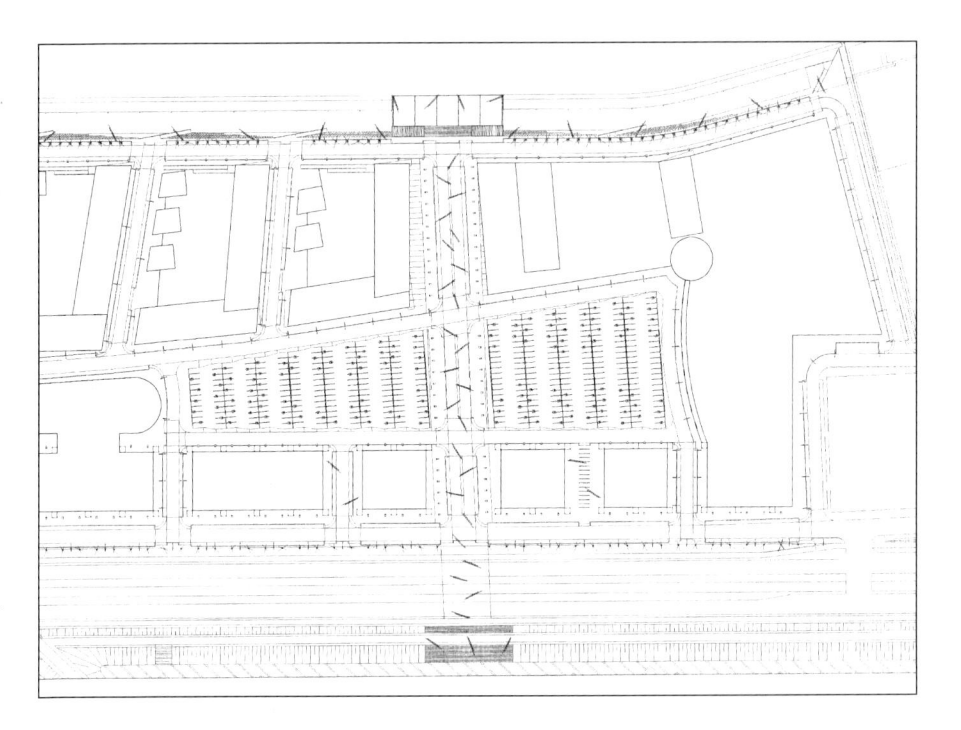

157 Urban spaces of Piet Smith plan 1996

whole. We proposed using the same material to pave both squares and pavements, configuring it into a variety of patterns according to the location.

The design of special elements like the Pitmit lamps helps fix the identity of the neighbourhood, while also monumentalising certain spaces like the central axis, helping it to become a genuine avenue linking the stadium with the waterfront. The main paving material will be brick – light red clay (terracotta), paving stone size for the parking spaces and 20 x 5 x 10 cm for the pavements. At certain points of particular significance, such as the central avenue, there will be a special surfacing of natural white granite for the road, the kerbs and the pedestrian ramps.

The walkway along the waterfront will be complemented by a system of floating steps composed of precast concrete slabs (approximate size: 60 x 120 cm). Similar slabs will be used for the access ramps to the walkway. Wooden boards will be laid at certain points along the walkway to signal zones of special interest, namely the ramps at both ends and the space coinciding with the axis of the central avenue in front of the kiosks for bars and restaurants with which we propose to finish the avenue.

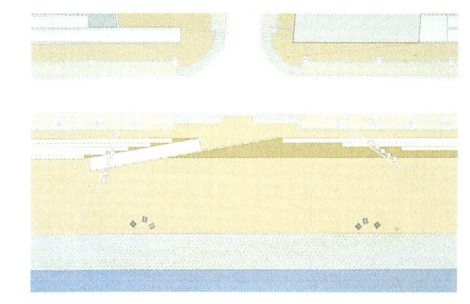

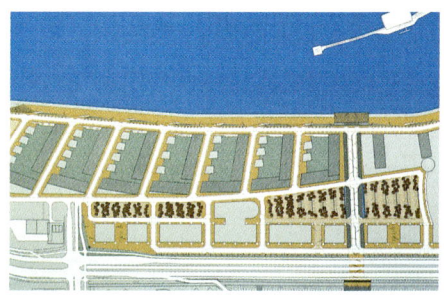

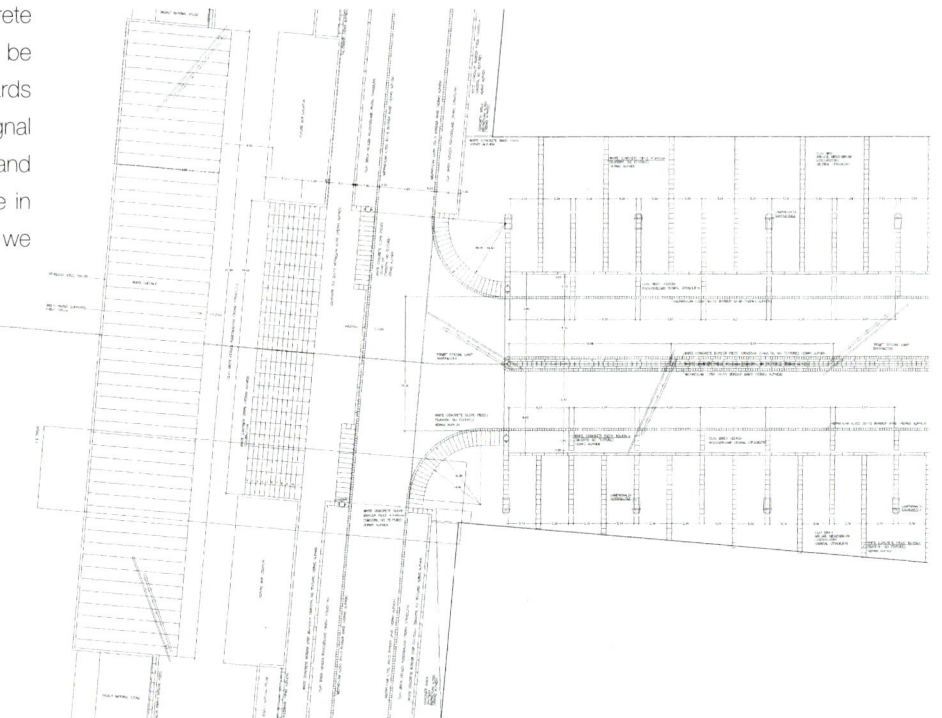

159 Urban spaces of Piet Smith plan 1996

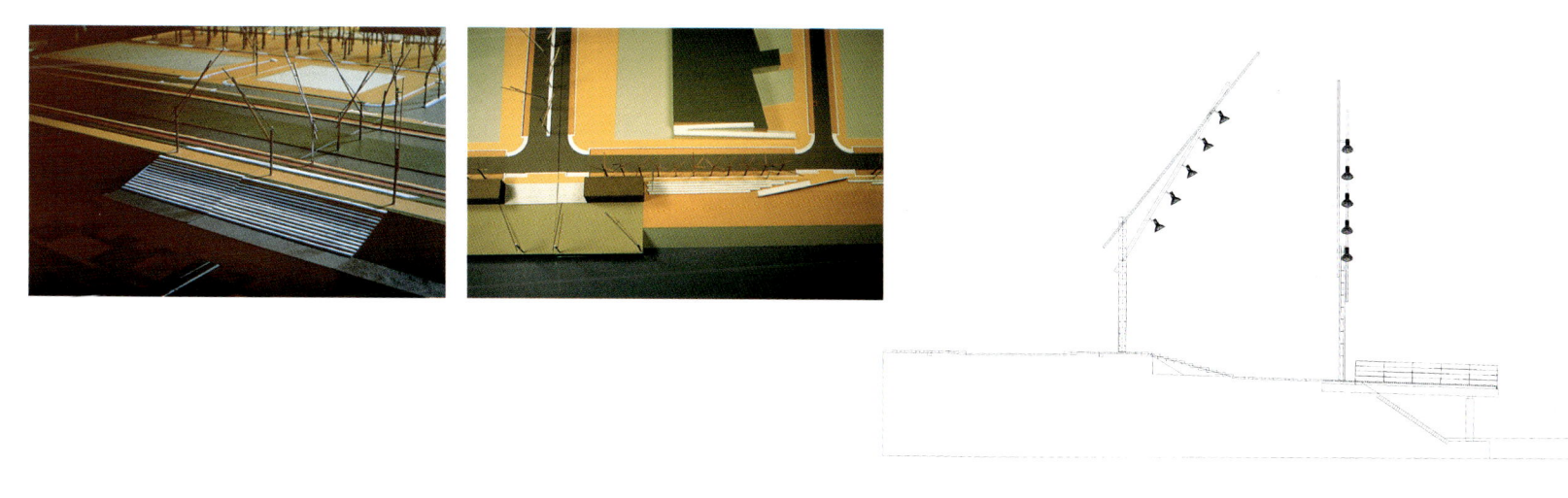

Pitmit outdoorlamp

Manufactured by Santa & Cole

With students: Jaume Benavent and Alex Giménez

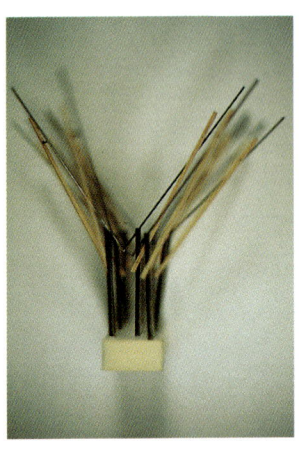

1997

Civic authorities often commission architects to draw up schemes that at first sight seem impossible. This was the case with the project for the public spaces in the Piet Smit Plan for the Veranda district in southern Rotterdam. The budget fell below any kind of acceptable minimum, which meant the materials would necessarily have to be the ones regarded as the cheapest in the Netherlands: concrete and brick. At the same time, the area had to exert a special attraction on people who might decide to move to the outskirts of the city.

The area already possessed a definite added value in being located close to the stadium of Feyenoord Football Club, one of the country's great sporting institutions. Consequently, the new neighbourhood had to express in terms of representative status what the area was to mean to its future inhabitants.

We concentrated our efforts on designing the lamps for the central axis linking the stadium with the quayside and the promenade running along it. They are very large lamps designed to illuminate large areas. The result is a gesture in the urban landscape consisting of two lines in the air – pit/mit – which can be organised in a range of very different forms.

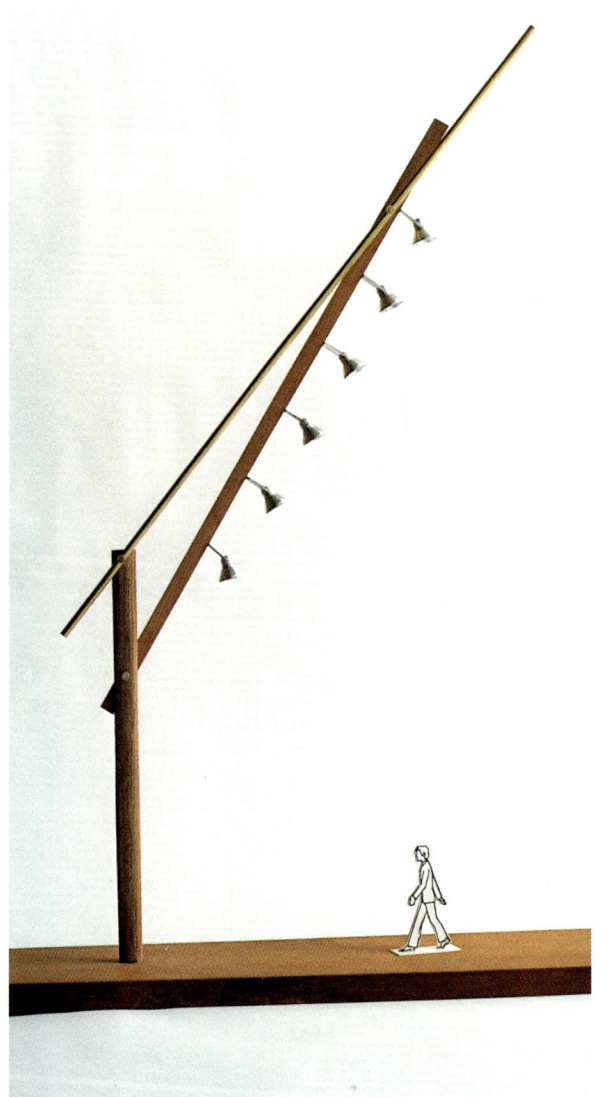

Photo Magneta

ALCAT FRONTAL

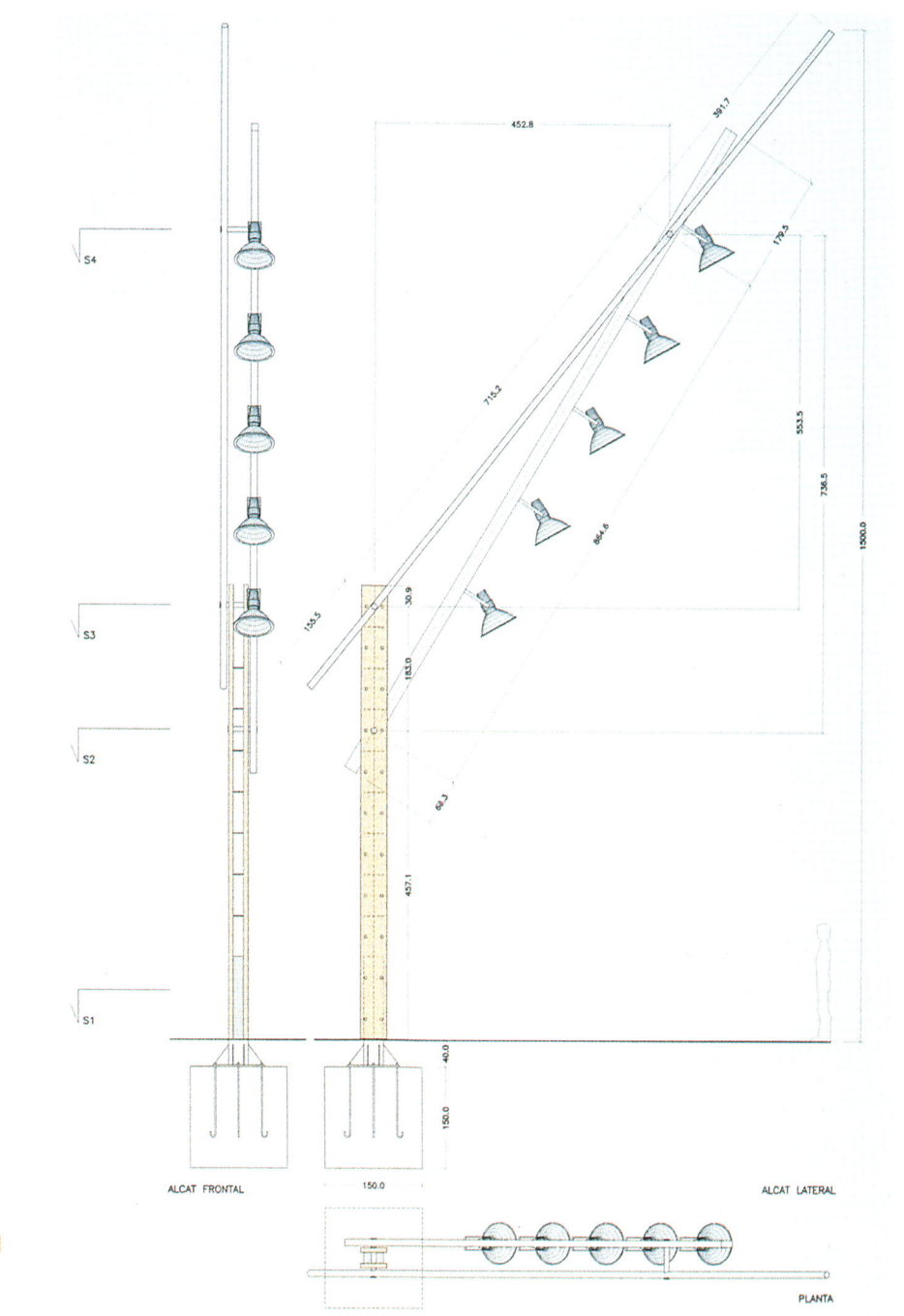

ALCAT LATERAL

PLANTA

161 Pitmit outdoorlamp

Neruda stool - Neruda bench

Manufactured by Santa & Cole

WITH JAUME BENAVENT AND PERNILLA MAGNUSSON
1998

This barstool was specially designed as part of the project for a café-restaurant that we recently carried out in Barcelona. We wanted it to be a very robust object that would be confused to a certain extent with the legs of the people standing at the bar. The legs of a person in a relaxed position are, of course, never perfectly vertical. They might be bent, they might be crossed, they might rest on a metal bar and so on. For that reason, we decided to give the legs of the stool a slight spiral movement.

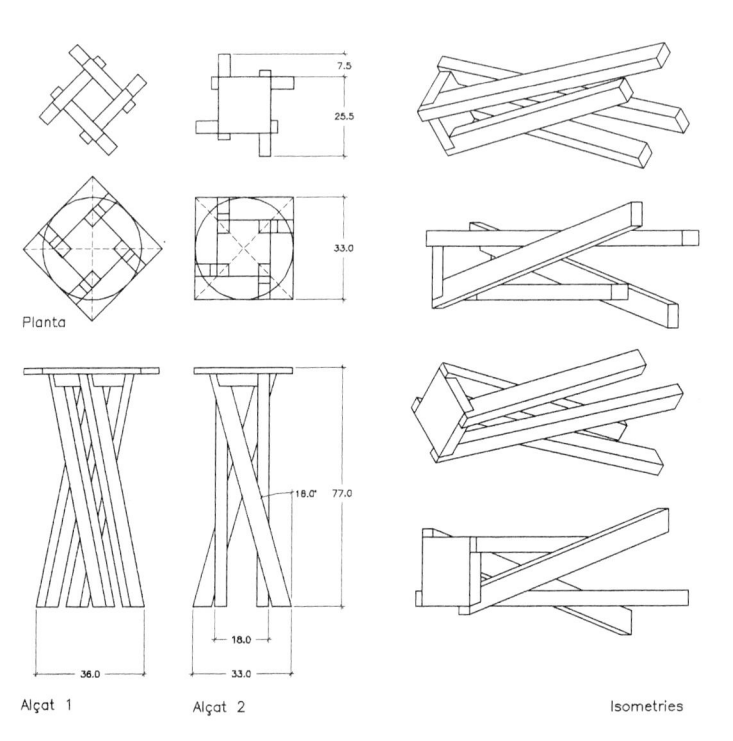

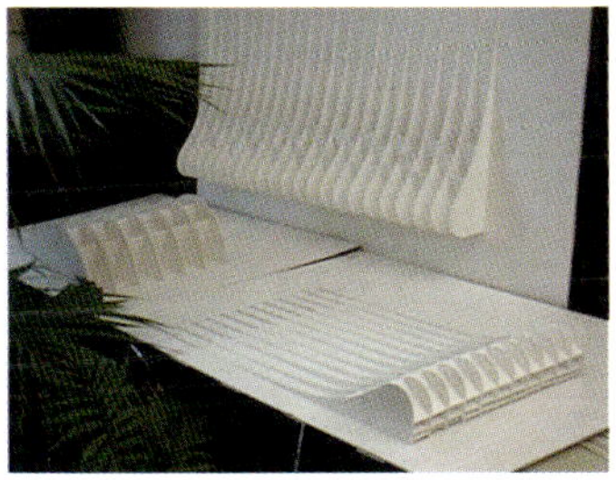

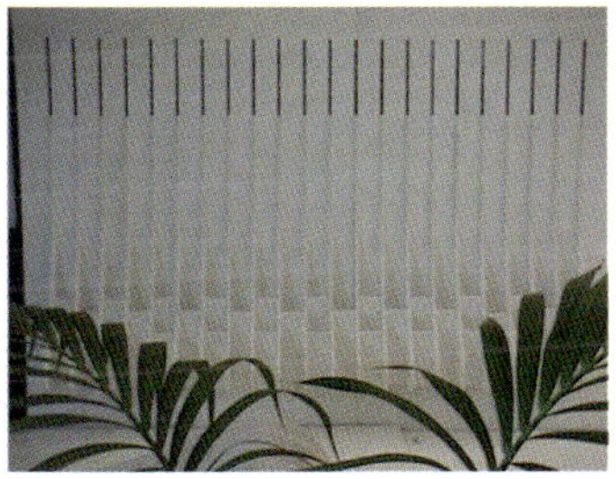

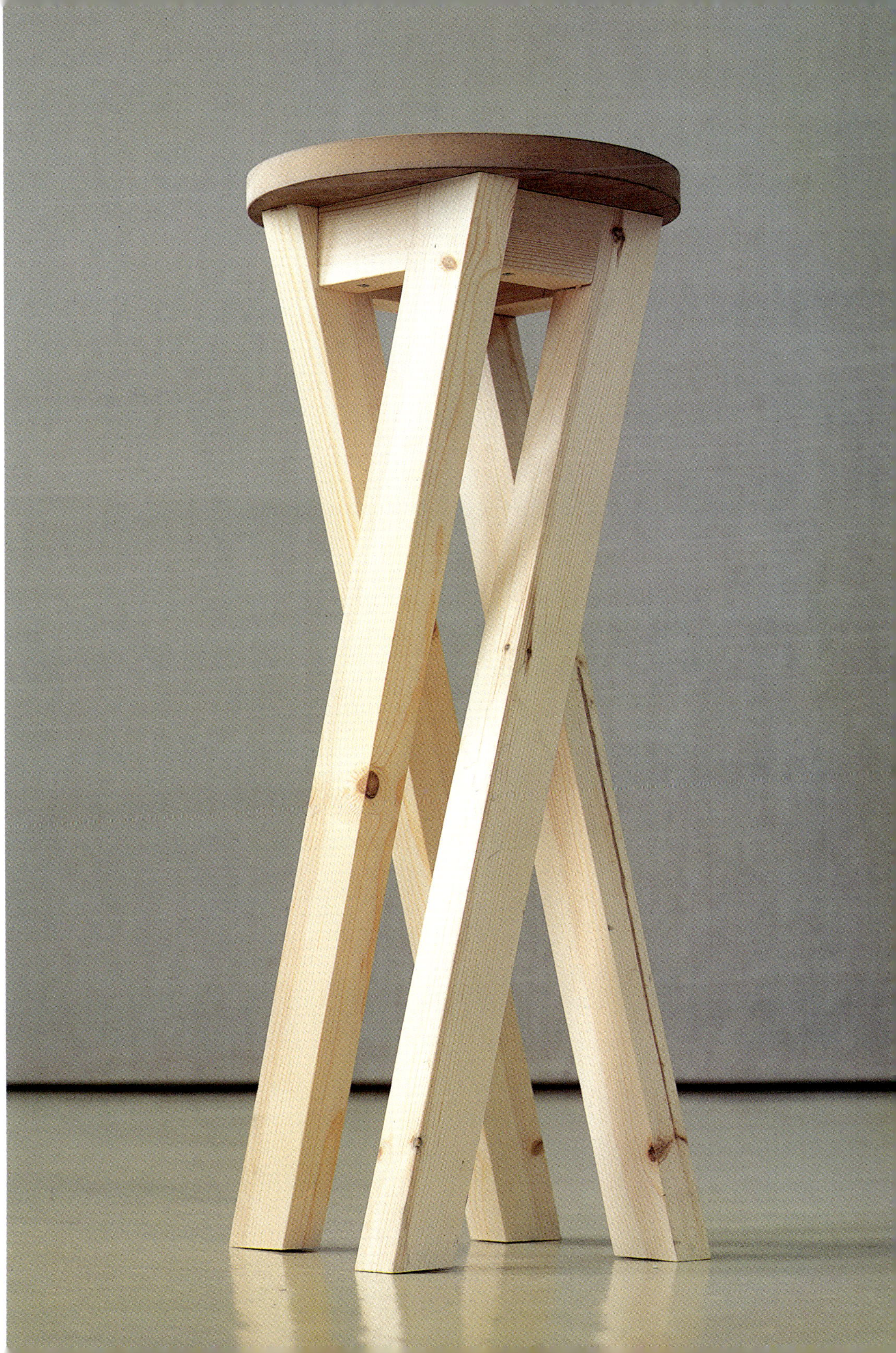

Collserola

Dwellings in Barcelona

With students: Jaume Benavent, Alex Giménez, Arola Tous, Andrea Tous, Nuria Cases and Paco Sert

1997

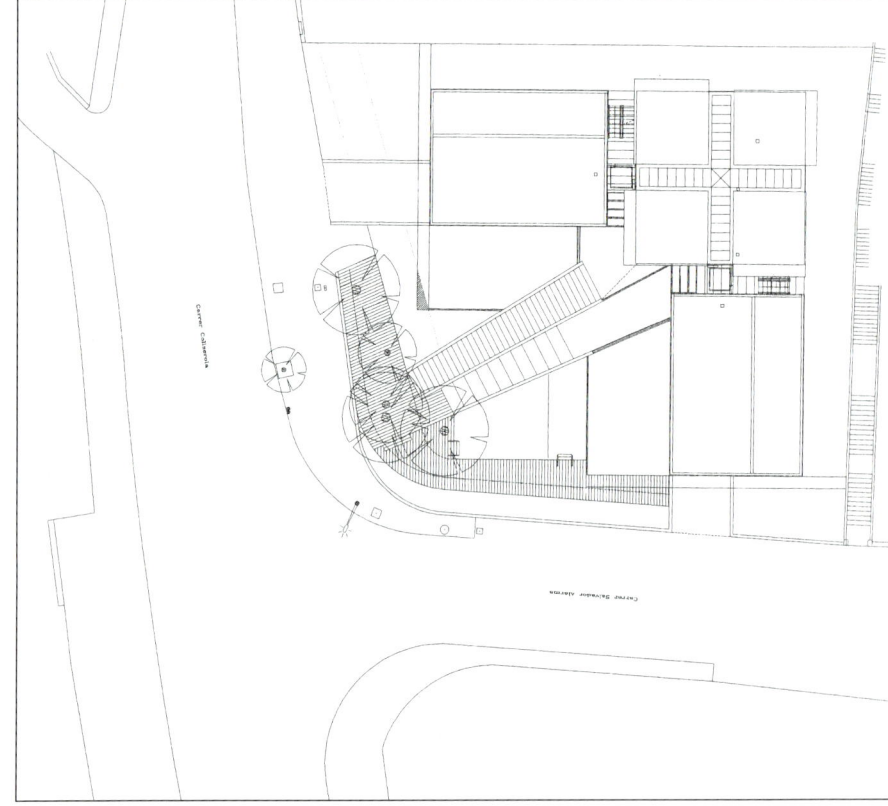

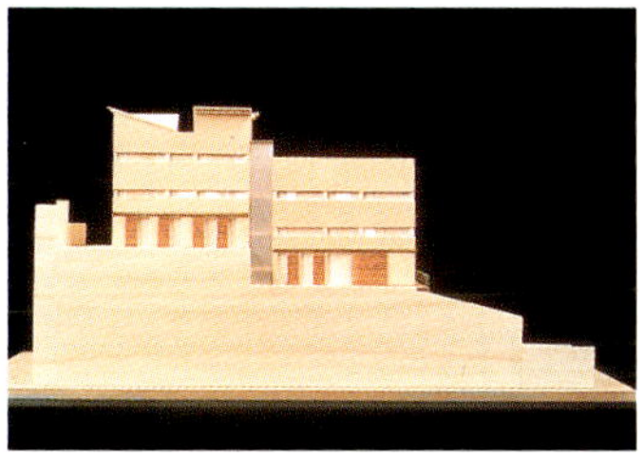
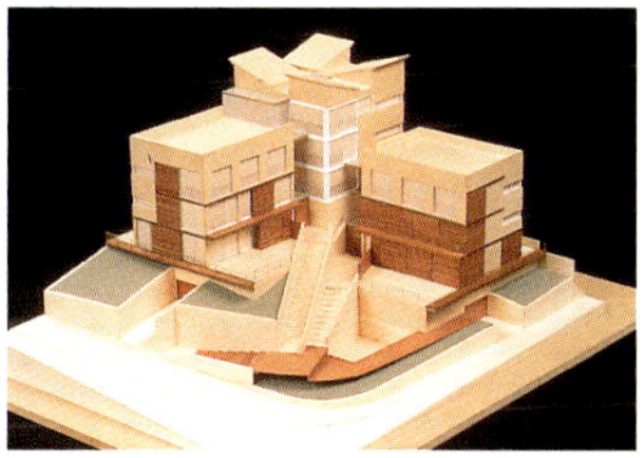
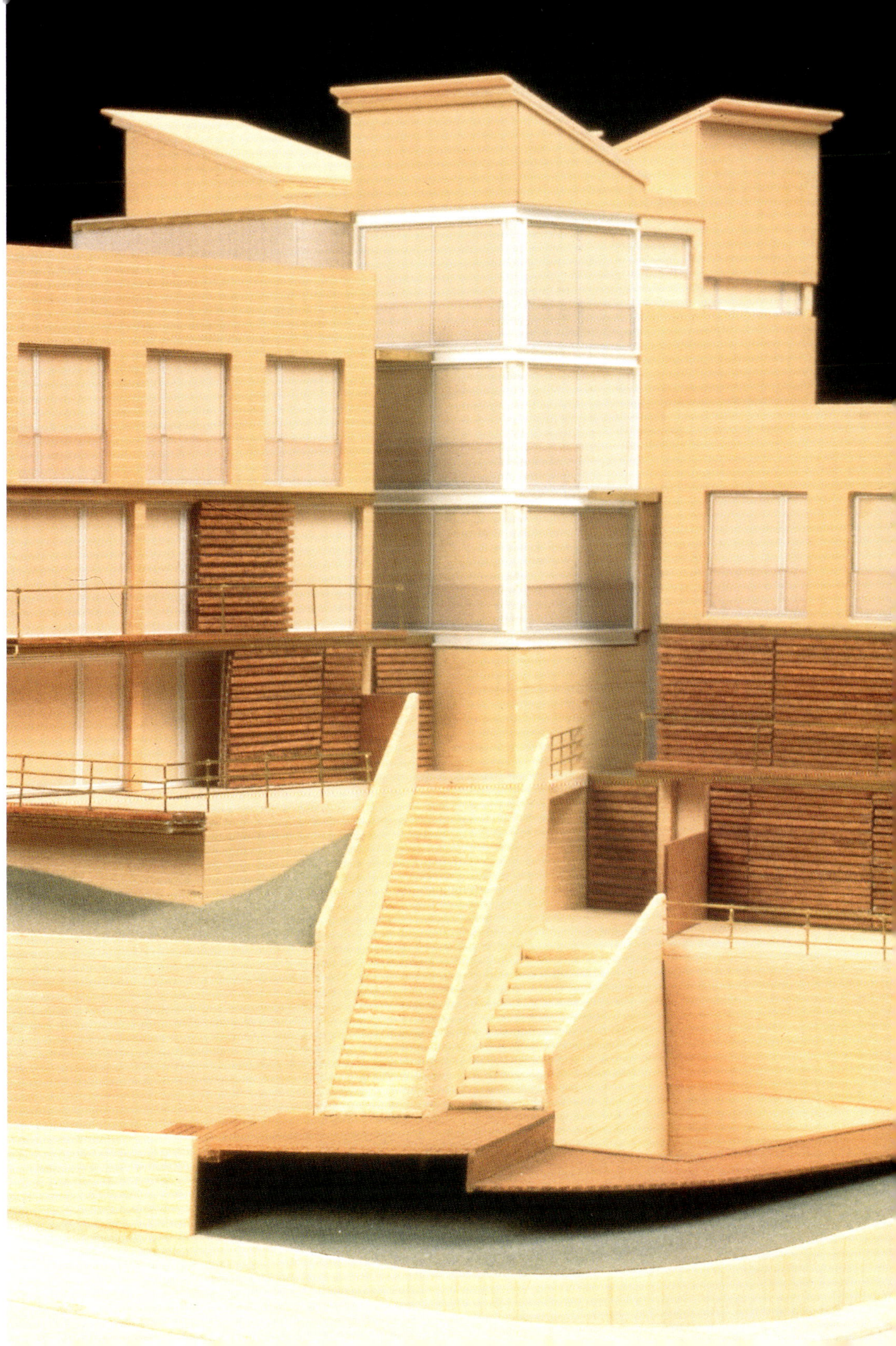

1th floor

2nd floor

3th floor

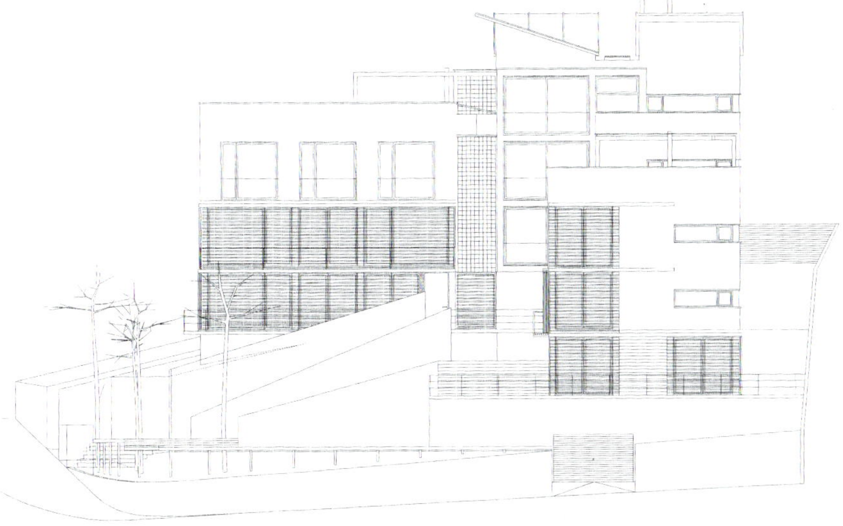

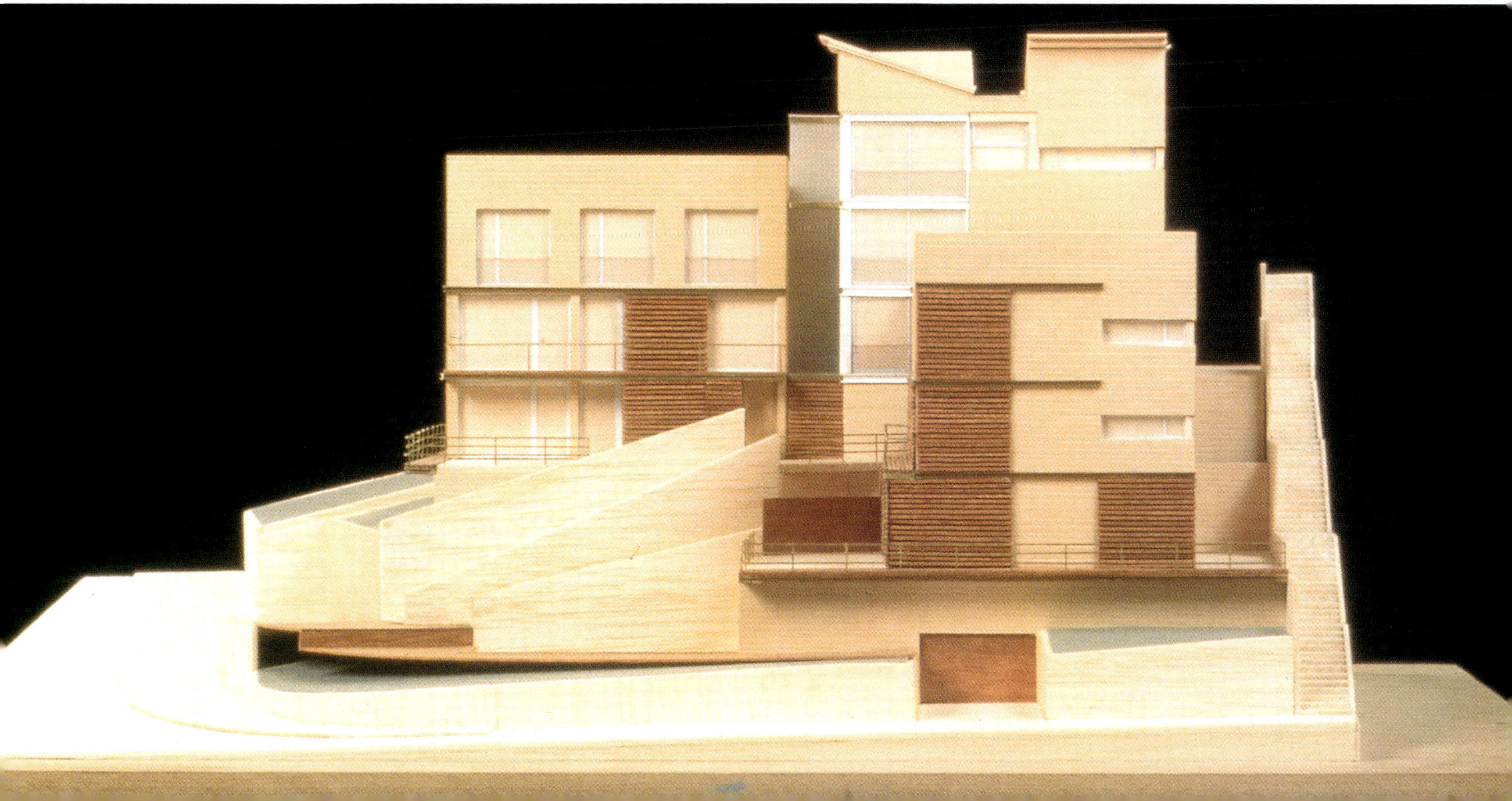

Jury Report
Nomination for Landscape Architecture Contest   Concurso Nacional de Arquitectura

Refurbishment of Vughterstraat, 's-Hertogenbosch
Reforma de Vughterstraat, 's-Hertogenbosch

The refurbishment of Vughterstraat stands out for its marked and coherent clarity, the near virtuosity of its elegance and its comfortable and appropriate use of materials. 's-Hertogenbosch takes the user of its public space seriously, and not only the pedestrian but also motorists and their cars and cyclists and their cycles. The dark-red thoroughfare meanders like a river in its bed, creating a flowing line along the varying width of the street cross-section. This enables the frontages to move back and forth, ideally framed by the enclosing bands of roughened pink granite, in a magnificent balance between height and width, the perfect, uniform detailing of driveways and transitions and a joyful encounter with the side streets. The pavement is marvellous, caressing the eye and the foot. It is taut, light, lucid and Mediterranean. It is pleasant to walk on, looks fresh and its subtle pattern lends it a dancing character. The tautness of the paving is gratifying, thanks to its black foundation mass. The clear lines of the pale-grey concrete paving blocks used for the gutters, the black parking spaces and the white stone markings for the cycle route reinforce the overall graphic image and perfectly delineate the different functions. The stainless-steel and vandal-proof street furniture is perfectly in keeping with its solidity, attractiveness and effectiveness. Beth Galí's cycle-racks are fabulous, a wonder of elegance, both with and without cycles (incidentally, all the members of the jury were persuaded of the beauty of the model, though not necessarily of its optimum functionality). The decision to suspend the lighting over the street reinforces the autonomy of the flowing profile of the road. The generous stainless-steel lampposts placed at a number of strategic positions along the pavement rightly put Vughterstraat under the spotlight.

Karin Daan - March 1998

La reforma de Vughterstraat destaca por su notable y coherente claridad, por el casi virtuosismo de su elegancia y por un uso contenido y apropiado de materiales. La ciudad de 's-Hertogenbosch se toma al usuario de su espacio público muy en serio, no sólo a los peatones sino también a los motoristas y a sus vehículos, y a los ciclistas y sus bicicletas. La calzada de color rojo oscuro serpentea como un río en su cauce, creando una línea fluida a lo largo de la anchura variable de la sección transversal de la calle. Ello permite el avance y retroceso de las fachadas, idealmente subrayadas por los bordillos de granito rosa sin pulir, en un magnífico equilibrio entre altura y anchura, el detalle perfecto y uniforme de los vados y las transiciones, y el alegre encuentro con las calles laterales. El pavimento es maravilloso, un regalo para la vista y los pies; es liso, luminoso, ligero, lúcido y mediterráneo; es agradable al andar, tiene un aspecto fresco y su sutil despiece le confiere un carácter asociado a la danza. La tersura del pavimento es gratificante, gracias a su base rígida. Las líneas claras del enlosado de hormigón claro en las alcantarillas, las plazas de aparcamiento de color negro y las marcas de piedra blanca para el carril de bicicletas refuerzan la imagen gráfica general y delinean perfectamente las distintas funciones. El mobiliario urbano, de acero inoxidable y antivandálico, combina perfectamente solidez, eficacia y atractivo. Los soportes para aparcar bicicletas de Beth Galí son fabulosos, un sueño de elegancia, con o sin bicicletas (a propósito, todos los miembros del jurado estaban convencidos de la belleza del diseño, aunque no necesariamente de su óptima funcionalidad). La decisión de suspender la iluminación sobre la calle refuerza la autonomía del fluido trazado de la calle. Las generosas farolas de acero inoxidable colocadas en lugares estratégicos a lo largo de la calzada sitúan a Vughterstraat bajo el foco de luz que se merece.

Karin Daan - Marzo de 1998

Biography

Elisabeth Galí i Camprubí
was born in Barcelona on 19 April 1950

ACADEMIC QUALIFICATIONS AND POSITIONS

- Studied piano at the Acadèmia Marshall through to final year, 1954-68.
- Baccalauréat Français, Lycée Français, Barcelona.
- 1st-year course in Fine Art, Escola Massana, Barcelona, 1964-65.
- Basic design (foundation course), Escola Elisava, Barcelona, 1965-66.
- Industrial design, studies in Industrial Design at the Escola Eina in Barcelona, graduated in 1969.
- Head of the industrial design department of the Metalplastica Española company, 1967-68.
- 1st-year course in Exact Sciences, Universitat Autonoma de Barcelona, 1971-72.
- Architecture, specialising in Urbanism, commenced studies at the Escola Superior d'Arquitectura de Barcelona in 1973-74, graduated as an architect in 1982.
- Vice-president of the Governing Body of the ADI-FAD (Associació de Dissenyadors Industrials i del Foment de les Arts Decoratives), 1976-79.
- Editor-in-chief of the first issue of the magazine IANUS, Old and New International Architecture, 1980.
- Worked as municipal architect with the Urban Elements and Projects team in Barcelona City Council's Department of Urbanism, 1981-88.
- Directs the Urbana collection for the Santa & Cole design firm, 1987-89.
- Responsible for the urban image of the Barcelona Film Festival, 1987-90.
- Deputy director of the Municipal Institute for Urbanistic Promotion and Olympic Games (IMPU'92), responsible for the Olympic Areas of Vall d'Hebron, Diagonal and Montjuïc, 1988-92.
- Maritime captain's licence, 1994.
- Member of the 'Commissie voor Welstand en Monumenten Rotterdam', Quality Team Kop van Zuid.
- Member of the 'Forum Catalunya demà: Els objectius i estratègies per un territori oganitzat sota criteris de sostenibilitat i cohesió territorial', Generalitat de Catalunya.

ACADEMIC ACTIVITIES

- Study grant from the Universitat Politècnica de Barcelona for academic year 1978 at the ILAUD (International Laboratory of Architecture and Urban Design), Urbino, Italy. Project: reordering of the Mercadale square.
- Member of the Final Year assessment jury 1987-88 at the Delft School of Architecture, the Netherlands.
- Worked during academic year 1978-79 with the Landscape Architecture Department, including publication of a booklet on 'Selection of Gardens'. (Course director: Elies Torres)
- Visiting tutor: Workshop 'Beschreven Leegte' at the Faculty of Fine Arts and Architecture, Rotterdam, the Netherlands, 1992.
- Visiting tutor: end-of-year assessments, École d'Architecture de Lausanne, Switzerland, academic year 1993-94.
- Visiting tutor at the workshop 'The planned void' at the Faculty of Fine Arts and Architecture, Rotterdam, the Netherlands, 1993.
- Visiting tutor at the School of Architecture, Barcelona. Urbanism V. Academic year 1993-94.
- Visiting tutor: end-of-year assessments, École d'Architecture de Lyon, France, academic year 1995-96.
- Workshop on 'Discovering the project', Barcelona, with 5th-year students from the Kampen Hogeschool, the Netherlands, 1996.
- Tutor for 'Urbanism III' at the Barcelona Architecture School since 1994.
- Professor of 'Masters in Landscape Architecture' at the Universitat Politecnica de Barcelona since 1994.

PAPERS GIVEN

1982 'Projectar des de l'Administració', Barcelona City Council, Barcelona, Spain.
1983 'Travaux rècents à Barcelone', Salle Audette, Strasbourg, France.
1984 'Parc de l'Escorxador', ETSAB School of Architecture, Barcelona, Spain.
1986 'Urban Projects', Architecture School, U.S.C., Los Angeles, USA.
1987 'Travaux Publiques', École Polytecnique, Paris, France.
1988 'Own Work', T.U. Delft School of Architecture, Delft, the Netherlands.
'Own Work', Academy of Architecture, Amsterdam, the Netherlands.
1989 'El parc de la Vall d'Hebron, el parc del Migdia i el Sot', lecture to the postgraduate course, Landscape Architecture Department, School of Architecture, Barcelona, Spain.
1990 'El fossar de la pedrera', lecture to the postgraduate course, Landscape Architecture Department, School of Architecture, Barcelona, Spain.
1991 'L'Arquitectura de Frank Gehry en l'art modern', Elisava School, Barcelona, Spain.
1992 'Montjuïc: el Parc i el Sot del Migdia', Project Complements course: urban space, design criteria, School of Architecture, Barcelona, Spain.
'Own Work', Universidad Internacional Menéndez Pelayo, Cuenca, Spain.

1993 'Own Work', Facoltà di Architettura di Genova, Italy.
'Un edificio, un'idea: Biblioteca Joan Miró', Facoltà di Architettura de Torino, Italy.
'Own Work', Facoltà di Architettura di Pescara, Italy.
1994 'Architecture as a transitional art', Institute of Contemporary Art London, England.
'Own Work', School of Architecture, Utrecht, the Netherlands.
1995 'Own Work', Royal College of Art, London, England.
'Rond Beth Galí', took part in the symposium on art in the street, Hogeschool 's-Hertogenbosch, the Netherlands.
'El fossar de la pedrera' Symposium ECLAS-95, School of Architecture, Barcelona, Spain.
Lecture and workshop, École d'Architecture de Lyon, France.
1996 '10 años de arquitectura', ETSAV School of Architecture, Valencia, Spain.
Communication on architecture schools to the UIA Congress, Barcelona, Spain.
1997 'Own Work', Minar Sinan University, Istanbul, Turkey.
'Pure details', Academie van Bouwkunst, Amsterdam, the Netherlands.
'Tra la Murgia e il mare', Andria, Italy.
'Territoires – Aménagements – Déménagements', Pavillon de l'Arsenal, Paris, France.
'Own Work', Architektur Fakultät, Stuttgart, Germany.

PARTICIPATED IN THE FOLLOWING COLLOQUIUMS

1989 'Paisatgisme Francés Contemporani', Col.legi d'Arquitectes de Catalunya, Barcelona, Spain.
1990 'Lluis Domenech-Josep Maria Jujol, dos vertientes del Modernismo', Universidad Internacional Menéndez Pelayo, Santillana del Mar, Spain.
1990 'Génere i identitat cultural', Comisió Internacional de la Difusió de la Cultura Catalana, Generalitat de Catalunya, Palau March, Barcelona, Spain.
1992 'Per la Igualtat', II Congrés de la Dona a Catalunya, Institut Català de la Dona, Generalitat de Catalunya, Antic mercat del Born, Barcelona, Spain.
1992 'Cultura i comunicació de masses', Comisió Internacional de la Difusió de la Cultura Catalana, Generalitat de Catalunya, Barcelona, Spain.
1998 Talks in Barcelona, 'Leopoldo Pomés: dones', Palau de la Virreina, Barcelona, Spain.

PARTICIPATION IN COMPETITIONS

1981 Design ideas for Parc Joan Miró, Barcelona, Spain.
1983 Design for Parc de la Devesa, Girona, Spain.
International competition to design Parc de la Villette, Paris, France.
1984 Preliminary design of a parliament building for the Autonomous Community of La Rioja, Logroño, Spain.
Preliminary design for the Gran Vía in Ceuta, Spain.
1985 Design for a health centre in La LLagosta, Spain.
1986 International competition to lay out La Cartuja Island for Expo' 92 in Seville, Spain. With Martorell, Bohigas and Mackay.
1987 Invited to take part in the international competition to design Parc de Bercy, Paris, France.
1990 Invited to take part in the 'Stad aan de Stroom' competition to lay out the Port of Antwerp, Belgium.
1991 Open competition for the new headquarters of the Colegio de Arquitectos de Andalusia Oriental in Granada, Spain.
1992 Open competition for the new headquarters of the La General savings bank, Granada, Spain.
1992 Open competition for Spreebogen, Berlin, Germany.
1994 Invited to take part in the competition to lay out Parc de Zafra, Huelva, Spain.
1995 Open competition for 'Parks am Potsdamer Platz', Berlin, Germany.

AWARDS FOR INDUSTRIAL DESIGN AND ARCHITECTURE

1966 Delta d'Or ADI-FAD for the design of connectable furniture modules.
1969 Delta d'Or ADI-FAD for the design of a portable shower.
Selecció ADI-FAD for the design of the Vieta AT 229 hi-fi amplifier.
1970 Selecció ADI-FAD for the design of an articulated bookcase.
1971 1st prize in the design ideas competition for Parc l'Escorxador.
1983 1st prize ex aequo in the international competition to lay out Parc de la Villette in Paris.
FAD Interiors award 1984 and FAD Opinion award for the refurbishment of the Information Office for Barcelona City Council.
1984 Delta d'Argent ADI-FAD for the design of an outdoor lamp.
3rd prize in the preliminary design competition for the Parliament of La Rioja, Logroño.
3rd prize in the preliminary design competition to lay out the Gran Via, Ceuta.
1985 Honourable mention in the competition to design a Health Centre
1987 FAD award for Ephemeral Architecture 1987 for the design of the exhibition: Eina, 20 anys d'avantguarda.

1991 FAD: finalist in the category 'New Architecture for Public Use' for the Joan Miró Library.
1994 1st prize in the competition to lay out Parc de Zafra, Huelva.
FAD award: finalist in the Ephemeral Architecture category for the design of the 'Corberò' exhibition at the Tecla Sala.

MEDALS

Barcelona 1992 Olympic Medal for contributions to the preparation of the Barcelona '92 Olympic Games.

PROFESSIONAL ACTIVITY

Industrial design
1966 Connectable furniture modules in the form of perspex cubes, manufactured by Tecmo G3.
1969 Portable shower, manufactured by Raydor.
AT 229 hi-fi amplifier, manufactured by Vieta Audioelectronica.
1970 Table lamp, manufactured by Metalarte S.A.
Table lamp, manufactured by Metalarte S.A.
Table lamp, manufactured by Metalurgicas Amat.
1971 Aladino, articulated book case, manufactured by Tecmo G3.
1972 'Construction' assembly game for children, manufactured by Pisa.
1973 'Elephan' assembly game for children, manufactured by Pisa.
1977 Medalla ADI, medal for design student competition.
1979 Design of door handles based on those on the doors of the Batlló, Milà and Calvet houses by Antoni Gaudí. Production: b.d. edicions de disseny.
1984 Lamparaalta outdoor lamp, manufactured by Santa & Cole.
1994 Park Bike bicycle stand, manufactured by Santa & Cole.
1997 Pitmit outdoor lamp, manufactured by Santa & Cole.
1998 Neruda stool, manufactured by Santa & Cole.

Ephemeral architecture:
designs for exhibitions and public events
1985 'Natura encara viva', design for the opening ceremony of the workshops on Homes i Dones d'esquerra, Hivernacle, Barcelona.
1986 'Homenatge secret a Oriol Bohigas', design for the party to celebrate the award of the City of Barcelona's Medal for Artistic Merit, Barcelona.
'La Pastoral, apunts per a un cuadre', design for the opening ceremony of the academic year, Escola EINA, Barcelona.
'150è aniversari de la Boqueria', exhibition design and setting for the commemoration of the 150th anniversary of the Boqueria market, Barcelona.
1987 'Vi a la Font de Canaletes', happening to mark the official start of remodelling work on the Rambla, Barcelona.
'EINA, 20 anys d'avantguarda', design of the survey exhibition devoted to the Escola EINA, Palau Robert, Barcelona.

From 1987 to 1990 directed and co-ordinated the urban image of the Barcelona Film Festival, taking part in the design of the following film sets in the street:
    'Hollywood-Hollywood' with Frank O. Gehry
    'La vie en rose' with Hans Hollein
    'Accident' with Dani Freixes
    'Cadires' with Joan Brossa
    'Entre bastidors' with Martorell, Bohigas and Mackay
    'L'erotisme' with Gae Aulenti
    'Llum de lluna' with Josep Ma. Civit
    'Manifest de Barcelona' with Bigas Luna, Claret Serrahima and Josep M. Mir
    'Homenatge a Busby Berkeley' with Federico Correa
    'Passatge anamorfic' with Tom Carr
    'Fred Astaire' with Antoni Llena
    'Marlène Dietrich' with Nestor Almendros
    'Charlot', design of exhibition on Charlie Chaplin

1994 Corberò a la Tecla Sala, design of exhibition on the work of the sculptor Xavier Corberò, Tecla Sala, l'Hospitalet, Barcelona.
1995 Monument, exhibition on the mayors of Barcelona, with Oriol Bohigas, constructed the monument to Mayor Pich i Pon, Casernes de Sant Agustí, Barcelona.

Architecture and urban spaces
1975 Tenis Brasco, Selva de Mar, Girona, Spain (completed in 1976).
1976 Group of four houses in Selva de Mar, Girona, Spain (completed in 1979).
1979 Vazquez Montalban house, remodelling of a private house, Barcelona, Spain (completed in 1979).
1982 Parc Joan Miró, Barcelona, worked with Joan Miró on the siting of the sculpture 'Woman and Bird' and the sculpture 'Forest' (completed in 1989).
Emili Vendrell gardens, Barcelona, Spain.
Casa Cases, two-apartment building in Barcelona, Spain (completed in 1989).

1983 Barcelona local authority information office, Barcelona, Spain (completed in 1984).
1984 Laying out of the Fossar de la Pedrera Park and Monument to Lluís Companys, Barcelona, Spain (completed in 1986).
Joan Miró Library in Parc Joan Miró, Barcelona, Spain (completed in 1990).
1985 Reyes house, private house in Cala Pregonda, Menorca, Spain (unbuilt).
Bernad house, remodelling of the interior, Barcelona, Spain (unbuilt).
Refurbishment of an apartment building in Vilafranca del Penedés, Barcelona, Spain (completed in 1990).
Llena house, private house in La Vansa, Lleida, Spain (completed in 1987).
1988 Park at the southern end of the Rovira tunnel, Barcelona, Spain (completed 1991).
Project for the conversion of the church in the Poble Espanyol into a music bar, Barcelona, Spain (unbuilt).
Migdia Parc, Barcelona, Spain (completed in 1992).
Open air auditorium in the Sot del Migdia, Barcelona, Spain (completed in 1992).
1990 Jover-Sala, private house in El Port de la Selva, Girona, Spain (completed in 1992).
Laying out of the public square at the junction of c/. Numància and c/. Viriato, Barcelona, Spain (completed in 1991).
1991 Ordering of the façade and new access to the South-West Cemetery, Barcelona, Spain (completed in 1992).
Escalators to the mountain of Montjuïc, Barcelona, Spain (completed in 1992).
Footbridge over c/. Rius i Taulet, Barcelona, Spain, (completed in 1992).
Restoration of the Av. Maria Cristina – Palau Nacional axis., Barcelona, Spain (completed in 1992).
1992 Teatre Nou, new building for a cultural centre, theatres and cinemas, Barcelona, Spain (unbuilt).
1993 Remodelling of the historic centre of 's-Hertogenbosch, the Netherlands (work in progress).
STOA, building for a shopping centre, 's-Hertogenbosch, the Netherlands, (completed in 1998).
1994 Indumentària, women's clothes shop, Barcelona, Spain (completed in 1995).
1995 Remodelling of the historic centre of Roermond, the Netherlands, (completed in 1998).
1994 Zafra Park, Huelva, Spain (work in progress).
1996 Urban spaces of Piet Smit Plan, Rotterdam, the Netherlands (planning phase).
1997 Apartments in Barcelona, Spain (planning phase).
Café Neruda, restaurant in Barcelona (work in progress).
Sert house, remodelling of the interior, Barcelona, Spain (planning phase).
1998 Bellavista residential development, Roses, Girona, Spain (planning phase).

CURATOR OF THE FOLLOWING EXHIBITIONS

1978 Gaudí Dissenyador, Les Drassanes, Barcelona, Spain.
1987 Gaudí in context, Cooper Hewitt Museum, New York, USA.
1988 Gaudí, Nagoya Castle, Japan.
1992 La Ciutat Retrobada, Pavelló de la República, Barcelona, Spain.

EXHIBITIONS OF OWN WORK

1983 La Ville et ses Jardins, Centre Georges Pompidou, Paris, France.
1984 Els Espais Verds, COAC, Barcelona and Girona, Spain.
1985 Arquitectures Retrobades, COAC, Barcelona, Spain.
1987 Espais Urbans, Fundació Joan Miró, Barcelona, Spain.
Area de Cultura, Palau de la Virreina, Barcelona, Spain.
1988 Barcelona, la Ciutat i el 92, Edifici de les Aigües, Barcelona, Spain.
1990 Espais Urbans, COAC, Barcelona, Spain.
Stad aan de Stroom, Antwerp, Belgium.
1991 Anvers, Barcelona, Rotterdam, Ciutats amb Port, COAC, Barcelona, Spain.
Barcelona, la Ciutat i el 92, Edifici de les Aigües, Barcelona, Spain.
Barcelona, a concise view of recent work by a Barcelona Architect, University of Waterloo, Ontario, Canada.
25 Anys de Premis Delta, Design Spring, B.D. Ediciones de Diseño, Barcelona, Spain.
Dissenys de Mobiliari Urbá, Design Spring, Rambla de Catalunya, Barcelona, Spain.
1992 La ciutat renovada, Pavelló de la República, Barcelona, Spain.
Kasa kit, Birdhouse in 'The inhabited garden' exhibition, Antonio de Barnola Gallery, Barcelona, Spain.
1993 Beschreven Leegte, exhibition of 5 Barcelona architects, Academie van Bouwkunst, Rotterdam, the Netherlands.
1996 Catalunya: arquitectura i ciutat, una visiò des del procès projectual, exhibition of contemporary Catalan architectural drawing,

Pati Llimona, Barcelona, Spain.
Arquitectura a Catalunya 1977-1996, l'Era de la democracia, Convent de Santa Mònica, Barcelona, Spain.

SOLO EXHIBITIONS

1995 Uitnodiging Rond Beth Galí, exhibition of architectural work produced between 1985 and 1995, Hogeschool, 's-Hertogenbosch, the Netherlands.
1998 Beth Galí, architecture & design 1966-1998, Het Kruithuis, Municipal Museum of Contemporary Art, 's-Hertogenbosch, the Netherlands.
Beth Galí, Landscape architecture, Galerie Renate Kammer, Architektur und Kunst, Hamburg, Germany.

ARTICLES AND BOOKS PUBLISHED

- 'Diez años de Arquitectura Española, 1966-1976', epilogue to the second edition of Arquitectura Moderna by Gillo Dorfles, Editorial Ariel.
- 'Los muros verdes del Ampurdan', Arquitecturas bis, no. 27.
- 'Can Jaume, la casa de Manolo Pertegaz en Pineda', Vogue, Spain – Nov. 1981.
- Interview with Federico Correa, Autrement, Paris.
- 'La calle, escenario real del cine', Vivir en Barcelona, no. 126.
- 'La cokteleria Bijoux y la joyeria Berao', Arquitecturas bis, no. 49
- 'Ricardo Bofill, 'socialista?', El Pais, 7/11/82.
- Contributor to the Architecture and Interior Design section of the magazine Gran Bazaar and Vogue.
- 'Ocupar a poc a poc la ciutat', Diari Avui, 29/6/88.
- 'Iniciativa privada versus iniciativa pública', Diari de Barcelona, La Ciutat i el 92.
- 'Biblioteca Joan Miró', Barcelona Metropolis.
- 'Fins i tot la plaça de les Arenes és imprescindible', Diari de Barcelona, 25/2/90.
- 'Tres alternatives per a la plaça de toros de les Arenes', Diari de Barcelona, 25/4/90.
- 'La Vall d'Hebron i la Diagonal, dues àrees olímpiques força desconegudes', Diari de Barcelona, 20/5/90.
- 'Una arquitectura banal', La Vanguardia, 20/5/92.
- 'Area olimpica de la Vall d'Hebron', essay in the book Barcelona, Ed. in Asa.
- 'Carles Buigas, técnico electricista', El País, 20/7/92.
- 'Proyectos a medida: muebles e interiores de Josep Aragall', Ardi, no. 28.
- 'Nel magazzino de tabacco', Abitare, no. 311.
- 'La música que escuchamos y el fantasma de la modernidad', El País, 10/2/94.
- 'Dibuixar per construir', Autobiografies, Federico Correa.
- 'L'Opera de Liò i el Liceu', Diari Avui, 23/5/95.
- 'Escoltar ópera a Barcelona', Escena opera magazine.
- 'Caminar pel fil de la navalla', Diari Avui, 12/3/96.
- 'Alfonso Milà', FAD no. 1.
- 'Dona i arquitectura', revista del col.legi de doctors i llicenciats en filosofia i lletres Catalunya.
- The invisible in architecture, book to be published by Rizzoli.
- Correa-Milà, arquitectura 1955/1997, book on the work of Federico Correa and Alfonso Milà, published by the Col.legi d'Arquitectes de Catalunya.
- Beth Galí, architecture & design 1966-1998, Museum Het Kruithuis, 's-Hertogenbosch, 1998.

MEMBERSHIP OF AWARD JURIES

1970 Competition for the design of kitchen utensils organised by Barcelona's Industrial Design schools, Barcelona, Spain.
1976 FAD awards for Architecture and Interior Design, Barcelona, Spain.
'Medalla ADI', annual competition for final-year students of industrial design, from 1976 to 1979, Barcelona, Spain.
1978 'Oscar for the best shoe designs' awarded by the Spanish stylists' professional association, Barcelona, Spain.
1990 Delta ADI-FAD awards, Barcelona, Spain.
1995 Prix de Rome 1995, Amsterdam, the Netherlands.

Bibliography

INDUSTRIAL DESIGN

- **Hogares Moderno**, (Feb. 1966)
- **El Correo Catalán**, (Nov. 1966)
- **Nobelart**, (Dec. 1969)
- **Nuevo Ambiente**, (Feb. 1970)
- **Enciclopedia Salvat de Arte Contemporáneo**
- **Els Altres Catalans**, in the chapter 'Art, Disseny Arquitectura' written by Alexandre Cirici i Pellicer

PARC JOAN MIRO

- 'Sobre el Concurso de l'Escorxador, **Quaderns** no. 146 (May-June 1981), Col.legi Oficial d'Arquitectes de Catalunya, Barcelona
- 'El concurso para el parque del antiguo Escorxador de Barcelona' Oriol Bohigas, **Arquitectura Bis** no. 40 (Nov-Dec 1981)
- 'Projecte d'Execució del Parc de l'Escorxador', **Quaderns** no. 149 (Dec. 1981), Col.legi Oficial d'Arquitectes de Catalunya, Barcelona
- 'Un programma per Barcelona' di Oriol Bohigas. **Casabella** no. 48 (Sept. 1982), Elemond Periodici, Milano
- **Skyline**, The Architecture and Design Review, (Apr. 1982), The Institute for Architecture and Urban Studies, New York
- **Plans i Projectes per a Barcelona 1981/1982**, Ajuntament de Barcelona, Area d'Urbanisme, (1983)
- 'Le Droit à la Ville, les espaces publics de Barcelone', **AMC Revue d'Architecture** no. 2, (Oct. 1983)
- **Lotus** no. 39, Milano, (1983)
- 'Regenerating Barcelona with Parks and Plazas', Peter Buchanan, **The Architectural Review**, vol. CLXXV, no. 1048 (June 1984)
- **La Biennal**, Produccions Culturals Juvenils De L'Europa Mediterrània, Ajuntament de Barcelona, (1985)
- 'L'art monumental et la cité', **L'Oeil**, Revue d'Art, no. 372-373, (July-Aug. 1986)
- **Barcelona Spaces and Sculptures (1982-1986)**, Ajuntament de Barcelona, Area of Urbanism and Public Works, Joan Miró Foundation, (1987)
- **AT Architecture Magazine**, (Feb. 1990), Delphi Research Inc., Tokio
- **Barcelona, la ciutat i el 92**, Barcelona Holding Olímpic S.A. (HOLSA), Olimpíada Cultural Barcelona 92, Ajuntament de Barcelona (1991)
- **Barcelone, dix années d'Urbanisme – La renaissance d'une ville**, Guy Henry, Editions du Moniteur, Paris, (1992)

PARC DE LA VILLETTE

- **L'Invention du Parc**, Parc de la Villette, Paris, Concurs International 1982 – 1983, Graphite Editions, (1984)

JARDINS EMILI VENDRELL

- 'Un programma per Barcelona' di Oriol Bohigas. **Casabella** no. 48, (Sept. 1982), Elemond Periodici, Milano
- **Plans i Projectes per a Barcelona 1981/1982**, Ajuntament de Barcelona, Area d'Urbanisme, (1983)

'LA CARTUJA', EXPO 92, SEVILLA

- 'Siviglia 1992, un concorso di idee per l'Esposizione Universale', Rafael López Palanco e Luis Marin, **Casabella** no. 528, (Oct. 1986), Elemond Periodici, Milano

BIBLIOTECA MIRO

- **Casabella** no. 573 (Nov. 1990), Elemond Periodici, Milan
- **El Croquis**, no. 46 (Enero 1991), El Croquis Editorial, Madrid
- 'A Ciencia Cierta', M. José Gómez Angelats, **Nuevo Estilo**, no. 156, (March 1991), Axel Springer Publicaciones, Madrid
- 'Biblioteca Joan Miró. Un refugio de paz en el centro de Barcelona', **Diseño Interior**, no. 3 (April 1991), Globus/Comunicacion S.A., Madrid
- 'Island Library', Peter Buchanan, **The Architectural Review**, no. 1133 (July 1991), MBC Architectural Press, London
- **European Masters/3**, vol. 1, Ediciones Atrium S.A., Barcelona, (1991)
- 'Een filter tussen park en stad', **Archis** no. 12-1991, Debussy Ellerman Harms BV, Amsterdam
- **d'Arquitectura** no. 10, Ed'A

FOSSAR DE LA PEDRERA

- **Barcelona Spaces and Sculptures (1982-1986)**, Ajuntament de Barcelona, Area of Urbanism and Public Works, Joan Miró Foundation, (1987)
- **Ottagono** 87 (anno 22, Dec. 1987), Ed. CO.P.IN.A. srl, Milano
- **Archis**, no. 11-1989, Van Loghum Slaterus, Deventer
- **AT Architecture Magazine**, (Feb. 1990), Delphi Research Inc., Tokyo
- 'Il Recupero della Memoria', Patrizia Falcone, **Abitare** no. 289 (Oct. 1990), Abitare Segesta, Milan

- **Barcelona, la ciutat i el 92**, Barcelona Holding Olímpic S.A. (HOLSA), Olimpíada Cultural Barcelona 92, Ajuntament de Barcelona, (1991)
- **Garten & Landschaft**, no. 1, (1991), Callwey Verlag, Munich
- **Barcelone, dix années d'Urbanisme – La renaissance d'une ville**, Guy Henry, Editions du Moniteur, Paris, (1992)
- **Jardins de Catalunya**, Edicions 62, Barcelona
- **Barcelona, arquitectura y ciudad**, Ed. Gustavo Gili
- **Spazi publici contemporanei**, Quaderni di AU. Ed. ASA
- **d'Arquitectura** no. 10, Ed'A
- 'Geläuterte Landschaftsarchitektur', Eric Luiten, **Topos** no. 21

EINA, VINT ANYS D'AVANTGUARDA

- **Premis FAD d'Arquitectura i d'Interiorisme 87**, Foment de les Artes Decoratives, (1987)
- 'EINA, veinte años de vanguardia', **ON Diseño** no. 93, Premios FAD de Arquitectura e Interiorismo 1987, Aram Ediciones, Barcelona

SURROUNDINGS AND SOUTH ENTRANCE OF THE ROVIRA TUNNEL

- **Barcelona Spaces and Sculptures** (1982-1986), Ajuntament de Barcelona, Area of Urbanism and Public Works, Joan Miró Foundation, (1987)
- **Barcelona, la ciutat i el 92**, Barcelona Holding Olímpic S.A. (HOLSA), Olimpíada Cultural Barcelona 92, Ajuntament de Barcelona, (1991)
- **Barcelone, dix années d'Urbanisme – La renaissance d'une ville**, Guy Henry, Editions du Moniteur, Paris, (1992)
- **Barcelona espai public**, Ajuntament de Barcelona, (1992)

CASA CASES

- 'Sotto un tetto leggero appena appoggiato' di Patrizia Falcone, Casa **Vogue**, (Feb. 1991), Milan
- **Architectural Houses**, Vol. 2 – City Houses, Ediciones Atrium S.A. Barcelona, (1991)

PORT OF ANTWERP

- **Antwerp – Reshaping a City**. The River and the City project, Blondé Artprinting International (1990)
- 'La ciutat com a material de projecte: projecte d'Anvers', AB no. 29

- 'Anversa: la città e il fiume', Marcel Smets, **Casabella**, no. 578, Elemond Periodici, Milan
- **Quaderns**, no. 191, Col.legi D'Arquitectes de Catalunya, Barcelona

CASA JOVER

- **Premis FAD d'Arquitectura i Interiorisme 1991**, Foment de les Artes Decoratives, Barcelona (1992)
- **d'Arquitectura no. 10**, Ed'A

PARC DEL MIGDIA AND AUDITORIUM DEL SOT

- **Barcelona Olímpica, la ciutat renovada**, HOLSA, Barcelona Holding Olímpic S.A., Barcelona (1992)
- **Barcelone, dix années d'Urbanisme – La renaissance d'une ville**, Guy Henry, Editions du Moniteur, Paris (1992)
- **Barcelona espai public**, Ajuntament de Barcelona
- **Premi FAD d'Arquitectura i Interiorisme 1992**, Ed.FAD, Barcelona.
- **d'Arquitectura no. 10**, Ed'A
- Beschreven Leegte, Barcelona (Publication expo. Rotterdam)
- **AU Arredo Urbano**, Editorial In Asa, Milano
- **ON**, Premis d'arquitectura i Interiorisme 1992, Barcelona
- **World of environment design**, Editorial Arco.
- 'Geläuterte Landschaftsarchitektur', Eric Luiten, **Topos** no. 21

BETH GALI OFFICE

- 'Nel magazzino del tabacco', **Abitare** no. 311, Editrice Sagesta, Milan

REMODELLING OF THE HISTORIC CENTER OF 'S-HERTOGENBOSCH

- 'Geläuterte Landschaftsarchitektur', Eric Luiten, **Topos** no. 21
- **Landschapsarchitectuur en stedebouw in Nederland 93-95** (Landscape architecture and town planning in the Netherlands 93-95), Uitgeverij TROTH
- 's-Hertogenbosch opmerkelijke stad, Waanders Uitgevers – Boekhandel Adr. Heinen
- **Beth Galí, architecture & design 1966-1998**, Museum Het Kruithuis, 1998

Collaborators

1. Beth Galí
2. Jaume Benavent
3. Alex Giménez
4. Armin Schäfer
5. Pepa de la Mora
6. Anna Birgisdottir
7. Pernilla Magnusson
8. Arola Tous
9. Maria Pella
10. Andrea Tous
11. Susana Guillermo
12. Laura Batalla
13. dog Tristan

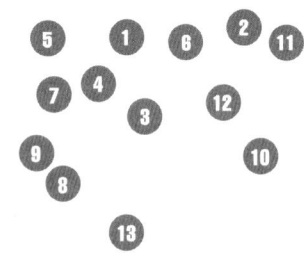

Xavier Arriola
Alain Aygalinc
Laura Batalla
Jaume Benavent
Gema Bernal
Anna Birgisdottir
Javier Brunello
Ramón Canals
Nuria Cases
Jaume Castellví
Josep M. Civit
Alessandra Dini
Ruth Egido
Inger Groeneveld
Susana Guillermo
Ramón Isern
Jordi Jansà
Alex Giménez
Margaret Koole
Ronald Kunh

Hubert van der Linden
Kathleen Lindstrom
Pere Llimona
Jaume Llongueras
Alfonso de Luna
Jeroen Luttikhuis
Pernilla Magnusson
Cristina Maragall
Inma Merino
Maura Monente
Pepa de la Mora
Vicenç Mulet
François Nordeman
Clemens Nuijens
Xavier Olivé
Maria Pella
Jaume Piñol
Marcos Roger
Valentina Rojas-Hauser
Javier Ruiz-Warnba

Joaquim San Joan
Juan Pablo Saucedo
Armin Schäfer
Willem Hein Schenk
Paco Sert
Willemijn Somers
Metchhild Stuhlmacher
Andrea Tous
Arola Tous
Alfredo Vidal

Photographers

Antoni Bernad 9/40/41/42/43/44/163/180

Anna Birgisdottir 124/125

Raimón Camprubí 87

Lluis Casals 92/93/94/95

Francesc Català Roca 47/55/69

C.B. Foto 58/60/61/62/67/68/70/72/73/86/90/98/108/110/111/113/116/117/118/121/122/123

Ferran Freixa 63/66/92/93/94/95/149

Fris 102/103/104/105

Beth Galí 21/22/57/71/73/96/100/101/107/109/137/144

Alex Giménez 15/16/17/42/58/75/78/106/129/134/136/138/139/140/141/145/146/147/148/150/152/153/154/155/162/165

Roberto Madrones 98/100

Toni Mateu 77/83

Eduard Maynès 96/97/99/100

Agustí Nubiola 120/164/165/166

Panorama 127

Lluis Sans 132/133

Jordi Sarra 79/80/81/82

Olaf Smit 135/140/151

Willemijn Somers 157/159

Hisao Suzuki 59/60/61/64/65

Tevisa 71/98

Foundation Friends of Museum Het Kruithuis

ABN/AMRO-bank, 's-Hertogenbosch

Alynia Lerou Architecten, 's-Hertogenbosch

Appèl Servicegroep, 's-Hertogenbosch

Croonen Adviseurs, 's-Hertogenbosch

CW Lease Nederland B.V., 's-Hertogenbosch

Faber Vastgoed B.V., 's-Hertogenbosch

The Greenery International B.V., 's-Hertogenbosch

Heineken Nederland B.V., 's-Hertogenbosch

Heijmans N.V., Rosmalen

Hogeschool, 's-Hertogenbosch

Huijbregts Beheer, Nieuwkuijk

ING-bank, 's-Hertogenbosch

Kamer van Koophandel & Fabrieken, 's-Hertogenbosch

De Keizer Assurantie B.V., Rotterdam

KPMG Accountants, 's-Hertogenbosch

Van Leeuwen/Van der Eerden advocaten, 's-Hertogenbosch

Uitgeverij Malmberg, 's-Hertogenbosch

Kunsthandel/Lijstenmakerij Monart, 's-Hertogenbosch

Jac. Mulders Electro B.V., Rosmalen

N.V. PNEM, 's-Hertogenbosch

PTT Telecom, 's-Hertogenbosch

Rieken & Oomen, Maastricht/'s-Hertogenbosch

Stienstra B.V. Bedrijfshuisvesting, 's-Hertogenbosch

Swinkels, Maas & Verhorevoort, 's-Hertogenbosch

Würth Nederland B.V., 's-Hertogenbosch

© 1998 All rights reserved with the authors

No part of this book may be reproduced in any form, by print, photoprint, microfilm or any other means, without the prior written permission of the publisher.

This book has been made possible by the positive enthusiasm of Yvònne G.J.M. Joris, Director of the Museum of Contemporary Art Het Kruithuis in 's-Hertogenbosch, and by the devastating efficiency of Alex Giménez and the talent and tenacity of Jaume Benavent, those indispensable members of my studio team.

edited by
Yvònne G.J.M. Joris
Museum Het Kruithuis

texts
Jaap Huisman
Oriol Bohigas
Antoni Llena
Antoni Mari

translations
Ted Alkins
Rita Barendse van de Berg
Dario Giménez
Bob de Nijs
Graham Thomson
Fabienne de Vilder

design
Scritto, Gent/B

lithography
Color Studio, Gent/B

printed by
Goff, Gent/B

published by
Museum Het Kruithuis
Citadellaan 7
NL-5211 XA 's-Hertogenbosch

ISBN 90 6538 182 1

with the support of:
Gemeente 's-Hertogenbosch
Heijmans Projectontwikkeling, Rosmalen
Multi Vastgoed BV, Gouda
Bouwbedrijf Pennings & Zn. BV, Rosmalen

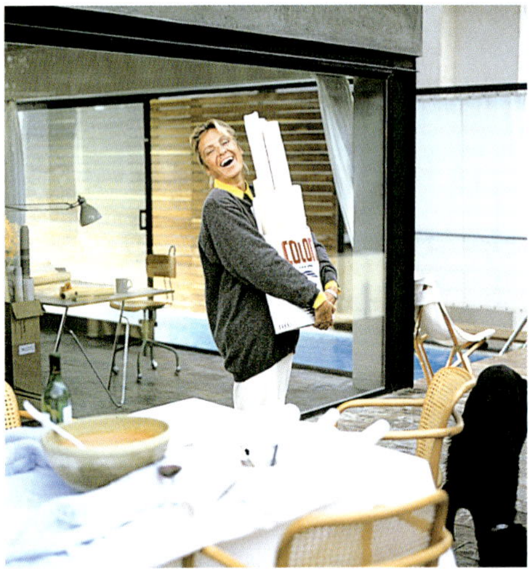